Palgrave Macmillan Studies in Banking and Financial Institutions

Series editor
Philip Molyneux
Bangor University
Bangor, UK

Aim of the series

The Palgrave Macmillan Studies in Banking and Financial Institutions series is international in orientation and includes studies of banking systems in particular countries or regions as well as contemporary themes such as Islamic Banking, Financial Exclusion, Mergers and Acquisitions, Risk Management, and IT in Banking. The books focus on research and practice and include up to date and innovative studies that cover issues which impact banking systems globally.

More information about this series at
http://www.springer.com/series/14678

To our family and beloved teachers

Preface

This book is on consolidation, restructuring and banking performance in post reform era of a quarter century. Idea of writing a book on banking reforms germinated with our research paper published on mergers and acquisitions of banks in Economic and Political Weekly, September 12, 2015. It got crystallized with further research on competition, cost efficiency and non-performing assets of banks in India, and some of these issues were explored in Ph.D. thesis of the second author. This became a fruitful and meaningful enquiry for update research and thus the idea of writing a book on this subject became concrete.

For past 25 years, banking industry was being transformed across the world to make it efficient enough to benefit from opportunities and deal with challenges of globalization. In the same way, Indian banking was also subjected to reforms since 1991 that led to gradual transformation on some dimensions of performance in the course of time, particularly with regard to efficiency, capitalization, technology, governance with equal emphasis on stability. Banking reforms became a positive political popular movement and forward looking measures in all academic and policy debates for a long time. Meantime global crisis of 2007–2008 led to bank failures in many countries and making others vulnerable to instability. However, Indian banks with limited risk exposure to overseas operation escaped from major catastrophic financial damages banks might have suffered. But it could not remain insulated from dampening effect of recession in Indian economy. Profits of banks slipped to lower level because of higher provisioning made against rising bad loans. Consequently, substantial banks' networth eroded and slide continued in post crisis period. All these events put a question mark on 25 years old banking reforms and its long term implications for banks in particular and for economy in general. Long term consequences of banking reforms were unknown except some research studies available on select issues or positive outlook projections described in scholarly lectures on the topic. Objectives of consolidation and restructuring, greater competition and lower concentration were attempted during progressive introduction of banking reforms. Consequently outcome of reform measures were expected to be tangible in terms of consolidation and restructuring of banks' operation. The question that whether these efficiency seeking reforms contributed to objectives is subject matter covered in various chapters of this book.

The question of optimal banking structure is elaborated and evaluated in first chapter. The discussion focused on criteria and indicators specified in literature and compatibility of emerging structure with developmental needs of Indian economy. Optimal structure of banking, though it is difficult to attain and maintain in view of multiple optima—is also necessary condition for efficient operation of the system. Market conditions of a service industry like banking is unlikely remain static in dynamic large economy like India. In view of banking deregulation and liberalization in general, market forces come into play to sharpen competition and discourage high concentration. These issues being a part of banking reforms are discussed in first two chapters. Despite reforms competition has not changed much but qualitative improvement in banking services is visible, concentration level marginally declined—all appeared to be constituents of oligopoly banking structure. Optimum size of firm grows with growth of economy, so was the case with banking entities in public sector having increased its efficient size over the period. Analysis of cost efficiency, economies of scale and diseconomies, if any, are presented in a chapter.

Equally important issue of productivity of inputs used by banks is scrutinized and given separately to validate cost efficiency. Unfinished consolidation and restructuring as examined in chapter on mergers and acquisitions proved that this objective did not materialize as recommended in Narasimham Committee Report. Deregulation of interest rates and liberalization in other operational aspects including variable reserve ratios contributed to performance that is seen in chapter on profitability. Also the issues of non-performing assets, technology innovations adding to efficiency are equally important and hence covered in this book.

This book would be useful reference to the academicians in teaching various post graduate programs in Economics and Finance. This book will serve as good reference text for research students, practitioners and policy makers for research, training and policy formulation in the area of banking in particular and economics in general.

Vadodara, India   T.R. Bishnoi
                                                                   Sofia Devi

Acknowledgements

We are greatly indebted to many scholars and colleagues for completion of this book. First of all, our grateful thanks to Prof. J.C. Sandesara, Emeritus Professor in Industrial Economics, Department of Economics, and University of Mumbai for initiating and orienting first author to work on banking sector performance while doing Ph.D. thesis under his guidance in 1980s. His work on "Economies of Scale in Indian Manufacturing Industry" (monograph) also proved to be very inspiring and helpful reference in one of the chapters in this book. We acknowledge with gratitude and reverence the benefits of mentorship from Prof. J.C. Sandesara.

This book was completed at the Reserve Bank of India Endowment Unit, Faculty of Commerce, the Maharaja Sayajirao University of Baroda, where we remain indebted to Professors Parimal H. Vyas initially Dean and currently Vice-Chancellor of the University, Sharad N. Bansal, Dean for their affectionate encouragement and administrative support in this academic work. We thank both of them for providing environment for research. Other colleagues in the Faculty of Commerce helped us immensely and immediately whenever demands were made on them and supported this work by an encouraging academic environment and fruitful interactions. We thank them all without naming any individual because of their numerous names makes a long list.

We are also thankful to publisher Palgrave Macmillan, London for publication of this book.

We solely remain responsible for inadequacies and errors, if any, in this book. Interpretation, views and suggestions mentioned in this book are entirely of authors and not of the institution where authors are currently employed.

T.R. Bishnoi
Sofia Devi

Contents

Abbreviations

AC	Average Cost
ARCIL	Asset Reconstruction Company (India) Ltd.
ATMs	Automated Teller Machine
BCBS	Basel Committee on Banking Supervision
BFS	Board of Financial Supervision
BIFR	Bureau of Industrial and Financial Reconstruction
BIS	Bank of International Settlements
BOB	Bank of Baroda
BPLR	Basic Prime Lending Rate
BR	Banking Regulation
BSR	Basic Statistical Returns
CAR	Capital Adequacy Ratio
CBS	Core Banking Solution
CC	Cash Credit
C-D	Credit-Deposit
CDR	Corporate Debt Restructuring
CPI	Consumer Price Index
CR	Concentration Ratio
CRAR	Capital to Risk Adjustment Ratio
CRR	Cash Reserve Ratio
CTS	Cheque Truncation Scheme

DCA	Debtor-Creditor Agreement
DRT	Debt Recovery Tribunals
ECGC	Export Credit Guarantee Corporation
ECS	Electronic Clearing Service
GDP	Gross Domestic Product
GNP	Gross National Product
HCS	Health Code System
HHI	Herfindahl-Hirschman Index
ICA	Inter-Creditor Agreement
IDRBT	Institute for Development and Research in Banking Technology
IMF	International Monetary Fund
IMPS	Immediate Payment Service
IOB	Indian Overseas Bank
IT	Information Technology
LABs	Local Area Banks
M&As	Mergers and Acquisitions
MC	Marginal Cost
MES	Minimum Efficient Size
MICR	Magnetic Ink Character Recognition
NACH	National Automated Clearing House
NEFT	National Electronic Funds Transfer
NIM	Net Interest Margin
NPAs	Non-Performing Assets
NPLs	Non-Performing Loans
OBC	Oriental Bank of Commerce
OC/TA	Operating Cost/Total Assets
OD	Overdraft
OLS	Ordinary Least Squares
PCR	Provisioning Cover Ratio
PEC	Pure Efficiency Change
PLR	Prime Lending Rate
PM	Profit Margin
PNB	Punjab National Bank
P-R	Panzar-Rosse
PSBs	Public Sector Banks
PSU	Public Sector Undertaking
PTLR	Prime Term Lending Rate
RBI	Reserve Bank of India
RDDBFI	Recovery of Debts Due to Banks and Financial Institutions

ReBIT	Reserve Bank Information Technology (ReBIT) Pvt. Ltd.
ROA	Return on Assets
ROE	Return on Equity
RRBs	Regional Rural Banks
RTGS	Real Time Gross Settlements
S4A	Scheme for Sustainable Structuring of Stressed Assets
SARFAESI	Securitization and Reconstruction of Financial Assets and Enforcement of Security Interest
SBI	State Bank of India
SCBs	Scheduled Commercial Banks
SCP	Structure-Conduct-Performance
SDR	Strategic Debt Restructuring
SEBI	Securities Exchange Board of India
SEC	Scale Efficiency Change
SICA	Sick Industrial Companies Act
SIPS	Systematically Important Payment Systems
SLR	Statutory Liquidity Ratio
TC	Total Cost
TCH	Technical Change
TEC	Technical Efficiency Change
TFPG	Total Factor Productivity Growth
UBI	Union Bank of India
WTO	World Trade Organization

List of Tables

1

Indian Banking Structure: An Overview

Introduction

This chapter deals with issues and changes in Indian banking structure during past a quarter century. It looks into a historical background and role of regulation in achieving intended structure to attain the multiple objectives of financial stability and operational efficiency coupled with autonomy for the purpose of financial inclusion. In this chapter, the historical background of modern commercial banking is elaborated along with subsequent developments up to nationalization of 14 major banks in 1969 and eight small banks in 1980. It also discusses regulation and optimal banking structure and explains criteria of optimal banking structure or particularly socially optimum banking structure that contributes towards the financial inclusion and economic development. It deals with the development in banking structure after financial reforms and provides an evaluation on the basis of relative size of banking system, accessibility and outreach of banking and credit allocation of the current banking system. Next, it defines the concepts of restructuring and consolidation and outlines the approach of analysis.

© The Author(s) 2017
T.R. Bishnoi and S. Devi, *Banking Reforms in India*, Palgrave Macmillan Studies in Banking and Financial Institutions, DOI 10.1007/978-3-319-55663-5_1

It is worthwhile to provide a critical discussion of market-friendly changes in Indian banking industry since 1991 when sweeping financial reforms were introduced to make banking efficient and vibrant enough to ensure systemic stability and greater optimality. The industrial organization perspective is important here as developments in banking system need to attain its size and composition optimally to minimize the problems of financial exclusions, credit deprivation and discrimination in the delivery of financial services to the needy firms and households. This perspective is exactly in line with the Reserve Bank of India (RBI) Annual Report 2013–2014 stating that 'It is important to review the banking structure in India with a view to enabling it to cater to the needs of a growing and globalizing economy as well as furthering financial inclusion. The global financial crisis of 2008 prompted many economies to review their banking structures'. Therefore, optimal structure of banking is an important and critical issue in regulatory reforms undertaken.

Historically, Indian commercial banking was subjected to several operational experiments in search of appropriate model suitable for India's mixed economy. The evolutionary development in banking was scrutinized to highlight questions relating to Indian structure and its operational efficiency (Basu 1978; Ghosh 1979; Bhatia 1983; Goldsmith 1983; Verghese 1983). Among many alternative banking models in use, some of them were the relevant choices available in designing the system such as organization type, ownership pattern, branch structure, composition, spread and credit portfolio allocation. Likewise there were the options in technology selection or capital–labour intensity in banking operation. Indian banking structure is policy determined and quite stable as regulation function and ownership of major banks both lie with central government, but it may not satisfy the criteria of optimal banking structure. Under each choice and option exercised by regulatory authorities and banking firms, resultant structure outcome is expected to be different. With long experience of private commercial banking for more than a century, India after Independence gradually shifted to a bank ownership pattern with public sector dominance and private sector keeping residual share in it. In order to provide banking cover to rural areas and marginalized sections of population in urban areas, cooperative banks (rural and urban) were simultaneously in existence to supplement functions of the commercial banks. In the 1970s, Regional Rural Banks (RRBs) were launched to strengthen the banking channels that were in operation. In a way, organization of Indian banking, it was a mixture of joint-stock companies, subsidiaries, cooperatives and corporations. Abundance of highly educated labour in India guided the appropriate choice of manual banking operation rather than software-driven automation that continued till computers arrived in the 1980s. In the beginning of the 1990s, computerization of banking services became a necessity, not for efficiency, but to survive against new entrants both domestic and foreign institutions in global competition. Branch licencing policy and loan policy of banks were suitably modified by new regulatory imperatives to cater to unbanked regions and credit-deprived sectors and other small economic activities.

The soundness of banking system is one of the prerequisites for financial stability and sustainability of the economy. The Indian banking system has undergone a series of reforms during the past two decades to enhance competition, productivity and efficiency, and dynamic operational flexibility with full autonomy in the sector. And to say, economic reforms in the real sectors of the economy will fail to realize their full potential without a parallel reform of the financial sector. Financial sector reforms are, therefore, a necessary concomitant of trade and industrial policy liberalization so that the competitive spirit and efficiency in the real economy could be ushered.

One such aspect of the reform process is consolidation as about a dozen of banks have been merged, amalgamated or restructured. An equal number of small banks were taken over by large ones prior to reforms (before 1991) to avoid bank failures. Apart from the eliminating weak and unviable bank units, the main purpose of consolidation of firms in banking industry was to realize the economies of scale, enable to earn more revenue and create the potentials for tax gains, thereby maximizing shareholders' value. There is no definite strategy or particular roadmap for bank consolidation in India. Rather, it is the result of a combination of internal and external factors that affected the operational environment of banks demanding healthy assets portfolio and financial health. Although certain objectives underlie the reforms process, policy constraints needed to be overcome. Strengthening banking structure, rehabilitation of the existing weak banks with various restructuring measures was the main thrust of the financial sector reforms. So, analysing the positions of banks in the post-reform period would be an interesting lesson for the future banking strategy. A brief overview of the Indian banking system before and after reforms serves to clarify the scope of bank consolidation and its impact on the commercial banks. It also helps to determine priority areas of reforms and strategy thereof for further restructuring the banking system. Before structural changes and consolidation are examined, it is worthwhile to present the historical background of Indian banking to understand the evolution of structure over the decades.

Historical Background of Indian Banking

Banking business in India has evolved within the framework of prevalent regulation over the past two centuries in response to economic opportunities and financial needs of modern organizations in commerce and industry. Nature of banking development in terms of organizational choice, spread of branches and degree of financial intermediation was very much influenced by macroeconomic environment and microlevel demand for banking services. There was a very slow progress of banking development during British India period as it served only to the interest of colonial regime benefiting from trade and commerce.

The banking functions in India were performed, some times in combination with mercantile pursuits, by Shroffs, Marwaris, Chettiars, Multanis, etc. These indigenous bankers continued to be singularly dominant until the English Agency Houses established financial firms based on modern organization and Western skill at Calcutta and Bombay. Next important events were setting up of the three Presidency Banks of Bengal, Bombay and Madras in 1806, 1840 and 1843, respectively—much before the principle of limited liability was introduced in Indian banking in 1860. Along with the functioning of these banks, the mushroom growth of small banks coupled with a recurrence of bank failure marked the progress of banking in India till 1920.

Amalgamation, a source of concentration of banking in other countries, was then difficult in India, because many banks were established to safeguard and promote different and conflicting communal, business and family interests. In such an environment, merger of the three Presidency Banks and formation of the Imperial Bank of India in 1921 marks the beginning of concentration in Indian banking. Between 1921 and 1945, the Imperial Bank stood singularly as the largest bank (with nearly one-half of the bank deposits under its control) among numerous small banks. In fact, the small banks perceived a logical philosophy of 'perpetual smallness' in view of some advantages available to them in the banking system.[1] The small banks maintained that 'with their knowledge of local trade and industries, they can give their customers better service than can the larger banks. With their greater personal knowledge of their customers and their affairs, they could accept business which to the larger institutions may seem to be too risky and beyond their province. Indeed, it has been argued that the existence of small banking institutions has had the effect of introducing the banking habit to those who live outside the cities'.[2] Thus, right from early times until recently the diverse character of the Indian economy has provided adequate scope for coexistence of small and large banks. However, of late, the distribution of deposits among the banks has become highly skewed in favour of the big banks. The number of banks in the large size category with deposits of Rs. 20 crores and more increased from 7 in 1945 to 11 in 1950 to 19 in 1961 and their share of banking deposits stepped up from 52% to 70% to 84% respectively, whereas the number of small banks with deposits of Rs. 10 crores or less varied from 356 in 1945 to 450 in 1950 to 276 in 1961 and their share in banking deposits declined from 30% to 24% to 9% over the same period.[3] The Reserve Bank's perception of the need of such a high concentration for stability in banking is clearly seen in its work on regulation and control of banks. The consolidation measures adopted by the RBI since 1950 have had, among other things, the effect of large banks having control over 80% of the banking business in 1960 relegating the small banks to a minor residual in the banking system.

A development of major significance for the banking industry was the nationalization of 14 major banks in 1969. Another nationalization of banks took place in 1980 when six more small banks were brought under state ownership. These two events led to the tightening of government control over banking system. Among the objectives of this change was to transform financial system on the basis of social objective consistent with physical and financial targets laid down in five-year plans. In other words, it was the need-based reorientation of the working of banking system for public or social interest, specified in rural banking policy as well as giving greater importance to the hitherto neglected areas and lines of business such as backward areas, agriculture, small industry, transport, professionals, exports and weaker sections. During the period since 1969, whereas there has taken place a phenomenal expansion of banking in rural and semi-urban areas and large strides have been made in lending to priority areas, these developments have also been accompanied by declining productivity and profitability of banks.

The decade of the 1980s recorded higher economic growth of 5% or above putting challenge for banks to finance accelerated growth without affecting the quality of their balance sheet. Banks were subjected to fixed interest rate regime, Cash Reserve Ratio (CRR) and Statutory Liquidity Ratio (SLR) reached their respective peaks and scope of credit targets was widened which adversely affected the revenue and profits of banks. Frequent loan melas, revised targets of directed credits and political interferences made banks more vulnerable to poor-quality portfolio and losses. Consequently, Non-Performing Assets (NPAs) increased and recycling of funds suffered a setback; operational autonomy was diluted to serve even unviable schemes to further political cause.

Regulation and Optimal Banking Structure

Apart from the financial stability perspective, there is also a dimension of optimal banking structure in banking regulation—economic optimal structure of banking consisting of commercial banking optimum and social banking optimum. Public regulation of banking activity stems from dual considerations. First, bank regulation for monetary policy consideration is traditional objective because banks serve as conduit through which monetary transmission takes place, attempting monetary stabilization. It means prevention of over-expansion or under-expansion of money and bank credit through monopoly or through excessive competition. Banks being custodian of public money, prudential regulation is also a necessity for ensuring systematic financial stability to support the monetary policy objective. Second, it pertains to the industrial organization of banking activities promoting competition. Regulation focuses on orderly development and growth of banks to avoid or minimize monopoly power and promote healthy competition and protection of the depositors against consequences of bank failures.[4] That is, regulation intends to promote banking structure that fosters allocative, distributive and technological ends for the society at large. It means central bank directs the regulation process for promoting socially optimal banking structure. In sum, banking regulation encompasses all types of central bank's controls or government's direct intervention in functional autonomy of commercial banks that covers entry barriers, branch licencing, mergers and amalgamations, joint ventures, credit allocation, portfolio composition and reserve requirements, prudential regulation of capital norms, assets quality and risk management, fixing interest rates on deposits, loans, refinancing facilities, range of products, services and its price band, etc.

Criteria of Optimal Banking Structure

Structure of banking is contingent on stages of economic development and macroeconomic policy regime guided by political philosophy and ideology. Thus, it varies over the time within the economy as well as across the countries. Changes in political establishment, market condition, technology, etc., are also other attributes of banking structure. Different aspects of structure can be analysed by looking at certain patterns such as ownership, organization and relative size of banking industry. More precisely, structure can be defined in terms of number and size distribution of banks, number of bank offices or branches, Automated Teller Machine (ATMs), mobile branches, extent of subsidiaries or holding firms, chain banking, etc.[5] Elaborating it further, Camron (1972) defined banking structure on various quantitative measures: (a) density—ratio of number of bank branches or offices to population, (b) size of banking system relative to macroeconomy—ratio of bank assets to Gross National Product (GNP) or wealth, (c) size distribution of banks within banking system—market share indicating degree of oligopoly or monopolistic power and (d) geographical concentration—regional distribution of bank branches, credit and deposit.[6]

Keeping aside the consideration of monetary policy regulation, Camron (1972) discussed characteristics of socially optimal banking structure and defined it on four criteria of needs of society. First characteristic of socially optimal banking structure is maximum productive efficiency. That means that social cost of producing banking service with an optimal structure is expected to be less than or equal to social cost of producing the same service with any other viable banking structure. Second characteristic of optimal banking structure is allocative neutrality meaning thereby that overall allocation of resources in the economy is not influenced substantially by the peculiarity of banking structure. It is reciprocally analogous to the concept of excess burden in taxation literature. Here, it must be noted that banks were promoted by business houses and were engaged in mobilizing resources from a large number of small and medium savers spread all over country and catering to their own needs by way of lending to few selected business houses. This feature of Indian banking has diluted the principle of allocative neutrality. Third characteristic of optimal banking structure is a derivative of allocative neutrality. It implies an absence of exploitation for all stakeholders (depositors, borrowers, employees and others), input suppliers and users of banking services. Banks avoid behaving like monopolist or monopsonist in their transactions with the public such as charging exorbitant lending rates and other fees, paying abnormally low deposit rates and paying casual contractual wages. Fourth characteristic of optimal banking structure is maximum responsibility to technological changes and market-based demand of the society. This criterion focuses on time needed for banks to adopt new technology and adjust its apparatus in order to shift in composition and magnitude of the public demand for banking services. These four characteristics of social optimal banking structure are maximum productive efficiency; allocative neutrality;

absence of exploitation of consumers and factors of production; and maximum responsibility to market needs and technology changes. Not satisfying the above criteria may produce distortion such as credit gaps and financial exclusion, emergence of special financial institutions outside banks, higher rate of innovations outside banking sector and labour-intensive technology in banking. Optimality in banking structure needs to be evaluated assuming that multiple objectives that banks expected to perform in India's transforming economy are policy dictates. For example, private sector banks consisting of foreign and domestic both pursue their profit maximization objectives subject to constraints of statutory obligations and regulations. Public sector banks also pursue same profit objective but in combination with that of social and development objectives mandated by larger public policy agenda. These subsidiary development objectives generate sustainability of long-term growth, profitability and efficiency shared by all types of banks.

There are several optimum concepts such as organizational, technical, managerial, cost, marketing and sales. The theory of optimal banking structure rests on consideration of maximization of public welfare. Since economy and society both are dynamic entities creating a steady demand for financial services and therefore banks need to be sensitive in their offerings by adapting and adjusting to new economic environment and developments. Thus, service firms such as banks need to change continuously to achieve optimality in its structure suitable to the economic system to serve the needs of society. Banking structure consisting of foreign and domestic private and public sector banks serves different niche in the market economy. For example, foreign banks are better equipped to serve the needs of foreign trade and multinational companies, and public sector banks are better positioned to provide services in rural, semi-urban segments along with catering to urban economic activities in the economy. Likewise, private sector banks can enter those many of the non-traditional high-risk areas which are not covered by foreign banks and public sector banks.

In contrast to the listed criteria of optimal banking structure as enumerated above, a distinct feature of Indian banking system in the pre-reform period was the prominence of public sector controlling over four-fifth of the banking assets (high concentration). Moreover,

Indian banks were subjected to high degree of regulation and controls motivated by nationalistic economic policy. Actually the Indian financial system of pre-reform period was designed to meet the needs of the planned development in a mixed economy framework where the public sectors had a major role to play in the economic activities. On the eve of the reforms in 1991, both the SLR and CRR were as high as 38.5% and 15%, respectively. These high rates adversely affected the operational flexibility of banks and depressed banks' income earnings. Above these, the system of directed credit programmes to priority sector at concessional lending rates also affected the profitability of banks. The banking sector as a whole in the pre-reform period was characterized by high cost of intermediation, low quality of banking services and fragile financial health of the institutions. To say, there was an urgent need for improving efficiency, productivity and profitability of the banking and financial sector so as to enhance their competitiveness, efficiency and profitability to withstand the challenges of globalization. Capital movement across the countries without barriers has created global environment of banking institutions with added significance to commercial objectives of bank operations.

Banking Structure After Financial Reforms

Narasimham Committee on Financial Reforms

Removal of these undesirable distortions and operational weaknesses in Indian banking of the pre-reform period was the basic objective of financial sector reforms, which indeed was taken up in the early 1990s. The basic priority in the early reform period was to remove the structural rigidities and inefficiencies in the financial system. The financial sector reforms in India took place in phases based on the recommendations of the Committee on the Financial System under the chairmanship of Shri M. Narasimham (Reserve Bank of India 1991). The first phase of financial sector reforms submitted its report in November 1991. Phase I, popularly known as the Narasimham Committee I, was initiated under the

Committee on the Financial System. Phase II, known as the Narasimham Committee II, was initiated in 1998 under the Committee on the Banking Sector Reforms. Narasimham Committee I defined its approach as to '…ensure that the financial services industry operates on the basis of operational flexibility and functional autonomy with a view to enhancing efficiency, productivity and profitability'. Narasimham Committee II was entrusted with the task of evaluating the extent of implementation of reforms recommended by the Narasimham Committee I with major focus on performance indicators of the banking sector.

Since the introduction of reforms, the Indian financial system has undergone radical transformation in many operational aspects, if not on all issues recommended. Financial sector reforms provided banks with operational flexibility and functional autonomy. Reforms have focused on altering the organizational structure, ownership pattern and domain of operations of banks. Entry and exit norms were relaxed. Foreign and new private sector banks were allowed entry to do business. As a result, the banks become slightly more competitive on non-price variables after reforms. Profitability of Indian banks in terms of operating profits as a ratio of total assets has increased. Productivity of the financial sector also improved as the lending rates showed a gradual decline from the range of 16 to 17% in most part of the 1990s to about 12% by 2006–2007 and further reduced to below 10% in 2015. This significant productivity improvement in the banking system lowered the intermediation cost of banks. Another performance indicator is the statutory pre-emption of banks, which have been lowered since 1991. The CRR has been reduced gradually from 15% in 1991 to 4.5% in 2003 although increased to 5% in October 2006. It was reduced to 4% in 2016. Similarly, the SLR has also been lowered from 38.5% in 1991 to 25% in 2006 and further to 20.75% in 2016. These changes in policy rates and ratios have released substantial amount of loanable funds for banks to profit from commercial lending opportunities, to which these funds can be channelized.

Another objective of banking reforms was to restructure and consolidate Indian banks for larger scale and competitive efficiency to attain suitable size distribution with a view to satisfy the financial needs of the economy. It needs to be mentioned here that there is an oligopoly character in Indian banking as revealed by size distribution of banks (in terms of assets and liability). Herfindahl-Hirschman Index estimated for deposits, credits of banks showed a slight decrease in concentration ratio, reflecting rising competition after reform as entry barriers tend to be lower than earlier one.[7]

India's Banking Structure: Relative Size of Banking

In Annual Report of 2013–2014, RBI has summarized data on the banking structure in select advanced and emerging market economies. In advanced countries, there is almost private ownership associated with high degree of concentration and penetration. Share of public sector controlling banks' assets was almost negligible with exception being the case of Germany (32%) and UK (26%). Concentration ratio in these economies varied from 58 to 82 with USA alone being outlier at 35%. Bank assets as proportion of Gross Domestic Product (GDP) were significantly high in the range between 84% in USA and over 600% in UK indicating penetration in advanced nations. As against it, emerging market and developing countries showed public sector dominance wherein India has government ownership of banks coupled with lower concentration, the lowest value of 29% in India. Emerging market and developing economies are gradually catching up with the banking features of advanced countries. Looking at the indicators of concentration, Net Interest Margin (NIM) and credit-deposit (C-D) ratios, Indian banking appeared to be better structured than that of many peer countries. It is important to note that financial stability of the economy is determined by the type of banking structure and public sector ownership of banks that is an important attribute to it. Weak banking structure is assumed to be poor optimal with greater systematic risk and the same is attributed to bad monitoring and inefficient regulations.

The European countries restructured their banking system mainly through vivid approaches of privatization process during the 1990s for a variety of reasons. American approach refers to privatization, competition and deregulation policy in order to redesign the state control on the economy. Privatization, according to European approach, refers to the change in banking company ownership and governance. In fact, European privatization (sale of public sector banks to private investors) is often just an initial step of wider process aimed at redesigning role of the state in the economy. This is in view of rising cases of banking crises in Asian countries in last quarter of the twentieth century (Khan and Bishnoi 2001).

Broadly, in banking structure there were five different categories of objectives pursued, namely systemic, macroeconomic, industry (microeconomic), political and social. In other words, sale of public sector firms in banking and finance was guided by transformation that included the achievement of competition between banks, to promote the entrepreneurial culture, tradition and right attitude towards risks and to drive for efficiency—allocative efficiency, technical (production) efficiency and managerial innovations. It is important to consider India's banking structure with a cross-country comparison based on some banking indicators capturing size, inclusiveness, ownership pattern, concentration and soundness. While the Indian banking sector compares favourably in terms of moderate concentration ratio and the reasonable soundness indicators, it has some distance texpected to covero cover in terms of inclusiveness, efficiency, size and ownership. The public sector owns a disproportionately large share of the total banking industry, thus diluting the advantage of moderate concentration. NIMs are also high in the face of low competition and come in the way of gaining efficiency improvement.

The relative size of Indian banking system indicated a positive change over the reform period. The ratio of aggregate deposits of scheduled commercial banks to GDP increased from 35% in 1991–1992 to 61% in 2006–2007 to 68% in 2014–2015, almost doubled. However, Indian banking with less than 70% deposit to GDP ratio of small size is no match to the record of China, Vietnam and developed countries. Its ratio is just one-half of these countries' values and therefore Indian banks have tremendous potential to improve this indicator. Likewise, though the credit to GDP ratio has improved from 19% in 1991–1992 to over 50% in 2014–2015, this ratio in the above-mentioned countries found to be in the range of 100–150%, indicating substantial gap between actual and desirable levels of banking development. This also reflects causal effect of bank credit input on the growth of the economy.

With the objective of sharing the high growth of certain sectors, scheduled banks started lending to sensitive sectors comprising capital market, real estate, commodity market—loans to the extent of 17% to GDP ratio in 2012–2013.[8] This exposure to high-risk sectors considered to be large given their relative contribution to GDP and employment.

India's Banking Structure: Accessibility and Outreach

Presence of banking infrastructure and availability of banking facilities in a region are reflected by number of population per branch, ATMs per branch, average branch size in terms of deposits and credits, penetration ratios—deposit and credit each per capita basis and share of priority sector credit in total outstanding credit. Since banking services act as catalyst in economic and commercial activities in the area, formal banks' accessibility and outreach has tremendous significance for the entire economy. Ideally, a bank branch is expected to cover 3–4 g panchayats with 8–10 villages, about 20,000 population assuming an average size of a village approximately 2000 persons. By this estimate, a branch can cater to 20,000 persons in its operational area and deliver financial services cost effectively if not cost efficiently. This arbitrary standard of 16,000 or less persons (8 villages multiplied 2000 persons per village) can be treated as good coverage yardstick by bank branch.

In recent years, number of Scheduled Commercial Banks (SCBs) including RRBs reported to decline from 276 in 1991–1992 to 222 in 2006–2007 to 151 in 2014–2015 as a result of consolidation by way of mergers and acquisitions. Many RRBs and some small commercial banks were either taken over by big ones or unviable and weak units were forced to merge with healthy banks in this period. Average population coverage per branch has touched a satisfactory level from 14,000 in 1991–1992 to 10,800 in 2014–2015 given considerable variation by state and regions. However, there are regions and states with considerable under-banking record of 20,000 or more populations per branch particularly in backward states and north-eastern region of the country. Deposits and credits each per branch (average size of branch) has increased from Rs. 33 million in 1991–1992 to Rs. 304 million in 2006–2007 to Rs. 675 million in 2014–2015. Likewise, there was a proportionate growth of average credit size of branch for the same years. Consequently, credit-deposit ratio has increased from 61% in 1991–1992 to 72% in 2006–2007 to 78% in 2014–2015 with a slide of corresponding proportion in investment ratio of all scheduled commercial banks. Added to this change, there was also a slight decline of 3% points in share of priority sector credit to total credit (from 38 to 35%) for these years. Per capita deposits have risen from Rs. 2368 in 1991–1992 to Rs. 19,276 in 2006–2007 to Rs. 62,252 in 2014–2015, thus a change of 26 times. In case of per capita credit, it was an increase from Rs. 1434 to Rs. 13,774 to Rs. 48,294—a jump of 34 times for the same durations (Table 1.1).

Above-mentioned phenomenal changes were originated mainly in newly created massive branch network across the country. As a result, there is a gradual shift in composition of bank branches or offices since 1991–1992 because share of rural branches drastically declined from 57% in 1991–1992 to 37% in 2014–2015. Some loss-making and unviable branches in rural areas were either closed or merged with nearest branches. Simultaneously, new branches were opened in urban and metropolitan areas. Likewise, relative share of rural deposit (15%) and credit (20%) in 1991–1992 declined to very low level (deposit 10% and credit 8%) in 2014–2015. It is a hindrance to rural banking development which is seen as a reverse trend of past policy. On the other hand, metropolitan branches with less than 10% share contributed more than 40% deposit and credit each in 1991–1992. Shares of metropolitan areas increased to 18, 54 and 65% in case of branches, deposits and credits, respectively, in 2014–2015. A combined share of metropolitan and urban branches stood at 24% with more than three-fifths share of deposits and credits each in 1991–1992. There was a substantial improvement in relative position of urban and metropolitan areas over these years. Their branches touched to a peak share of 37% with 76% of deposits and 81% of credits in 2014–2015. Average deposit balances in account found to be about Rs. 3000 in rural, Rs. 4500 in semi-urban, Rs. 6600 in urban and Rs. 14,000 in metropolitan areas in 1991–1992 and correspondingly average credit outstanding for them

Table 1.1 Changes in structure of Indian commercial banking: 1991–1992 to 2014–2015

Item	1991–1992	2006–2007	2014–2015	Remarks
No. of commercial banks including RRBs	276	222	151	Some RRBs closed and merged with parent or other banks
Population per branch (000)	14	16	10.8	Ratio falling in the past 8 years
Deposits per branch (Rs. million)	33	304	675	Average size doubled in the past 8 years
Credits per branch (Rs. million)	20	217	524	Increased by 203%
Credit-deposit ratio	60.6	71.5	77.6	Increased by 20%
Investment-deposit ratio	37.7	35.5	28.3	Decreased by 40%
Per capita deposits (Rs.)	2368	19,276	62,252	Increased by 26 times from 1991–1992 to 2014; 3 times over 2006–2007 to 2014–2015
Per capita credits (Rs.)	1434	13,774	48,294	Increased by 34 times from 1991–1992 to 2014–2015; 3.5 times over 2006–2007 to 2014–2015
Share of priority sector credit to total credit (%)	38	37	35	Decreased by 2%

Source RBI: Basic Statistical Returns of relevant years

was Rs. 8000, 13,000, 32,000 and 104,000. Deposit size and credit outstanding per account increased considerably in 2014–2015. The figures of deposits were about Rs. 19,000, 33,000, 74,000 and 1,74,000 per account and those of credit were Rs. 101,000, 173,000, 528,000 and 1,227,000, respectively. Average credit outstanding per account far exceeded the deposits by over five times, indicating pre-emption of bank resources from small population centre to metropolitan sectors. Despite the socialist policy guiding rural expansion and credit targets of public sector banks, emerging scenario of post-reform Indian banking particularly in branch network and credit distribution was far from satisfactory. A notable feature of post-reforms banking was a skewed distribution of credit and deposits among population groups across states and enhanced deprivation of institutional finance and deficit of banking facilities in many regions. In sum, share of rural branches in total branches is shrinking and that of others is increasing. Average deposit and credit per account by population category reveal the tendency of fund transfer from rural to urban and metropolitan areas. This may vitiate banking exclusion in rural sector which is already deprived of its rightful claims on financial services and institutional credit (Tables 1.2 and 1.3).

Accessibility and extension of banking services across regions were always an issue for regulators and challenge for banks since the 1960s. Because of RBI's aggressive rural orientation in branch licencing policy since the 1960s, opening of new bank branches, particularly that of the Public Sector Undertaking (PSU) banks, received a big push enhancing visibility of bankers in areas not covered so far by them. It was a haphazard planning of branch network—substantial number of branches opened in rural and semi-urban areas since the 1970s; faced shortage of trained and experienced manpower to staff them; many were poorly staffed and unable to scale up; and failed to cross breakeven in branch-level banking business. By the end of 1990s, many branches were reported to be unviable and loss-making requiring branch consolidation through swaps, merging two or more branches or closing loss incurring units. Thus, aggregate number of branches was more or less stabilized in 1990–1991 and future expansion of banking led to adopt technology-driven alternative channels. In the recent decade, extension of banking activities is more through ATMs and franchises as indicated by the ratio of ATMs to branches. It is more than one for all scheduled commercial banks in 2013. Among banks, foreign banks (Citibank, HSBC, Standard Chartered Bank, DBS Bank, Deutsche Bank and The Royal Bank of Scotland) and new private banks added fairly large number of ATMs. These banks began to operate their services considerably more through ATMs than PSU banks did by these channels. However, PSU banks also have reasonable ATMs network as its ratio of ATMs to branch

Table 1.2 Share of deposits and credit of SCBs by population group: 1991–1992

Population group	No. of offices	Deposits (Rs. million)			Credits (Rs. million)		
		Accounts	Amount	Average size of account	Accounts	Amount	Average size of account
Rural	35,134 (57)	114.8 (31)	357,497 (15)	3114`	33.9 (51)	275,201 (20)	8118
Semi-urban	11,566 (19)	102.0 (28)	465,914 (20)	4568	17.2 (26)	228,421 (17)	13,280
Urban	8833 (14)	83.4 (23)	552,894 (23)	6629	9.4 (14)	301,287 (22)	32,052
Metropolitan	6191 (10)	69.6 (19)	994,767 (42)	14,293	5.4 (8)	562,150 (41)	104,102
All	61,724 (100)	369.8 (100)	2,371,072 (100)	6412	65.9 (100)	1,367,058 (100)	20,744 (100)

Table 1.3 Share of deposits and credit of SCBs by population group: 2014–2015

Population group	No. of offices	Deposits (Rs. million)			Credits (Rs. million)		
		Accounts	Amount	Average size of account	Accounts	Amount	Average size of account
Rural	44,653 (37)	407 (33)	7,871,511 (10)	19,340	47 (35)	4,754,155 (8)	101,151
Semi-urban	31,663 (26)	340 (28)	11,410,772 (14)	33,561	38 (28)	6,580,224 (11)	173,164
Urban	23,386 (19)	231 (19)	17,140,100 (22)	74,200	19 (14)	10,032,993 (16)	528,052
Metropolitan	21,263 (18)	248 (20)	43,134,829 (54)	173,931	33 (23)	40,478,050 (65)	1,226,608
All	120,965 (100)	1226 (100)	79,557,212 (100)	64,892	139 (100)	61,845,422 (100)	444,931

is approximately one. It commands a share of 61% of all ATMs in the country. New private banks accounted for 31% of ATMs which comes one-half of all PSU banks' ATMs. To some extent, skewed distribution of branches as indicated above is compensated or corrected by ATM installations by private banks. It indicated greater use of technology in banking operation. The branch structure is shaped predominately by public sector banks (including RRBs) accounting for almost 90% branches in 2005 and rest claimed by private sector (old and new) banks. With aggressive strategy of new private banks, this group was able to double their share in short span from 3% in 2005 to 11% in 2013. Local banks and foreign banks were left with a very little space in 2013. In short, this existing branch structure reflected the dominance of public sector banks and skewed distribution among banks of different ownership (Table 1.4).

India's Banking Structure: Allocation of Credit

Allocation neutrality is another characteristic of optimal banking structure. It is measured in terms of credit allocation by organizational ownership and occupation or activity. In 1991–1992, private corporate sector and households claimed majority share of credit and remaining sectors received residual credit. As against this, household sector with 98% share of borrowing accounts claimed 43% of outstanding credit in 2014–2015. Astonishingly, household sector and individuals add up to 75% of outstanding bank credit in which individuals claimed 35.6% of credits. Public sector organizations accounted for 0.1% of borrowers' accounts and 18% of credit outstanding where major share went to non-financial public sector firms. More or less same pattern is visible in case of large borrowers' accounts and outstanding of credit in 2014–2015. The next category of microfinance institutions maintained a share of less than a per cent in credit. The decline in share of PSU organizations with corresponding increase in share of private sector reflects restructured credit allocation over the period (RBI, Basic Statistical Returns (BSR)).

Credit allocation is subjected to RBI intervention under SLR and priority sector credit targets. Credit outstanding by occupation showed that industry with 2% share in total borrowing accounts had 42% of total credit outstanding in 2014–2015. Relative share of accounts and

Table 1.4 Branches and ATMs of SCBs: 2005 and 2013

Bank group	March 2005			March 2013		
	Total branches	ATM	ATM per branch	Total branches	ATM	ATM per branch
Public sector banks	47,288 (88.0)	9992 (56.6)	0.21	72,661 (82.0)	69,652 (61.1)	0.95
Old private banks	4511 (8.4)	1241 (7.0)	0.28	6047 (6.8)	7566 (6.6)	1.27
New private banks	1685 (3.1)	5612 (31.8)	3.33	9522 (10.8)	35,535 (31.2)	3.73
Foreign banks	242 (0.5)	797 (4.5)	3.29	332 (0.4)	1261 (1.1)	3.80
SCBs	53,726 (100.0)	17,642 (100.0)	0.33	88,562 (100.0)	114,014 (100.0)	1.26

Source RBI: Report on trend and progress of banking in India, 2004–2005 and 2012–2013

credit outstanding are sliding over the years as firms are permitted to mobilize resources directly from public and abroad and reduce dependence on bank debt. Personal loans were new category introduced after reforms and emerged as next big borrowing category in 2014–2015, with 36% share in number of accounts and 16% share of credit outstanding. It has doubled its share because banks consider it more secure and high return portfolio. Agricultural credit under priority sector has 18% subtargets and commanded a share of 42% in accounts and 15% in amount outstanding in 1991–1992. The relative share of agriculture was 50% in accounts and 13% of credit outstanding in 2014–2015. Trade and professional loans are also priority sector credits, and these had a share of 9 and 7%, respectively, in 2014–2015. Transport operators have constant share at 2% in both accounts and credits all these years. Finance claimed a share of 3 and 8% of credit outstanding in 1991–1992 and 2014–2015, respectively. The pattern of credit outstanding reveals uneven allocation given the contribution of each activity in output, GDP and employment in the economy (Table 1.5).

Restructuring and Consolidation of Banks: Concepts

Restructuring

Restructuring of banks around the world has taken place for a wide variety of reasons. Some nations adopted as a policy either on account of efforts to restructure inefficient banking systems or rehabilitation from the financial crises or distortions. But the motives and purposes of restructuring have changed over time. Motives will also vary among the countries with country-specific circumstances. Recapitalizing and restructuring banks in the aftermath of a systemic crisis is a complex process that typically requires significant government intervention and takes several years to design and implement (Enoch et al. 2001). In the case of China, which has a predominance of state-owned banks such as India, the main thrust behind the restructuring is to restructure the weak financial institutions, which is facing difficulties in terms

Table 1.5 Credit outstanding of SCBs by occupation, 1991–1992 and 2014–2015 (%)

Activity	1991–1992		2014–2015		Remarks
	No. of accounts	Credit outstanding	No. of accounts	Credit outstanding	
Agriculture	42	15	50	13	Priority sector target is 18% of the previous year outstanding credit
Industry including small	10	48	2	42	Small industry covered under priority sector
Transport operators	2	2	2	2	Covered under priority sector
Professional and other services	6	3	2	7	Covered under priority sector
Personal loans	11	8	36	16	Started after 1991 reforms
Trade	18	14	5	9	Part of priority sector
Finance	0.03	3	0.4	8	Not covered in priority sector
All others	11	7	3	2	Not classified above
Total credit	100	100	100	100	

Source RBI: Basic Statistical Returns (BSR)

of making payments, insolvent or making losses or to mitigate financial risk or to exit from the market. In the USA, where banking system accounts for higher proportion of mergers, deregulation has been an important force in altering banking structure. Most Asian countries are in the middle of a major process of bank restructuring. In Malaysia, consolidation programme was important in order to survive following the Asian financial crisis. However, consolidation could also be driven by non-value maximizing motives such as empire-building by corporate executives or by government's objective to make the banking system more stable (Mohan 2005). Many countries around the world have used consolidation as a strategy to either realign the structure of banks through mergers and acquisitions or recapitalize distressed institutions after a major financial crisis or shocks. In the case of Indian banking, restructuring prior to the sixties was an important event to consolidate the system, followed by nationalization of major banks to align institutional credit allocation according to plan priorities. In post-reform era, restructuring of banks has a different objective in the context of globalization of financial markets and need a proven strategy to implement in future.

Consolidation

The term 'consolidation' is not a new phenomenon and a derived outcome of restructuring process of banks. Consolidation is defined as a decrease in the number of firms in an industry, along with a simultaneous increase in average size of the continuing firms. Consolidation also implies larger sizes, larger shareholders' bases and larger number of depositors. The main aspect of consolidation is the synergy effect that firms could gain after combination and thereby maximize shareholders' value. The main synergies to be derived through consolidation of firms in an industry are the ability to enjoy economies of scale, ability to earn more revenue, profits and the potentials for tax gains.

There are several methods of consolidation with each method having its own strengths and weaknesses, depending on the economic circumstances or exigencies. However, the most commonly adopted method of consolidation by firms has been through Mergers and Acquisitions (M&As), liberalizing entry of new firms or combination of both. Consolidation of banks through M&As is not a new phenomenon for the Indian banking system. Since then, there were mergers and amalgamations of select banks to protect depositors' interest. In post 1991, there were more frequent M&As in Indian banking either to eliminate weak banks or to attain inorganic growth in new banks, which will be discussed later on in a separate chapter.

Approach of Analysis

As discussed above, there are significant changes in structure and assets composition of the entire banking system during post-reform period. This is a result of deregulation of interest rates and entry barriers in financial markets, innovative products, growing customer sophistication, stricter regulations, diversification in their activities, etc. Banks have begun to strengthen and consolidate their operation by using various restructuring strategies. Strategies cover branch and business consolidation, adopting new mode of transaction such as outsourcing of business processes, franchise and deploying technologies such as ATMs, net banking, phone banking, electronic money transfers, and adding retail loans (housing loans, vehicle loans, education loans, etc.) in portfolio. Therefore, it is opportune to study and evaluate the performance of banks in the post-reform period on various banking parameters. This book covers the existing structure, competition, mergers and acquisitions, non-performing assets (NPAs), profitability, cost and economies of scale, productivity and technology use. Thus some important questions are relevant to explore here:

1. Does the Indian banking attain optimal banking structure over the years?
2. Were the banking reforms comprehensive enough to cover all functional dimensions of banks? What is the progress record of banking reforms since 1991?
3. Do mergers and acquisitions strengthen bank consolidation and improve performance of banks?
4. Does competition among banks increase and concentration decline in the post-reform era?
5. Does size matter for cost efficiency of Indian banks?
6. What is change in total factor productivity of banks in post-reform period? What are the sources of change in productivity?
7. It is expected that profitability of banks increase in the post-reform period. What is the trend in profitability of banks since 1991?
8. Do prudential regulations help in controlling NPAs of banks? Do NPAs are explained by a slowdown in growth (systematic risk) or asymmetric information?
9. What is the role of technology in banks in post-reform period?

This book is on restructuring, consolidation and performance of Indian banks during the reforms that were initiated in 1991. In general, scheduled commercial banks are covered in discussion and in some specific cases, all 27 public sector banks were considered. Certain bank-specific variables such as assets, income, net worth, expenses, advances and deposits were taken as the main banking variables. Data on number of branches, number of employees and various selected financial ratios of banks were also taken according to the requirement of analysis. Banking reforms were elaborated with reference to deregulations of entry barriers, interest rates and other statutory requirement. Prudential regulations relating to capital norms, non-performing assets and corporate governance were equally important here. Analysis of mergers and acquisitions were carried out for the banks that went for mergers during the period. A pre-merger performance and post-merger performance were compared to these banks in order to see whether mergers improved performance of the banks (Bishnoi and Sofia 2015). Competition and concentration are the fascination of banking reforms and therefore need a space in the book. Whether reforms have changed the degree of competition and concentration in banking sector? Economies of scale and productivity of banks were other performance parameters of cost efficiency. Profitability was considered in terms of three important measures of profits, namely return on assets (ROA), return on equity (ROE) and profit margin (PM). Non-performing assets, being a very complex and debatable issue in policy implementation, were taken up in the context of macroeconomic slowdown and information asymmetry problem. Given the data constraint in technology in banks, some aspects of technology use particularly in payment and settlements were highlighted in this volume.

Select appropriate statistical tools and methodologies were employed to study performance of the banks after reforms. Paired sample test is used to measure pre-merger and post-merger performance of the banks. In order to measure the degree of competition among firms and their positions of market shares, the k-firm concentration ratios and the Herfindahl-Hirschman Index (HHI) were used. For the economies of scale, a linear cost function was a good fit and thus used here. This cost function was estimated for each bank group and for all banks together by using Ordinary Least Squares (OLS) regression method. Economies of scale were analysed for different years. For profitability trend of the banks, time trend and panel regression were fitted for three different measures of profitability. In the case of non-performing assets, statistical range, correlation and regressions were used appropriately wherever applicable. Technology in banks and its trends were used in order to trace the progress of electronic payments and digital banking in India. In the last chapter, summary and conclusions along with policy suggestions were given for future policy inputs.

The study was conducted on the basis of data available from secondary sources. Data were compiled from the time series data of RBI, various annual reports and occasional publications for different time periods.

Conclusion

Optimum banking structure is always an important issue for banking policy. India's banking structure as examined on the criteria of relative size in relation to GDP, accessibility, outreach and allocation neutrality reflects progressive improvement since 1991. The tremendous potential to grow in relative size to cover the gap between actual and desirable levels of banking development is the first challenge. Despite the socialistic objective banks pursue for past couple of decades, the substantial financial exclusion in rural and semi-urban areas remains yet to be addressed with suitable policy adjustment. Though allocation neutrality is broadly taken care in credit distribution to priority sector and marginalized sections, credit allocation according to contribution of each activity in output and employment is yet to be achieved. These gaps can be treated with technology penetration in service delivery and appropriate banking model involving a proper mix of in-house operation and outsourcing process.

This book contains the text on banking reforms and its achievements. First four chapters highlighted various aspects of restructuring and consolidation, concentration and competition in Indian banking in the post-reform era. The other chapters deal with performance evaluation on cost efficiency and productivity, profitability, non-performing assets, technology use, etc. Lastly, summary, conclusion and some suggestions are given at the end.

Notes

1. Panandikar, S.G. (1963, p. 26).
2. Sayers, R.S. (ed.) (1952, p. 160).
3. Bishnoi, Tulchha Ram (1988, Chap. I).
4. Meltzer, Allan, H. (1967, pp. 482–501).
5. Greenbaum, Stuart I. (1967).
6. Camron R. (ed.) (1972, p. 9).
7. Sofia Devi Shamurailatpam (2013, Chap. VI).
8. RBI (2013): Report on Trend and Progress of Banking in India, Appendix Table IV.

References

Basu, C.R. 1978. *Central Banking in a Planned Economy: The Indian Experiment*. New Delhi: Tata McGraw-Hill.

Bhatia, R.C. 1983. *Banking Structure and Performance*. Bombay: NIBM.

Bishnoi, T.R., and Sofia Devi. 2015. Mergers and Acquisitions of Banks in Post-Reform India. *Economic and Political Weekly* 50 (37): 50–58.

Bishnoi, Tulchha Ram. 1988. *Size and Performance of Commercial Banks in India—1961 to 1982*. Ph.D. thesis, Department of Economics, University Of Mumbai.

Camron, R. (ed.) 1972. *Banking and Economic Development—Some Lessons of History*. New York: Oxford University Press.

Enoch, Charles, Gillian Garcia, and V. Sundararajan. 2001. Recapitalizing Banks with Public Funds. *IMF Staff Papers* 48 (1): 58–110.

Ghosh, D.N. 1979. *Banking Policy—An Evaluation*. New Delhi: Allied Publishers.

Goldsmith, Raymond W. 1983. *The Financial Development of India, 1860–1977*. Delhi: Oxford University Press.

Greenbaum, S.I. 1967. Competition and Efficiency in Banking System—Empirical Research and Its Policy Implications. *Journal of Political Economy* 75 (4): 461–479.

Khan, M.Y., and T.R. Bishnoi. 2001. Banking Crisis and Financial Reforms: Lessons for India. *Chartered Secretary*, January.

Meltzer, A.H. 1967. Major Issues in the Regulation of Financial Institutions. *Journal of Political Economy*—Supplement August, 75 (4): 482–501.

Mohan, Rakesh. 2005. Financial Sector Reforms in India. *Economic and Political Weekly* 40 (12): 1106–1112, 1115–1121.

Panandikar, S.G. 1963. *Banking in India*. Bombay: Orient Longmans Ltd.

Reserve Bank of India. 1991. *Report of the Committee on the Financial System*, November, Mumbai.

Reserve Bank of India. 2013. *Banking Structure in India—The Way Forward.* Mumbai, India: Discussion Paper.

Reserve Bank of India Annual Report 2013–2014.

Reserve Bank of India: *Basic Statistical Returns*, various issues.

Reserve Bank of India: *Report on Trend and Progress of Banking in India*, various issues.

Reserve Bank of India: *Statistical Tables Relating to Banks in India,* various issues.

Sayers, R.S. (ed.). 1952. *Banking in British Commonwealth.* Oxford University Press.

Shamurailatpam, Sofia Devi. 2013. *Reconstruction and Consolidation of Banks.* Ph.D thesis in Economics, The M S University of Baroda, Vadodara, Gujarat.

Verghese, S.K. 1983. *Profits and Profitability of Indian Commercial Banks.* Bombay, India: NIBM.

2

Banking Reforms

Introduction

This chapter discusses banking reforms that were introduced as a part
of broad economic reforms in post 1991 years as real sectors are closely
integrated with the financial sector. It provides a critical view of banking
reforms that crystallized Indian banks' challenges and opportunities from
1991–1992 to 2015–2016 to steer the path in globalized Indian economy. It also delineates the unfinished agenda of banking reforms needed
for a vibrant and healthy financial system. The main objectives of banking
reforms are financial stability and efficiency of banks; both are prerequisites of monetary stability and economic development. Financial stability
exists when the financial system is able to perform financial intermediation task properly—attracting latent savings and allocating capital and
has the capacity to withstand panics, shocks and crisis. Central bank is
assigned the task of ensuring stability of financial system, defending it as
a whole by appropriate intervention either be the prudential regulation
or be the lender of last resort. Sometimes this responsibility is shared
between the central bank and government, if large-scale intervention is
needed in special circumstances. Efficiency of a bank is attained when

© The Author(s) 2017   31
T.R. Bishnoi and S. Devi, *Banking Reforms in India*, Palgrave Macmillan Studies in
Banking and Financial Institutions, DOI 10.1007/978-3-319-55663-5_2

it is capable to produce output or service by using the minimum inputs per unit, given other things constant. In other words, it refers to the least cost level of operation at which cost of output or service is minimum and profit is maximum (efficient or optimum size). Banks are highly regulated because of high leverage entities, their well-recognized role in minimization of information asymmetry in financial markets, conduit of monetary policy, etc. Tight regulations were a necessity during the evolutionary phase of banking system for attaining its optimal structure. Moreover, socialist policy implementation demanded new financial regulations or targets particularly since the 1970s focusing banking expansion in rural areas along with redistribution of credit, both changes took the toll of efficiency, that proved to be adverse for and inconsistent with India's market economy. Dismantling controls began to appear selectively in trade and financial services in post 1985 years, signalling necessity for other interrelated sectors to follow liberalization. Thus banking deregulation was sought for efficiency and stability of the financial system in globalization mode of economy (Singleton 2011).

During evolutionary phase, Indian banking regulations were gradually tightened, accompanied by nationalization of the existing private bank entities, in the 1960s and 1970s with a strong belief that these produce public goods, so-called financial health of banking firms, needed for then-planned development strategy execution, which in turn demanded credit allocation in favour of public sectors and priority sectors (credit-deprived economic sectors), institutional credit to hitherto neglected areas, regulations and controls as supplements to other macropolicy measures. The experience of 3 decades of pervasive state intervention in financial markets led to reverse the belief of regulator that too much and many regulations breed inefficiency and distortion in the financial system. Progress of public sector banks under such controlled regime was mixed with positive developments and negative features in the form of certain unwarranted operational rigidities (organization inefficiency), loss of competitiveness and weak structure (financial repression). Other negative effects of such welfare-oriented regulations emphasizing social banking are also clearly acknowledged (Joshi and Little 1994). Populist regulation led to distortions and dilution of commercial principle in bank credit and investment that supported the contrary perception, 'regulation cannot do good all the times', and therefore reforms were inevitably proposed to attain optimality and dynamism in banking structure consistent with democratically governed Indian market economy (Goodhart et al. 1998). Strategy of banking reforms was based on a gradual approach to avoid jerks and pitfalls of policy change, a disastrous feature noted in reforms of some of the Latin American countries and African continent as well as East Asian region.

Major Indian commercial banks initially set up as private firms were nationalized (large and small banks from 1955 to 1980 to create public sector undertakings) to strengthen the socialistic pattern of the economy. Commercial banks were nationalized, starting with Imperial Bank of India in 1955 and Provincial banks in the 1960s to form the State Bank Group, followed by nationalization of 14 large banks in 1969 and further six small banks in 1980, to convert class banking into mass banking, and thus a sizable shift of above four-fifths India's banking assets under state ownership and control. It facilitated a big push in rural banking and credit allocation in favour of major sectors so far bypassed by banks, namely agriculture, small-scale industries, and transport; all were credit-deprived till the end of fourth five-year plan, 1974. Along with this transformation in ownership and structure of assets, there were loan grabbing political interventions to benefit vote constituency and other several concomitant developments that led to the loss of flexibility and market discipline in banking operation. Some of the prominent developments include interest rate regulation, steady rise in wages mediated by Indian Bank Association, disregard to productivity, profitability in guise of social banking and use of labour-intensive technology making banks prone to frauds and coordination failure in bank management. Since 1970, Indian commercial banks made commendable strides in outreach by way of geographical spread and functional diversity irrespective of cost escalation and productivity loss and consequently suffered erosion in profitability and net worth. Substantial proportion of loan assets were gradually became non-operative, not because of recession but on account of poor due diligence process, lack of monitoring of end-use of sanctioned credit and poor recovery law. As a consequence and also due to the absence of loss provisions, banks' capital diminished to very low level, or turned negative in case of few banks. Thus the main characteristics of Indian commercial banking have been public sector dominance with growing state intervention leading to operational rigidity, inefficiency, poor assets quality, weak organization, poor work culture and financial bankrupt, awaiting a trigger in policy to shift gear in reverse for U-turn to escape from the collapse of financial system. Thus banking reforms became urgent imperative to avert bigger crisis emanating from further financial repression, systemic weakness and global financial integration. Then banking reforms, following economic crisis in 1991, were based on the Narasimham Committee recommendations on a number of diverse issues such as capitalization and risk management, directed investment and credit programmes, accounting policy and transparency, assets quality and loss provisions, organization methods and procedures, interest rate liberalization, and supervision and regulation (RBI 1991). Reserve Bank of India responded timely and swiftly on reform mechanism as suggested in the Report to strengthen the banking system in 1991. Market principle-based incentives were built into new regulatory provisions to be implemented in a progressive manner to cope with a weak banking system and restore the public confidence in banks. Banking reforms were sequenced with adaptive process, keeping pace with other sector reforms, to enable the banks to adjust with new environment and overcome external constraints to move towards flexibility and independent attitude untouched by intervention (Rangarajan 2007).

Observing that the main concern of the regulation of banks is solvency (the relation between equity, debt and asset risk), the RBI set up an autonomous authority in 1994 called Board for Financial Supervision (BFS) in order to perform the monitoring functions of on-site inspection and off-site surveillance. The main functions of BFS include: (i) restructuring of the system of bank inspections, (ii) introduction of off-site surveillance, (iii) strengthening of the role of statutory auditors and (iv) strengthening of the internal defences of supervised institutions.

Since its inception, BFS has taken several initiatives relating to its supervision function. It is engaged in supervision and monitoring of the financial health of banks. In addition, its main focus is on consolidation of accounting system, identification of bank frauds, assessment of NPAs and substantiation of necessary legal and technical processes.

Deregulation

Liberalizing Entry Barriers and Interest Rates

According to the theory of banking firm, high entry barrier for banks is common feature across the countries as these institutions serve as custodian of public saving and conduit of monetary policy (Klein 1971). High entry barriers in banking were also useful in maintaining and strengthening existing structure of banking industry for long enough to attain maturity, stability and financial deepening. Moreover, economic systems with public sector dominance tend to experience difficult entries, if not impossible in the financial industry. Examples of this type of experience are from banking sectors of central European countries, Russia, France, Germany and many more countries (Hanson 2004). Entry barriers consist of bank licensing, minimum equity capital, promoters' contributions, and foreign holdings in voting equity capital, eligibility and management quality benchmarks, and business plan requirements for new entrant banks. In Indian economy, social objectives embedded in planning process made banking entry almost impossible under Banking Regulation Act 1949 with an exception being only setting up of Regional Rural Banks under state sponsorship. A complete ban on new private banks' entry remained as a policy imperative because of doubt about the contribution that such banks can make in planned economic development of the country in view of poor performance record of past banking history of pre-Independence and immediately thereafter. For restructuring and competition, liberalization of new entry as well as consolidation through M&A on market principle and profitability consideration was recommended by the Narasimham Committee in 1991 which were carried out during next 25 years. The RBI's adopted slow-motion banking reforms due to its conservative attitude in opening the banking for private entry as well as foreign multinational banks. RBI issued guidelines in 1993 and again revised in 2001 for the issue of new bank licenses, listing certain norms such as minimum equity capital paid-up, promoters' contribution and management background in banking for entry of new banks. Minimum capital for new entrant was fixed at Rs. 200, to be increased to Rs. 300 during the first three years of operation wherein promoters' contribution needs to be not less than 40% for 5 years from the operation. Later on, the voting equity capital for new bank entity was raised to Rs. 500 crores (RBI 2016).[1] For improving the degree of competition and increasing productivity as well as efficiency in banking, RBI issued twelve bank licenses in the private sector between 1994 and 2005, 10 of them on the basis of 1993 guidelines and two on revised guidelines of 2001. Almost half of these local banks set up by professional individuals were either failed or merged with others or muted growth, making non-competitive and unviable a real concern.[2]

RBI also set up High-Level Advisory Level Committee (Chairman: Bimal Jalan) in 2010 to examine the applications of new banks to strengthen the structure of banking system and suggested issue of licenses. After 25 years of experience of gradual testing the contribution made by new private banks and their performance, Reserve Bank of India recently issued fresh guidelines for licenses and permitted new banks on the line of Giro banks in USA, deposit banks and payment banks (as called differential banks) in 2015 for experiment. Now easing entry further from the financial year 2016–2017, bank license began to be available on tap within the framework and guidelines determined by the Reserve Bank of India. It is a U-turn from the past banking policy of restricting fresh entry of banks. Because of these new entries, it certainly introduced non-price competition based on the offering of new financial products and services, setting quality-oriented service benchmarks, use of information technology (Internet or phone banking, electronic fund transfers, etc.), ATMs and mobile branches—all positive steps in attaining the objective of financial inclusion. Though the substantial change in structure of banking industry was yet to come or price competition yet to take place, commercial principle in bank operation is openly visible in cost cutting, technology use, restructuring of business portfolios, branches and staffing. Perhaps it is so because there is a trade-off between price competition and stability of banking system. Gradually all these new practices and initiatives are likely to contribute to efficiency and productivity.

Reserve Bank of India adopted a pragmatic approach in allowing M&As to facilitate inorganic growth, restructuring and consolidation of banks. Under Section 44(A) and Section 45 of Banking Regulation Act 1949, Reserve Bank of India has discretionary powers to approve amalgamation by mergers either of compulsory type for reconstruction or of voluntarily between two or more weak bank entities with strong banking unit. In terms of Section 66 AE of Banking Regulation Act, Central Government with RBI consent can acquire or nationalize private banks in the interest of depositors or national interest. Unlike compulsory mergers directed for weeding out weak banking units prior to 1990, there is quite liberal approach in permitting such M&As on compulsory and voluntary basis in post-reform period since 1991. During the period from 1991 to 2010, 22 banks were approved for M&As by the RBI—a half of these cases were enforced on compulsory mergers and rest half on a voluntary basis. In two cases namely, ICICI and IDBI both development banks, had done reverse mergers—merging with its own newly established subsidiary companies (commercial banks). Apart from the weeding out weak banking units, these M&A cases in banking were expected to serve many objectives: (i) change in management and control, (ii) substantial acquisition and (iii) consolidation of the firms for efficiency and enlarging of size. Major considerations in recent M&As in Indian banks were inorganic growth, size increase for economies of scale, change in management and control to remove inefficient promoters and clean the system, and transformation of development banks into commercial banks. Accordingly, these market-oriented liberalization approach of mergers and amalgamations in Indian banking regulations contributed positively for the efficiency of banks over the years. In the long run, consolidation and restructuring of banking operation is likely to strengthen financial performance, structure optimality, customer-centric attitude and global vision of Indian banks.

The second important deregulation was of interest rates. Interest rate is a price of funds. Capital deficit Indian economy needed modest regulation of interest rates for allocating investible funds according to development priorities of 5 year plans rather than commercial criteria for profit maximization of banks. Therefore, free interest rate regime gradually became history when the Reserve Bank of India began fixing the minimum rate of interest on advances of Scheduled Commercial Banks with effect from 1, October 1960. It was made the maximum rate of interest in 1968 followed by reintroduction of minimum loan rate in 1972. After 1976, loan rates were prescribed following the multiple considerations, of specific sector, specific programme, specific purpose, type of borrower, size of loan, etc. Likewise, regulation of interest rate on deposits began in October 1964 and reached to peak level in 1980; Reserve Bank of India was fixing all interest rates—minimum floor and maximum ceiling—at different point of time in order to implement government directives on this aspect. Consequently, the prevailing structure of interest rates by 1991 appeared to be complex to monitor due to a multiplicity of rates and complicated to administer. It became difficult for branch managers to comply with owing to the conflicting considerations of rate determination. However, there is theoretical rationale for interest rate regulation and other state intervention on the ground of market failures in financial markets. That is to set interest rate high enough to incentivise saving mobilization and contain demand for credit by the private sector. Control on interest rates was not without trade-off in credit allocation. In information asymmetric environment, control of interest rate to curtail the demand for credit leads to credit rationing as well—depriving adequate credit to the genuine borrowers undertaking commercially sound projects and allowing the excess credit at high interest to borrowers undertaking high-risk projects (adverse selection problem). Apart from this, public sector banks were lending to state enterprises, even to those loss-making ones purely on ownership criterion (Joshi and Little 1996). It affected not only demand but also quality of loan portfolio due to the presence of poor-quality projects funded by banks. This behaviour of bank lending to risky projects gave rise to moral hazard problem and often took toll of efficiency of banking institutions.[3]

As mentioned above it was during 1964 and subsequent years, one after another interest rates were successively put under regulation with detail administrative and discretionary controls, culminating into more than 80 short-term rates and over 60 long-term rates fixed by 1980 (Bishnoi 1995). As a result, prevailing interest rate regime had

the following characteristics during pre-reform years: (i) large interest spread (about 100%) due to low rates of interest on deposits and
high interest rate on lending, (ii) a ceiling or floor of one interest rate
led to another ceiling or floor and (iii) RBI also applied quantitative
ceilings or restrictions on a wider scale in allocation or distribution of
finance and fighting inflationary pressures. Thus, the system of administered interest rates comprises the presence of discretionary controls on
the level and variations of interest rates, impacting the quality of banks'
assets, profitability and eventually net worth (owners' capital). Initially
up to the end of fourth five-year plan, it served the intended purpose of
successfully diversifying credit allocation including lending to marginalized sections and small enterprises but prolonged full-range regulation
thereafter began to create distortion in deposit market and rationing of
credit allocation. It had an element of cross-subsidization among sectors and concealment of the true fiscal deficit by reduced interest burden on public debt. Subsidized priority sectors loans claimed 40% of
the credit outstanding while its burden transferred through high interest
rates charged to other borrowers particularly industry and trade. Viewed
in negative real interest rates and inverted yield pattern, administered
interest rate system became an important attribute of financial repression in Indian financial markets (Bhole 1985). Fixed interest rate tends
to be an insensitive or inelastic policy instrument, ceased to be price
signal for investment decisions and thus does not provide any guidance in the allocation of scarce credit and financial resources. Also monetary policy, instead of using interest rates, depended on other direct
quantitative instruments to manage liquidity at macrolevel. In view of
this, Reserve Bank of India (1985), so called Chakravarty Committee
Report, commissioned a study on administered interest rates with a view
to overhaul this complex structure of interest rate with inverted yield
pattern and suggested its liberalization to end financial repression.[4]
Translating theory into practice, the Committee also made a strong
case for better coordination between monetary and fiscal policy, a new
interest rate structure with fewer slabs but greater freedom for banks to
decide rates, with the maximum lending rate pegged at 3% above the
maximum nominal deposit rate to ensure decent margins—measures
for a positive real rate of return to depositors and a change in rates

consistent with market conditions for government securities and their maturities. Though the Committee favoured cutting number of interest rate slabs but it fell short of recommending a complete dismantling of administered rates. In 1986–1987, the government began to implement some of these recommendations paving the way for new thinking in policy design—modern monetary policy framework in the globalized economy leading to the Urjit Patel Committee report advocating Consumer Price Index (CPI)-based inflation targeting.

Recognizing the importance of interest rate as credit allocation mechanism in market economy, its deregulation was initiated after reforms and quickened liberalization thereafter so as to set all rates free from control in alignment with market condition. In this context, the RBI instructions were issued to scheduled banks regarding the interest rates on advances for progressively deregulation with effect from 18, October 1994, and their greater functional autonomy for freely determining lending rates on advances of different maturities. As a result, interest subsidy in bank credit reduced except in the case of agricultural loan up to Rs. 2 lakhs. Allowing flexible market linked, if not market determined interest, rates had a simultaneous positive effect on macroeconomic balance—fiscal deficit pruned and discipline in government borrowing observed. This made investors to subscribe government securities unlike previous feature of public debt subscribed and held only by banks. Liberalized interest rate structure in post-liberalization era bears steady relationship with Bank Rate or Repo—an anchor in Indian money market.[5]

It started with freedom allowed to individual commercial bank for setting its minimum base deposit and loan rate called Bank Prime Lending Rate (BPLR). BPLR was the rate at which banks were giving loans to its most trustworthy, very low risk and first rate borrowing clients. In practice, banks were found to be pragmatic in charging much lower interest rate on housing loans as well as wholesale advances to big corporate firms, an incentive offered to lure good customers at the subprime rate.

During the 1990s, there was a complete deregulation of bank lending rates, exception being agricultural loan up to Rs. 2 lakhs. Initially, the structure of lending rates had six size-wise slabs in September 1990 that compressed into four in April 1992 and further into three a year later (April 1993). Lending rates for loans with credit limits of over Rs. 2 lakhs were deregulated in October 1994 with simultaneously declaring the Prime Lending Rates (PLRs) by concerned bank. Banks allowed prescribing separate PLRs and spreads over PLRs, for both loan- and cash-credit components effective from February 1997. In October 1997, for term loans of 3 years and above, separate Prime Term Lending Rates (PTLRs) were required to be set by banks. In October 1999, banks were given flexibility to charge interest rates without reference to the PLR in respect of certain categories of credit. In April 2000, banks were allowed to charge fixed or floating rate on their lending for credit limit of over Rs. 2 lakhs. Effective from April 2001, the PLR ceased to be the floor rate for loans above Rs. 2 lakhs. Simultaneously, in order to match deregulation of loan rates, interest rates on all maturities of deposits were gradually freed from RBI control during this period, except saving bank interest rate freed a decade later. In October 2011, RBI deregulated interest rates on savings bank deposit accounts to eliminate skewed benefit enjoyed by banks at the cost of depositors, completing the task of dismantling interest rate regulation that process began 3 decades ago. This also made deposit market conducive for competition unlike in the past with single interest rate stipulated by the RBI for very long period. There is strong possibility for savings bank deposit rate to serve as anchor rate for policy purposes.

One of the objectives of banking sector reforms was to ensure that the financial repression inherent in administered interest rates is removed. For this to happen, Reserve Bank of India freed from control all lending rates of scheduled commercial banks except one; in case of loans up to Rs. 2 lakhs, the RBI continued to fix lending rate in order to protect the interest of these borrowers at the appropriate level in a manner that the lending rates of banks should not exceed the Benchmark Prime Lending Rate (BPLR) of the respective banks. In sum, deregulated market-linked interest rates generate advantage in competitive pricing of deposits of different maturities as well as determining risk premium in interest rates on various categories of loans consistent with bank credit regulation. Banks were expected to benefit from positive impact of interest rate deregulation in terms of lower operating cost and higher income and profits than otherwise would have occurred.

Variable Reserve Ratios

Among the most popularly discussed and used policy ratios are Cash Reserve Ratio (CRR) and Statutory Liquidity Ratio (SLR). Under fractional reserve banking system, commercial banks are required to keep a fraction of deposits in cash form with central bank of the country or in the vault with a view to ensure liquidity for banks in the event of emergency or crisis. There are different views regarding utility and imposition of reserve requirements across the countries and according to this, all the countries can be grouped into three categories—first group of countries those believing in free banking opted for zero reserve requirement or eliminated this requirement such as Australia, New Zealand, Sweden, UK and Canada; second group of countries with low cash reserves ratio limited to single digit such as Eurozone, South Africa and Switzerland; and third category of countries with double-digit reserve ratio. At different times, countries are free to introduce, eliminate or re-impose and vary its ratios upside in double-digit level if policy warranted. Compliance of CRR implies foregone interest income on cash that can be advanced as interest-bearing loan. Statutory reserve is maintained in terms of cash as it is deposited by banks with central bank or its designate bank, impacting directly the capacity of bank lending. Compliance of SLR requires bank deposits to be invested in government bonds or government-approved securities only; it is also termed as an investment ratio imposing allocation of bank funds in favour of public sector. However, initial function of the former ratio is the first line of liquidity for banks, whereas the latter ratio is the second line or supplementary liquidity for the banks. Over the period, central banks discovered the utility of both reserve ratios in monetary management and used very actively with frequent variations, particularly after the 1970s till the end of the twentieth century.

For the first time, at Federal Reserve Board in 1931, apart from immediate liquidity reason, the reserve ratio was suggested as an instrument to control credit expansion, scarcely to be used in combination with other instrument of monetary policy in special circumstances and be imposed in the range from the minimum of 5% to the maximum of 15% of total deposits (Watkins 1936).

In India, CRR and SLR each as a fraction of deposits—different ratio for demand deposits and time deposits separately—was introduced as an immediate line of liquidity for banks according to RBI Act 1934 in the initial stage and subsequent following the Banking Companies Act, 1949, for commercial banking regulation. The minimum CRR of 5% of demand deposits and 2% of time deposits was operating from July 1935 to Mid-September 1962. Following an amendment to the Banking Companies Act, a minimum CRR was fixed at 3% of total demand and time liabilities combined in 1962. With several modifications relating to CRR and SLR in the Banking Regulation Act and Reserve Bank of India Act over the years, regulator-approved CRR came to be at minimum of 3% of time and demand deposit liabilities and maximum of 15%. With some experiment searching appropriate level of CRR since 1949, it was raised in stages to 7% in 1973 and, further with variations, revised upward to 8% in 1983 in order to curb inflationary trend. Subsequently as inflationary expectations became strong with double-digit growth of money supply, more frequent changes in CRR became routine in the years followed ultimately touching 15% with additional incremental CRR in 1989. Monetized fiscal deficit became a regular way to finance development activities in public sector over the years, leading to the high growth of high-powered money (new money creation) contributing to inflationary trend. In order to neutralize the inflationary potential of this additional liquidity, frequent increase in CRR from the minimum level was necessitated, i.e. from 3 to 15% plus incremental CRR. Discovery of twin functions of CRR as an instrument of liquidity and a tool of monetary regulation made RBI to use this ratio more actively with upward revisions for inflation control since 1973. It was used in conjunction with other instruments of monetary control for the better effect of policy ratios.

In post-reform period, CRR was reduced in pari passu with weakening inflationary pressures. Its reduction began from peak to 14% in 1993 to 10% in 1997 to 5% in 2002 and to 4% in later years. To complete the monetary policy reforms, it is argued that it needs to be adjusted downward further to the minimum level of 3% of demand and time deposits.

SLR, which stipulated as a secondary source of liquidity for banks to begin with, was found to be popular later with RBI's credit policy to support financing of expansion of the public sector. It was kept constant at 20% for a long period from 1949 to 1964. Following an amendment in Banking Regulation Act in 1962, the ratio was raised first time to 25% in September 1964. It was frequently stepped up sometimes more than once in a year to reach 30% in 1972 and further 35% in 1981. The upward trend in SLR continued as well in the 1980s, eventually to touch 38.5% in 1990. The higher ratio implied government pre-empting larger bank credit by way of sale of securities to banks for which secondary market was undeveloped. Hence, banks served as a captive market for parking government bonds and securities in compliance with SLR stipulation—a default may attract penalty. Needless to mention, low coupon rate of SLR bonds and securities resulted in the loss of interest income, thus affecting adversely the profitability of banking system as a whole.

From 1970 to 1990, CRR and SLR remained the most important measures of monetary policy which was guided by three factors. Control of inflationary pressures was the major concern of monetary policy that required direct freezing liquidity through frequent and often steep increases in CRR to the last limit of 15% with incremental CRR. Added to this was RBI credit to government leading to growth in reserve money fuelling unexpected liquidity to be contained in effect to manage price line. Consequently, this substantial growth in government borrowing from RBI at subsidized rate, as mentioned above, created a captive market for public debt funded through increased SLR requirement for banks. Both the variable reserve ratios touched their ceiling or exceedingly high level, impacting banking system with substantial erosion in profitability.[6] Reversal of trend in these ratios in post 1991 period proved to be a boon in freeing bank funds and deploying them in more profitable avenues. It may be possible to reduce the CRR to the lowest level of 3% if inflation targeting monetary policy becomes a successful hit and slash in SLR becomes a reality if fiscal deficit is adhered to the lower level and public borrowing becomes modest in decades to come.

Banking Prudential Regulations

'Report of the Committee on Financial System', submitted by M. Narasimham in November 1991, laid down the roadmap for banking reforms for smooth transformation from a weak and financially fragile system into an efficient, stable and dynamic development catalyst. It provided an overview of major forces accounting for declining productivity, efficiency and erosion of profitability in the banking sector. As identified by the Committee, the major factors among others were: (a) directed investment programmes (enhanced SLR), (b) directed credit programmes (priority sectors credit targets), (c) poor quality of loan portfolio, (d) inadequacy of capital associated with the absence of loan loss provisions, (e) the absence of income recognition, proper accounting and disclosure practices, (f) erosion of profitability, (g) outdated manual technology accompanied by lack of customer-centric services, (h) over staffing, trade union pressures and weak management and (i) inadequate internal control as well as deterioration in balancing of books (reconciliation of inter-branch and inter-bank entries). These reforms were intended to reverse the existing regressive financial regulations. The reform measures include elimination of unnecessary controls and regulations and adding new dynamic ones, set up of new complementary agencies and competitive institutions, introduction of organizational efficiency benchmarks, enactment of new laws dealing with insolvency and credit recovery, granting operational autonomy to better manage institutions, etc. In this regard, Reserve Bank of India enjoined banks to comply with prudential regulation norms of capital adequacy, asset classification, income recognition and provisioning rules, risk exposure limits and asset liability management systems, that have helped to identify and contain risks, contributed to greater financial stability, competition and freedom of banks to take credit decisions independently.

The traditional view was that government ownership is a good substitute for bank capital and in the event of a financial panic and crisis, government can act as assurance agency and the lender of last resort when there are bank failures. Having capacity to intervene, government can restore public confidence in the panic moments and assure the safety of principal amount of depositors and creditors of banks through either deposit insurance or credit guarantee or return them their money on demand. Goldstein (1997) found that deregulation or liberalization of financial system resulted in banking crisis in economies with poor quality of institutions and government ownership, which extenuated it in certain situations.

In pursuance of the Narasimham Committee recommendations, India began to adopt Basel norms for commercial banks in 1992. The Committee endorsed the internationally accepted prudential norms relating to capital adequacy, assets classification and income recognition, disclosure and transparency in operation, assets and liability management, risk control and management, NPAs, corporate governance, corporate debt restructuring, etc.

During 15 years from 1992 to 2008, Reserve Bank of India implemented capital norms at 9% to be adequate enough, a higher level than Basel norm of 8%. It adopted three-track approach, justified by its own risk profile and type of regulation, to include (a) minimum capital, (b) supervisory review, transparency, and accountability, and (c) market discipline.

Capital to Risk-Weighted Asset Ratio

Main focus of the banking reforms is strengthening capital structure of commercial banks for the reason of financial stability. Protection of the net worth of banks is assumed to insulate the institutions against insolvency. Prescription of capital norms, risk exposure norms, classification of assets and provisioning for loan loss are some of the measures highlight this intent of bank regulator. Following the recommendations of the Narasimham Committee Report and also in consonance with international practice and Basel norms, new capital adequacy ratio adjusted for risk of assets was introduced for different commercial banks in 1992. Capital adequacy standards so-called Basel I norms, developed by the Basel Committee on Banking Supervision (BCBS) in 1988, considered to be the first move towards risk-weighted capital adequacy norms. Indian commercial banks were required to be fully compliant with respect to capital adequacy, as well as credit and market risks. Prudential capital regulation enjoins to enforce capital adequacy norms, to minimize risks of accounting manipulations and to insulate bank managers from macroeconomic shocks, which are beyond their control (Dewatripont and Tirole 1994).

Among many objectives of capital regulation by the bank regulators, some of these are: (a) to prevent or reduce bank failures and promote banking stability and (b) to reduce losses to depositors and the deposit insurance company or insurer of lender of last resort when the bank fails. Capital norms were narrowly understood till 1980, when utility of bank capital in the crisis and financial panics as Kindleberger calls them was seen in guidelines issued by USA Federal Deposit Insurance Corporation in 1981 for banks and further adoption of Basel Capital Norms for most of the countries during the 1990s (Nachane et al. 2000).

Since 2008, USA financial crisis took toll on many financial institutions including banks in North America and Europe continents, emphasizing need for recapitalization of banks exposed to risk of insolvency. Views on market generated capital requirement differ from that of regulatory requirement or historical requirement (Berger et al. 1995). In India, Banking Regulation Act, 1949, stipulated the minimum paid-up capital requirement for banks of different types, irrespective of risk exposure. Recently, the RBI has been pressing its importance in consideration of high NPAs, bank exposure to securitization and off-balance-sheet activities and limited budget allocation (Nair 2017).

Basel I was a framework for calculating 'Capital to Risk-Weighted Asset Ratio (CRAR)'. It defines a bank's capital as two types: core capital termed as Tier-I Capital which consists of paid-up capital, statutory reserves and other disclosed free reserves not for any specific liability and capital reserves (surplus generated from sale of capital assets). Second tier is non-core termed as Tier-II Capital which consists of undisclosed reserves and paid-up capital perpetual preference shares, revaluation reserves (at discount of 55%), hybrid (debt or equity) capital, subordinated debt, general provisions and loss reserves. Subordinated debt is in the form of fully paid-up, unsecured debt instrument subordinated to the claims of other creditors and redeemable at the expiration or option of issuing bank. An important stipulation here is that Tier-II Capital cannot exceed 50% of Tier-I Capital for arriving at the prescribed Capital Adequacy Ratio.

While implementing Basel I norms it indicated some inadequacies and regulatory flaws in prudential regulation and thus Basel II was introduced for a comprehensive framework of banking supervision. Besides, CRAR calculation it mandated supervisory review and bank assets to market discipline. Thus, Basel II stands on three pillars, namely (a) minimum capital, (b) supervisory review, transparency and accountability, and (c) market discipline.

Minimum regulatory capital (Pillar 1)—the RBI introduced a revised and extensive framework for capital adequacy standards, where CRAR is calculated by incorporating credit, market and operational risks.

Supervisory review (Pillar 2)—it provides key principles for supervisory review, risk management guidance and supervisory transparency and accountability.

Market discipline (Pillar 3)—it encourages market discipline by developing a set of disclosure requirements to be used by market participants to assess key information on risk exposure, risk assessment process and capital adequacy of a bank.

In the year 1992–1993, the Narasimham Committee submitted its first report and recommended in compliance with Basel Norms I that all the banks are required to have a minimum capital of 8% to the risk-weighted assets of the banks. Capital Adequacy Ratio is defined as the ratio of bank's capital (net worth) to its risk assets and known as CRAR. All the 27 public sector banks in India (except UCO and Indian Bank) had achieved the Capital Adequacy Norm of 8% by March 1997. The Second Report of Narasimham Committee was submitted in the year 1998–1999. It recommended the CRAR to be raised to 10% in a phased manner. It recommended an intermediate minimum target of 9% to be achieved by the year 2000 and 10% by 2002.

In February 2005, the RBI issued the first draft guidelines on Basel II implementations in which an initial target date for Basel II compliance was set for March 2007 for all commercial banks, excluding Local

Area Banks (LABs) and Regional Rural Banks (RRBs). According to the RBI guidelines on Basel II implementation, Indian banks were required to maintain a minimum CRAR of 9% on an ongoing basis as against international benchmark of 8% initially suggested. The undercapitalised Indian banking companies faced challenges of full implementation of Basel II guidelines—the revised capital norms mandated by the Bank for International Settlements (BIS) by 31, March 2009, in order to maintain adequate capital reserves in each year (Chandrasekhar 2008). Basel II mandates CRAR of 8%. However, for keeping a slight cushion in bank capitalization, the RBI prescribed a CRAR of minimum 9% for Indian commercial banks effective from 31, March 2009. Further enlarging this cushion of net worth, the Government of India stated that public sector banks must have a capital cushion with a CRAR of at least 12%, higher than the threshold of 9% prescribed by the RBI. Significantly, the level of capital ratio in the Indian banking system compares quite well with the banking system in many other countries. However, although all Indian commercial banks complied with this statutory requirement with a CRAR of more than the stipulated requirement, a few banks had to seek capital from the Union Government or raise capital from the market through public issues to meet this requirement.

Advantage of capital adequacy standards is clear in the sense that it deemed to control risk appetite of the bank by aligning the incentives of bank owners with depositors and other creditors. Capital adequacy is an indicator of the sound financial health of banking system. Since banks are the main pillars of financial system, it has traditionally been regarded as a sign of strength of the financial system. Minimum capital standards are thus a vital tool to reduce systemic risk. According to Section 17 of the India's Banking Regulation Act (1949), a banking company incorporated in India is required to transfer a minimum of 20% of declared profit to a reserve fund in each year while the RBI has advised to transfer 25–30% to the reserve fund. The RBI advised the banks to operate above the minimum regulatory capital ratios to withstand any unexpected panic-driven crisis. It also initiated appropriate preventive measures to prevent capital from falling below the minimum.

Under Basel Norms I, all the commercial banks irrespective of risk class attained double-digit capital ratio and maintained with 1% band around the mean and so was the case under Basel Norms II. In 2015, each bank maintained about 8% of core capital (Tier-I) as against 6% desired, slightly above 10–12% of total capital, obviously keeping an excess of minimum stipulation.

Bank credit was growing in excess of 15% on annual basis since 1995 and hence banks required additional capital to maintain CRAR stipulation. Setting aside provisions for loan defaults out of profits, there was no consistency in maintenance of CRAR across banks every year and hence, variation in net worth became a common feature. It is a noteworthy revelation of the fact that banks were not uniform in applying health code to corporate credits leading to concealment of the quality of loans and risk inherent in such assets. Hence, true net worth of banks may be at variance with those declared values in balance sheet and needs uniformity in mechanism to reflect true adjustment of real risk of assets.

Governance: Transparency and Disclosures

Assets Quality: In view of state ownership of banks, political intervention became common after 1970 from controlling interest rates to loan disbursal on various discretionary criteria. Specific factors were responsible for deteriorating loan quality of banks. For instance, absence of monitoring the repayment of bank loans, poor legal and administrative mechanism for loan recovery, compliance with politically determined credit targets and occasional loan waiving schemes were some of the major issues in quality of loan assets. Accounting rule followed the concepts of 'income earned' instead of 'income accrued' to overstatement of profits in income and expenditure statement of banks. The RBI introduced 8 health codes for bank loan accounts in November 1985, signalling useful information relating to irregularity, quality of loans and extent of recovery problem. Loan accounts were classified as satisfactory, irregular, sick and viable, sick and non-viable, advances recalled, suit filed accounts, decreed debt and bad and doubtful debt. Though this guideline created awareness, information and initial framework to deal with the loans in defaults, it proved to be inadequate for the purpose in view of complex and cumbersome legal framework of loan recovery.

The theory of NPAs is based on fundamentals of risk associated with credit. Among others, the two main factors that explain the credit risk are recession in growth and asymmetric information. Unforeseen recession in growth adversely affects sales (cash flow) of commercial firms characterizing slowdown or delayed or defaults in repayment of bank debt. Defaults or irregular servicing of loan, therefore, attributed to persistent low growth. Another attribute is projects' information unevenly shared between bank and borrower firm—the former knowing very little about project risk as against the latter knowing all about it (information asymmetric problem). Tendency of the borrower firm to undertake projects with greater return involving high credit risk (moral hazard) induces bank to lend more for such projects in order to maximize profits (adverse selection). Theoretical origin of bad loans (NPAs) lie in the presence of these two factors in credit market that means credit default problems arise from enhanced systematic (market) risk and non-systematic (assets specific) of borrowed credit.

Following the Basel norms of international practices, the Committee on the Financial System (Chairman, Shri. M. Narasimham) recommended and the Reserve Bank of India accordingly introduced prudential norms for greater transparency and consistency in the statement of income and expenditure as well as in balance sheet items (assets and liabilities). Hence, income recognition on an accrual basis, asset classification according to health codes and risk-related provisioning for the credit portfolio of the banks all became mandatory since 1992 and were implemented gradually over the feasible time frame objectively determined by the RBI in consultation with other stake holders. In order to ensure consistency, uniformity and objectivity, the RBI defined Prudential Norms on Income Recognition, asset classification and provisioning pertaining to Advances.

Classification of Non-performing Assets

An asset, including any loan or an advance, treated non-performing when it fails to generate income for bank. For detailed specifications in definition, it stated that an asset is treated NPAs in the following cases: (i) overdue of interest and or instalment of principal for more than 90 days in a term loan, (ii) the account remains 'out of order' (if the outstanding balance remains continuously in excess of the sanctioned limit and drawing power for 90 days) in respect of an Overdraft and Cash Credit, (iii) the overdue bills (purchased discounted) for more than 90 days, (iv) overdue of the principal or interest for two crop seasons for short-duration crops and for one crop season for long-duration crops, (v) the amount of liquidity facility remains outstanding for more than 90 days, in respect of a securitization transaction undertaken in terms of guidelines on securitization dated February 1, 2006, and (vi) in respect of derivative transactions, the overdue receivables representing positive mark-to-market value of a derivative contract, if these remain unpaid for a period of 90 days from the specified due date for payment.

Categories of NPAs: According to the RBI circular, effective from 31, March 2005, banks are required to classify non-performing assets (based on duration of non-performance and potential for dues realization) into the three categories, namely

1. Substandard Assets: NPA for a period less than or equal to 12 months and likely to sustain loss due to credit weakness.
2. Doubtful Assets: Asset remained in the substandard category for a period of 12 months.
3. Loss Assets: Loss of assets identified by the bank, or auditors or the RBI as uncollectible, unbankable with salvage value but not written off in accounts of bank.

Banks accumulated NPAs due to recession as happened in post 2008–2009 periods. In other countries, it happened because of the financial crisis in 1997 such as Czech Republic (Cimburek et al. 2009). Banks in South East Asian countries also reported high NPAs during crisis of 1996–1997. Indian public sector banks showed very high ratio, some of them more than 20% during first phase reforms from 1993 to 2000. Since then there were fluctuating NPA ratio for individual banks with considerable variation among public sector banks, private domestic banks and foreign banks. Emphasis on cleaning balance sheet of banks by the RBI affected public sector banks as viewed in increasing NPA ratio into double-digit range: a concern to be addressed in various ways including securitization, Corporate Debt Restructuring (CDR), provisioning, legal method (seizure and auction of assets to recovery of NPAs), etc.

Securitization of debt is a process of pooling together bank loans with common characteristics (size, maturity, type of borrower and interest rate) and assets involved can be sold for cash to other banks or investors, Asset Reconstruction Company (India) Ltd. (ARCIL). According to the RBI guidelines, banks can sell NPAs to ARCIL or other investors in cash only. But securitization in India has a short history since 1992 and remained narrowly developed in view of institutional constraints. First initiative by setting up of Assets Reconstruction Company in public sector in 2002 was indeed a long-felt need to promote securitisation base. In discrete market with few participants, there were mixed trend visible in securitisation transactions over the years. Recently there was a slowdown in securitization as volume declined to Rs. 17,200 crores in 2015 from Rs. 28,800 crores in 2014 and from Rs. 37,876 crores in 2012. Banks in India were reluctant to opt for securitization deals in view of poor institutional set-up, inadequate incentives mechanism and little concern for transparency in assets classification and preferred to adopt Strategic Debt Restructuring (SDR) route or retain bad loans on the balance sheet.[7] Whenever banks found their large amount of funds locked with poor recovery in loans advanced for financing housing, consumer goods purchases, credit card transactions, etc., securitization deals helped banks to get liquidity through sale of such non-performing loans from 1991 to 2015. Sometimes high discount was used to make transaction return attractive.

CDR is available to bank creditors to resolve the NPAs in cases of heavily indebted firms. It is quite challenging and equally difficult for creditors' to convince borrower firms to participate in CDR and the debt obligations mutually acceptable. The CDR mechanism is a voluntary non-statutory system based on custom-tailored contract and consent of lenders. These are Debtor-Creditor Agreement (DCA) and Inter-Creditor

Agreement (ICA). The principle of approvals is sought by majority decisions of 75% creditors (in value) that are binding on the remaining 25% creditors. The CDR mechanism covers debt amount outstanding Rs. 10 crores and more in multiple banking accounts, syndication and consortium accounts. It covers all categories of assets in the books of member-creditors classified in terms of the RBI's prudential asset classification standards. Besides, it has also court cases filed for recovery in various agencies. The cases of restructuring of standard and substandard classes of assets are covered in Category-I, while cases of doubtful assets are covered under Category-II.[8]

In order to protect the erosion in the net worth of banks, provisioning for loan loss was required. Consequently depending on classification grade of loans, provision norms were applied ranging from 0 to 100%.

Income Recognition and Provision Policy

As suggested by the Narasimham Committee to add transparency in income and expenditure statement, accounting in banks was changed to eliminate missing income and assets. For this, banks were directed to follow income recognition concept and strictly adhered to it, in reporting income on the 'income actually received' basis unlike 'income earned and accrued' basis in past till 1991. It is suggested as an important internationally accepted practice in Basel norms. The Basel norms intended to clean balance sheet from the burden of non-performing assets of banks and introduce provisioning of NPAs as a compensating measure for loss of quality of assets and loss of income of such assets. Its provisioning is ranging between 25% in case of doubtful assets up to 1 year to 40% for such assets beyond 1 year but up to 3 years and 100% in case of more than 3 years. Similarly provisions were required to be made by the banks for other loan assets and foreign exchange exposures as well as country risk from less than 1–100% according to Export Credit Guarantee Corporation (ECGC) classification of country risk. It is monitored by Provisioning Cover Ratio (PCR)—ratio of provisioning to gross non-performing assets.

This ratio indicates the proportion of funds kept aside by a bank to cover loan losses due to NPAs.

From a macroprudential perspective to maintain sound health of banking system, banks are expected to build up provisioning reserves and capital buffers in good times and use the same to absorb losses of bad years. Accordingly, it was determined to attain at least 70% PCR by September 2010 in order to augment the provisioning buffer for the soundness of individual banks as also the stability of the financial sector. Progress in attaining 70% PCR is proved quite challenging in view of surging NPA level into double digit and beyond this range.

Legal Approach to Assets Recovery

In order to minimize the delays and cost of recovery of bad loans, banks take recourse to all feasible approaches. In addition to Lok Adalat, compromise settlements and recovery tribunals, banks were approaching civil courts to file recovery suits for NPAs. Civil recovery suits were very costly in terms of time delays, fees and legal charges, and cumbersome procedural mechanism. Thus, following the Adhyarujina Committee's recommendation, Securitization and Reconstruction of Financial Assets and Enforcement of Security Interest (SARFAESI) Act, 2002, was passed to enable banks without recourse to civil courts, recover long-term assets, manage the problem of liquidity, reduce asset liability mismatches and improve recovery by taking possession of securities, selling them and reducing NPAs. To supplement the SARFAESI Act, certain other reforms were undertaken to accelerate loan recovery process which was hindered earlier under BIFR and SICA. In order to eliminate unnecessary legal constraints and also to improve recovery process further, the SARFAESI Act 2002 and Recovery of Debts Due to Banks and Financial Institutions (RDDBFI) Act 1993 have been amended by the Parliament. Besides, Scheme for Sustainable Structuring of Stressed Assets (S4A), the Insolvency and Bankruptcy Code were introduced during 2015–2016 for facilitating resolution of rising bad loans. All these legal initiatives, securitization, provisioning, etc., proved effective in curtailing the rampant wilful defaulters' problems and improving the quality of assets.

Conclusion

Since bank nationalization in 1969, Indian banking has been subjected to dominance of government ownership along with development seeking credit allocation experiments and controls impacting the quality of balance sheet, income and cost. In addition, it gradually acquired distinct features of operation rigidity, inefficiency stemming from administered interest rate system and peak-level reserve ratios locking assets in cash and low yield, poor or negative net worth, low productivity from manual (labour-intensive) technology, and dismal governance record from lack of transparency and disclosures. In view of these adverse and distorting characteristics, banking reforms were called for urgent implementation in order to infuse flexibility and improve the working performance with functional diversification, adapting to global service benchmarks and practices, restructuring business segments and branches to ensure financial soundness and better technology. Since 1991, interest rate liberalization completed, variable reserve ratio slashed to the near statutory minimum level, disclosures and transparency introduced, and entry barriers lowered for new banks. Though the banking reforms covered substantial areas but further reforms needed to capture the unexplored areas such as to restructure branches and business for reason of efficiency and competitive organization, minimize information asymmetric hazard to keep NPAs under control, introduce greater transparency and disclosures for uniformity in financial statements, upgrade ATMs, computerization and technology software for real-time bank service delivery. Challenges of financial globalization need to be converted into new banking opportunities by suitable reforms dealing with risk and cyber security, competition in urban and coordination in rural areas of bank operation, scale advantages, product innovation, governance-related best banking practices and service delivery benchmarks. Changes in banking regulation consistent with new developments in banking sector have also added stability and dynamism in the economy.

Notes

1. RBI (2016, May 5).
2. RBI (2010, August 11).
3. Joshi and Little (1996, Chap. 4, pp. 109–169).
4. Reserve Bank of India (1985, Chap. 10, pp. 173–183).
5. RBI Master Circular DBOD. No. Dir. BC. 13/13.03.00/2014-15 dated July 1, 2014 (RBI 2014).
6. Reserve Bank of India (1985, Chap. 13, pp. 245–256).
7. RBI norms to hit loan securitization market: ICRA, MINT May 13, 2015 (ICRA 2015).
8. www.cdrindia.org.

References

Berger, Allen N., R.J. Herring, and G.P. Szego. 1995. The Role of Capital in Financial Institutions. *Journal of Banking and Finance* 19 (3): 393–430.

Bhole, L.M. 1985. Administered Interest Rates in India. *Economic and Political Weekly* XX (25/26): 1089–1104.

Bishnoi, T.R. 1995. Empirical Evidence on Fine Tuning of Monetary Policy and Economic Fluctuations in India. In *Indian Economy During the Eighties*, ed. V.N. Kothari. Vadodara: Department of Economics, The Maharaja Sayajirao University of Baroda.

Chandrasekhar, C.P. 2008. India's Sub-Prime Fears. *Economic and Political Weekly* 43 (32): 8–9.

Cimburek, J., M. Kollar, L. Komarek, and P. Ez Abek. 2009. *Resolving Nonperforming assets in the Czech Republic: Theory and Practice*. CESifo DICE Report 3/2009.

Das, Ashish. 2011. A Rational Savings Bank Deposit Interest Rate in India. *IIT Bombay Technical Report*. Mumbai.

Dewatripont, Mathias, and Jean Tirole. 1994. *The Prudential Regulation of Banks*. The Walrus-Pareto Lectures. December, MIT.

Goldstein, Morris. 1997. *The Case for an International Banking Standard*. Washington, DC: Institute for International Economics.

Goodhart, Charles, Philipp Hartmann, David Llewellyn, Liliana Rojas-Suarez, and Steven Weisbrod. 1998. *Financial Regulation: Why, How and Where Now?* London and New York: Published in Association with Bank of England, Routledge.

Hanson, J.A. 2004. *Public Sector Banks and Their Transformation*. World Bank.

ICRA. 2015. RBI Norms to Hit Loan Securitization Market. *MINT*, May 13.

Joshi, Vijay, and I.M.D. Little. 1994. *India: Macroeconomics and Political Economy, 1964–1991*. Washington, DC: The World Bank and Oxford University Press.

Joshi, Vijay, and I.M.D. Little. 1996. *India's Economic Reforms 1991–2001*. New Delhi: Oxford University Press.

Khan, M.Y., and T.R. Bishnoi. 2001. *Banking Crisis and Financial Reforms: Lessons for India*. Chartered Secretary, January.

Klein, Michael A. 1971. A Theory of the Banking Firm. *Journal of Money, Credit and Banking* 3 (2): 205–218.

Nachane, D.M., Aditya Narain, Saibal Ghosh, and Satyananda Sahoo. 2000. Capital Adequacy Requirements and the Behaviour of Commercial Banks in India: An Analytical and Empirical Study. Department of Economic Analysis and Policy, Reserve Bank of India, Mumbai, September, Development Research Group Study No. 22.

Nair, V. 2017. Rajan Calls for Revamp of Bank Regulations. *MINT*, August 17.

Rangarajan, C. 2007. *The Indian Banking System—Challenges Ahead*. Mumbai: Indian Institute of Banking and Finance, July 7.

Reserve Bank of India. 1985. *Report of the Committee to Review the Working of Monetary System*. Mumbai, India.

Reserve Bank of India. 1991. *Report of the Committee on the Financial System*. Mumbai, India.

Reserve Bank of India. 2010. *Entry of New Banks in the Private Sector—A Discussion Paper*, August 11.

Reserve Bank of India. 2014. *Master Circular—Interest Rates on Advances Refer to the Master Circular DBOD. No. Dir. BC. 13/13.03.00/2014-15 Dated July 1, 2014*.

Reserve Bank of India. 2016. *Draft Guidelines for 'on tap' Licensing of Universal Banks in the Private Sector*, May 5.

Singleton, John. 2011. *Central Banking in the Twentieth Century*. New York: Cambridge University Press.

Watkins, Leonard L. 1936. The Variable Reserve Ratio. *Journal of Political Economy* 44 (3): 339–373.

www.cdrindia.org.

3

Restructuring and Consolidation—Mergers and Acquisitions

Introduction

This chapter provides a complete historical account of mergers and acquisitions (M&As) strategy of Indian commercial banks since 1991 and its impact on performance of banks involved. In addition to this, a brief sketch of pre-reform M&A activities in Indian banking from 1969 to 1990 also added to complete the scenario. This M&A process was a desired step in the direction to have few mega banks in the post-reform structure as envisaged by Banks Bureau Board and Central Government to cope with challenges of globalization and achieve growth for new banks as suggested by Narasimham Committee.

The M&A activities and the determinants thereof in the Indian banking gained more importance after reforms and thus adopted as a method of consolidation and restructuring of banking system. The terms M&As are often used interchangeably in financial literature though both are different type of transaction in legal and financial arena. In the case of merger, two separate entities combine and both parties involved in the deal merge their equity shares with common stock in a single, combined entity. In the case of an acquisition,

© The Author(s) 2017
T.R. Bishnoi and S. Devi, *Banking Reforms in India*, Palgrave Macmillan Studies in Banking and Financial Institutions, DOI 10.1007/978-3-319-55663-5_3

the acquirer entity buys the equity stocks or assets of the firm being acquired (seller or target entity). Choice of merger or acquisition depends on opportunities of such deals under prevalent regulation and economic environment.

Currently the Reserve Bank started working on the framework for on-tap licensing as well as differentiated bank licenses. The intent is to expand the variety and efficiency of players in the banking system while maintaining financial stability. To say, a major perspective is that the Reserve Bank will also open to banking mergers, provided competition and stability are not compromised.

In microeconomics literature, M&As have been considered as one of the measures of consolidation, restructuring and strengthening of banks. Motives of M&As in the banking sector generally vary from change of ownership to enhancing size for efficiency gains; that is, to enlarge the size to tap economies of scale in banks or to prevent the bank failure. In the context of this process becoming a very popular in financial sector and particularly for Indian banking, the policy of M&As needs to be examined on the basis of acquirer's performance that is necessary for survival in the global economic environment.

This chapter examines the RBI's policy of M&As of the banks from the perspective of efficient banking structure. The focus of this chapter was to evaluate performance of the banks that went for mergers during and after the financial sector reforms. The main emphasis is to see whether M&As by the banks contribute to overall growth and economies of scale and efficiency of the banks. In the next section, a brief theory of M&As is discussed. The regulatory framework of M&A in India is provided in another section. It is relevant here to provide a review of literature followed by trends of M&As and impact thereof to know efficacy of this measure.

Mergers and Acquisitions: Theory, Objectives and Empirical Evidences

According to the Securities and Exchange Board of India (SEBI), the objectives of the firms that opted for mergers may be as follows: (i) to change in management, (ii) to change in control, (iii) substantial acquisition, (iv) consolidation of the firms, (v) merger or buyout of subsidiaries for size and efficiency, etc.

There were several theoretical prepositions to justify M&As in an industry. According to Hay and Morris (1991), different motives drive mergers and takeovers activities that can be classified on the basis of type of transactions or type of markets involved. Among the type of transactions involved, four subcategories are agreed mergers, management buyouts, divestments and contested takeovers. Regarding the type of markets, three subcategories are horizontal mergers, vertical integration mergers and conglomerate mergers. The agreed mergers are voluntarily in approach, having the benefit of growth in size, realization of cost economies and tax gains. It could be within group to enlarge the size of firm relevant in globalized economy. In management buyout, managers often take over distressed firms to protect employment and avoid insolvency of firms. Divestments take place in the form of spin-off or split-off of the company assets and sold to others in order to restructure business for competitiveness. Sale of firm's entire assets is also treated as divestments. These help in revenue generation or achieving core competency in business. Core competency of firm by restructuring process is a common method in emerging market economies as well as in transition economies. Contested takeovers are hostile acquisitions of equity of firms when these are highly undervalued due to stock market imperfections. Undervalued firms in marketplace become the takeover targets as these are likely to generate benefits in future. Horizontal mergers are primarily a route to inorganic growth to gain the market size and to achieve cost economies and profits, obviously without capacity addition (Marris 1964; Manne 1965). Vertical mergers are integration of businesses to create forward and backward linkages for transaction cost advantage and tax saving purposes. In banking, independent subsidiaries, dealing in housing finance, infrastructure finance, project finance, financial technology or software, etc., are merged with parent banks. Conglomerate acquisitions are helpful in creating large business group, for example in financial sector universal banking business (Lintner 1971; Levy and Sarnat 1970; Lewellen 1971). Rezaee (2001) in an overview study of USA banking M&As provided a list of motivations for M&As, justification and reasoning drawn from empirical researches there. These include economies of scale (reduction in cost, increase in productivity, output and efficiency), inefficient management (buyout inefficient by efficient management), re-engineering and market power, and geographic and product diversification (enhanced revenue and profitability and risk moderation). Jensen and Ruback (1983) reported evidence of economies of scale resulting from several M&A deals in USA. In a different view, Grossman and Hart (1981) give the argument that takeover occurs due to undervaluation of a company in the stock market.

Implications of these M&As are many and varied depending on the type of markets and economic development of the country. Among the positive benefits, some of the notables are improvement in capacity utilization leading to fall in cost per unit, large-scale operation associated with research and development, and risk diversification in business and faster growth. In contrast, increase in market power enhancing monopoly element in prices and supply constraints, hostile takeover and change in management, elimination of rival firms and the absence of competition are important negative consequences adversely affecting public welfare (Bishnoi and Rajamohan 2004).

A recent research has also highlighted economic, financial, cultural and psychological factors which together contribute to the performance of the twenty-first-century M&As. Among the several waves of M&A mostly was confined to US market, the wave of mergers during 1991–2001 and from 2003 to 2008 was a global phenomenon as it spreads from North America to Asian market countries due to deregulation, technological and financial innovations, low interest rates (cheap money) and globalization (Killian and Dolfsma 2013). Another study focused on domestic and cross-border transactions of M&As in banks of European Union in post-deregulation era particularly since 1996 indicated a wave-like acceleration to reach peak level in such activities in 1999 leading to formation of few mega banks or financial conglomerates in Euro countries. Obvious implication was an enhanced banking concentration in few big financial firms. These M&As found to be spread across Euro countries that reflected a structural shift towards the big size of both domestic and pan-European mega-banking groups. The underlying trend revealed a profound and dynamic response to deregulation and formation of common banking market. When examined effectiveness of M&As in terms of value creation for shareholders, the large majority of M&As carried out at global level in Europe or in the USA fail to report expected value creation in the short run of 2 years duration. Almost three-fifth of the M&As completed were failures in stock market performance and 70% of mergers were unsuccessful in producing any business benefit as regards shareholders' value is concerned. However, banks of similar size and also banks with domestic retail business involved in M&As gained cost efficiency. In case consolidation of banks reached saturation limit or when concentration level peaked to over 70%, then banks explored M&A opportunities abroad for enlarging revenue scale and enhancing profitability. Conclusion of the study is that 'big is beautiful' is not an absolute criterion for efficiency and profitability, but it is rather a product mix, and target consumers (retail loans to individuals/wholesale credit to firms) are important attributes (Ayadi and Pujals 2005). In M&A literature, an equally debatable issue is the target companies those are either poorly managed entities or highly undervalued ones. Hannan and Rhoades (1987) rejected the hypothesis that poorly managed firms are more likely acquisition targets than other firms. There exist evidences of acquiring firms used mergers as a vehicle to increase their market share and profits (Phillips and Pavel 1986), or M&As occur to overcome geographical limits on bank expansion (Piper and Weiss 1974). Also it was found that profitability measured by return on equity and core-deposit growth of acquired banks had consistently important effects on a merger premium (Hunter and Wall 1989). Rose (1988) found that important factors driving mergers' activities were increases in profitability, market share, growth rate, market power, and stock price and a decrease in tax liabilities. Besides, new business opportunities make takeover of banks a viable option to enter and penetrate in segment (Cheng et al. 1989). However, there was no clear evidence supporting the diversification for risk reduction (Asquith and Kim 1982) and no synergy effect (Mueller 1980) arising from M&A actions in few other cases studied.

Among the many determinants of bank M&A, the important identified by the studies were deregulation, easing entry restrictions, fair value standards, technological development facilitating better communication, risk management, internet banking and data processing.

Because of rising concentration level in financial sector, expanding range of financial services leading to earning power, low interest rates and abundant funds in the form of monopoly capital (private equity, venture fund, etc.) rising economic growth, all created a favourable environment for mergers and takeovers in banks across continents.

Two important issues of M&As deals were: (1) What bank(s) are potential targets for acquisition and (2) what prices were paid for acquired banks. It was discovered that motivation and determinant by value maximization factors such as profitability, sales and earnings growth (Palepu 1986). Studies of the prices paid (premiums) in bank M&As (Cheng et al. 1989; Rhoades 1987) found that the price-to-book paid for a bank increased with the profitability of the acquired and decreased with the acquired bank's capital-to-asset ratio and return on assets. Other empirical studies of M&A transactions found evidence in support of the several hypotheses that: (1) seller earned positive abnormal returns while acquirer (bidding) bank experience negative abnormal returns; (2) banks that made larger acquisitions perform better than banks making small acquisitions; (3) bank takeover valuations (price-to-book) have increased; and (4) number of banks has declined, concentration increased but size of M&A deals has increased.

Various studies on the effect of bank mergers on performance have been conducted in many countries with mixed results. Mixed evidences were reported on the costs and benefits analysis of bank M&As. Different tools and banking parameters were used by analysts for measuring the bank performance. Some studies (Shaffer 1993; Akhavein et al. 1997) found that mergers can potentially lower costs and increase profit efficiency, while others (Berger and Humphrey 1994; Rhoades 1993) concluded that mergers have not resulted in any significant post-merger improvements in efficiency and accordingly found that horizontal mergers during 1980–1986 did not improve the total cost efficiency.

In an earlier study, Alhadeff and Alhadeff (1955) examined bank mergers completed in 208 US banks between January 1953 and mid-1954. They analysed the causes of mergers and attempted to determine their relative importance in the ongoing merger movement. Bank-by-bank basis data shows that the causes initiating mergers were management, cost and profit ratios, branch banking, growth rates, legislation, antitrust laws and market structures. The study shows that acquisition by large and middle size banks were of mainly small banks during the period.

Rhoades and Yeats (1974) analysed US commercial banks with a stratified random sample of 600 commercial banks over the period 1960–1971. It was an attempt to update the Alhadeff's findings to see whether their major conclusion still holds and also to determine the impact of mergers on growth. Their findings supported the Alhadeff's findings that large banks grow less than the system as a whole. The regressions fitted for bank consolidation yielded unambiguous results and concluded that deconsolidation occurred in the banking industry over the period 1960–1971.

Peristiani (1997) investigated the effect of bank mergers on the efficiency and financial performance of merger survivors. This study utilized translog flexible functional form to estimate the cost structure of banks and derive measures of efficiency. Empirical findings indicated that X-efficiency was fairly constant across all other size, except for large banks. In contrast to X-efficiency, scale efficiency was more variable across the different size groups. Therefore, it appeared that mergers were not beneficial to banks in terms of X-efficiency during the1980s.

Focarelli et al. (2002) analysed all the M&As, both as separate events, among Italian banks for a period of 1985–1996. Profitability for mergers increased because of the efficient use of capital, although the increase in income from services is offset by the higher staff costs. For acquisitions, the increase in profitability for the acquired banks was linked to the improvement in the quality of their loan portfolio. Their findings are consistent with the hypothesis that expanding revenues from financial services is a strategic objective for the mergers.

Kalhofer and Badreldin (2010) analysed the performance of Egyptian banks that had undergone M&As during the period 2002–2007. The study concluded that M&As were without clear effect on the profitability of banks in the Egyptian banking sector. However, there were minor positive effects on the credit risk position.

To say, various studies have given varied conclusions. While some adds value to the performance of the banks after mergers, others are of the view that mergers retard growth, reduces profitability and raise credit risk position level of the merger banks.

Regulatory Framework and Trend in Mergers and Acquisitions

The regulatory framework for M&As in the banking sector in India is provided by the Banking Regulation (BR) Act, 1949. The Act provides for two types of amalgamations, namely (i) voluntary and (ii) compulsory. The RBI has the discretionary power to approve the voluntary amalgamation of two banking companies under Section 44(A) of the BR Act. As per the compulsory amalgamations are concerned, these are induced or forced by the Reserve Bank under Section 45 of the BR Act, in public interest, or in the interest of the depositors of a distressed bank, or to secure proper management of a banking company, or in the interest of the banking system. In this regard, the amalgamation will become effective on the date indicated in the notification issued by the government. In the case of voluntary M&A of any financial business by any banking institution, there was no provision under the BR Act for obtaining approval of the Reserve Bank. Guidelines regarding the process of merger proposal, determination of swap ratios, disclosures, and buying and selling norms of shares before and during the process of merger are laid down by the RBI for voluntary mergers involving banking companies as well as between non-banking and banking companies.

Till 1960, banks' amalgamations took place on voluntary basis under Section 44A of the BR Act, 1949, as there was no other provision of law. Though there was urgent need to strengthen banking system by eliminating the unviable small and weak banks, the result in respect of voluntary bank amalgamation was very poor and discouraging. In view of this, RBI acquired statutory powers through an amendment in Act in 1960 for reconstruction or compulsory amalgamation of banks. Since then, amalgamations were on voluntary basis with approval of the RBI (Section 44A of Act) wherever possible, and compulsion wherever necessary (Section 45 of the Act). Section 45 of the Act specifies the provision under which a bank to be reconstructed or amalgamated compulsorily, by the RBI in consultation with Central Government in the case of banks which are weak, unsound or not possibly managed.

The RBI's policy is to encourage amalgamation to protect generally the interest of depositors in particular and strengthen the banking structure in the area in general. RBI also encourages banking integration through the transfer of assets and liabilities of small and unsound, weak and small units into larger and strong banking units.

In terms of Section 36 AE of the BR Act, the Central Government has power, with the consent report from RBI, to acquire or nationalize any banking unit in the interest of the depositors, in the interest of banking policy or for the better provision of credit generally of any particular section of the community.

Thus, 14 big banks were nationalized in 1969 to strengthen Public Sector Undertaking (PSU) dominance and alter structure on ownership criterion. It was assumed that this process might contribute to a more efficient and optimal banking structure. Thus, the restructuring and consolidation through strategy of M&As is a continuous process to improve the working of Indian banking towards optimal structure in terms of size distribution, multiple ownership and organizational diversity.

From 1960 to June 1982, 20 voluntary amalgamations; 49 compulsory mergers; 18 mergers with SBI and its associates; and 130 transfers of assets and liabilities were completed. Prior to 1969, Indian banking system was very weak and dominated by small unviable banks owned by various business houses. So, in 1960, the RBI was empowered to bring compulsory mergers and integrations. In post 1960 period, there were a large number of compulsory mergers (particularly 30 in 1961) and integration (transfer of assets/liabilities for 62 in 1964). The elimination of weak banks helped to boost economic efficiency and financial integrity leading to an improved banking structure. It is to be noted that the RBI policy is quite objective in that it allows the development of both sizes of banks simultaneously as small and large banks are equally efficient. The M&A activities in Indian banking are directed to consolidate the system to attain optimal structure, i.e. rationalize, decentralize, reallocate and reorganize the banking units.

Table 3.1 shows the list of banks merged after banks nationalization of 1969 till the period before the financial sector reforms. Twelve cases, all involving public sector banks, were allowed to merge during the period. The main motive here was to strengthen the banking sector through

Table 3.1 Banks amalgamated since nationalization of banks in India: 1969–1990

S. No.	Date of merger	Merging bank	Merged with	Motive of merger	Type of merger
1	08/11/1969	Bank of Bihar Ltd.	State Bank of India	Restructuring of weak bank	Compulsory
2	02/20/1970	National Bank of Lahore Ltd.	State Bank of India	Restructuring of weak bank	Compulsory
3	29/07/1985	Miraj State Bank Ltd.	Union Bank of India	Restructuring of weak bank	Compulsory
4	24/08/1985	Lakshmi Commercial Bank Ltd.	Canara Bank	Restructuring of weak bank	Compulsory
5	26/08/1985	Bank of Cochin Ltd.	State Bank of India	Restructuring of weak bank	Compulsory
6	19/12/1986	Hindustan Commercial Bank Ltd.	Punjab National Bank	Restructuring of weak bank	Compulsory
7	13/05/1988	Traders Bank Ltd.	Bank of Baroda	Restructuring of weak bank	Compulsory
8	31/10/1989	United Industrial Bank Ltd.	Allahabad Bank	Restructuring of weak bank	Compulsory
9	20/01/1990	Bank of Tamilnadu Ltd.	Indian Overseas Bank	Restructuring of weak bank	Compulsory
10	20/02/1990	Bank of Thanjavur Ltd.	Indian Bank	Restructuring of weak bank	Compulsory
11	20/02/1990	Parur Central Bank Ltd.	Bank of India	Restructuring of weak bank	Compulsory
12	29/08/1990	Purbanchal Bank Ltd.	Central Bank of India	Restructuring of weak bank	Compulsory

Source RBI: Report on trend and progress of banking in India, 2008

Table 3.2 Mergers and amalgamations of Indian commercial Banks: 1991–2010

S. No.	Date of merger	Merging bank	Merged with	Motive of merger	Type of merger
1	04/09/1993	New Bank of India	Punjab National Bank	Restructuring of weak bank	Compulsory
2	01/01/1996	Kashi Nath Seth Bank Ltd.	State Bank of India	Restructuring of weak bank	Compulsory
3	08/04/1997	Bari Doab Bank Ltd.	Oriental Bank of Commerce	Restructuring of weak bank	Compulsory
4	08/04/1997	Punjab Cooperative Bank	Oriental Bank of Commerce	Restructuring of weak bank	Compulsory
5	03/06/1999	Bareilly Corporation Bank Ltd.	Bank of Baroda	Economies of scale & scope	Voluntary
6	22/12/1999	Sikkim Bank Ltd.	Union Bank of India	Restructuring of weak bank	Compulsory
7	26/02/2000	Times Bank Ltd.	HDFC Bank Ltd.	Economies of scale & scope	Voluntary
8	10/03/2001	Bank of Madura Ltd.	ICICI Bank Ltd.	Economies of scale & scope	Voluntary
9	03/05/2002	ICICI Ltd.	ICICI Bank Ltd.	Universal banking	Voluntary
10	20/06/2002	Benares State Bank Ltd.	Bank of Baroda	Restructuring of weak bank	Compulsory
11	01/02/2003	Nedungadi Bank Ltd.	Punjab National Bank	Restructuring of weak bank	Compulsory
12	25/06/2004	South Gujarat Local Area Bank Ltd.	Bank of Baroda	Restructuring of weak bank	Compulsory

(continued)

Table 3.2 (continued)

S. No.	Date of merger	Merging bank	Merged with	Motive of merger	Type of merger
13	14/08/2004	Global Trust Bank Ltd.	Oriental Bank of Commerce	Restructuring of weak bank	Compulsory
14	02/04/2005	IDBI Ltd.	IDBI Bank Ltd.	Economies of scale & scope	Voluntary
15	01/10/2005	Bank of Punjab Ltd.	Centurion Bank Ltd.	Economies of scale & scope	Voluntary
16	02/09/2006	Ganesh Bank of Kurundwad Ltd	Federal Bank Ltd.	Restructuring of weak bank	Compulsory
17	03/10/2006	United Western Bank Ltd.	IDBI Bank Ltd.	Restructuring of weak bank	Compulsory
18	31/03/2007	Bharat Overseas Bank Ltd.	Indian Overseas Bank	Economies of scale & scope	Voluntary
19	19/04/2007	Sangli Bank Ltd.	ICICI Bank Ltd.	Economies of scale & scope	Voluntary
20	29/08/2007	Lord Krishna Bank Ltd.	Centurion Bank of Punjab Ltd.	Economies of scale & scope	Voluntary
21	23/05/2008	Centurion Bank of Punjab Ltd.	HDFC Bank Ltd.	Economies of scale & scope	Voluntary
22	13/08/2010	The Bank of Rajasthan	ICICI Bank Ltd.	Economies of scale & scope	Voluntary

Source RBI: Report on trend and progress of banking in India, various issues

compulsory amalgamation in order to weed out unviable banks by liquidation or by taking over of assets of the non-functioning banks by other banks. It is the prevention of bank failures to avoid panic and elimination of unviable banking units. This way, so the RBI carried out consolidation through compulsory amalgamation and merger before the reform period.

Table 3.2 shows the list of banks that went for mergers during the reform period from 1991 to 2010. In all, there are 22 cases of bank mergers—11 cases of compulsory mergers and the rest 11 mergers of voluntary type. A special case of voluntary mergers is that of ICICI Bank and IDBI Bank where the process is of reverse merger to strengthen a case of universal banking. M&A were used in Indian banks as a long-term effective strategy in their restructuring process since 1991.

Analytical Framework

It covers the hypotheses, methodology comprising data and indicators, and the results.

Hypotheses The main objective is to examine whether the performance of banks has increased after mergers. Accordingly, below-mentioned hypotheses are formulated.

H_0 There is no significant change in the performance of banks after mergers.

H_1 There are significant changes in the performance of banks after mergers.

Methodology: The performance of the banks is analysed in terms of financial ratios such as profitability ratios, solvency ratios, efficiency and earning capacity of banks and growth rate of total assets. The financial performance indicator and its use are defined as:

1. Profitability Indicators: Measure overall performance.
2. Capital Adequacy Indicators: Measure bank's ability to meet its obligations relative to its exposure to risk.
3. Efficiency Indicators: Measure bank's ability to generate income, pay expenses and measure the productivity of employees.
4. Growth Indicators: Measure changes in bank's assets.

Table 3.3 Definition of performance ratios

Ratio	Definition
(i) Profitability indicators:	
• Return on Assets (ROA)	Ratio of profit after tax to total assets
• Return on Equity (ROE)	Ratio of net profit to average shareholders' equity
(ii) Solvency indicator:	
• Capital Adequacy Ratio (CAR)	Ratio of Tier-I Capital and Tier-II Capital to risk-weighted assets
(iii) Efficiency Indicators:	
• Spread	Net interest income as a percentage of total assets
• Operating cost/Total Assets	Total operating expenses as a percentage of total assets
• Profit per employee	Ratio of net profit to number of employees
(iv) Growth indicator:	
• Asset growth rate	Percentage change in book value of total assets in the previous year

The specific measures used to represent these factors are defined in Table 3.3. These indicators are used to identify whether merger has any improvement or bearing on the performance of the banks.

A comparison of the performance of post-merger with that of pre-merger allows measuring impact of the mergers. A benchmark of 3 years prior to merger and 3 years after the merger took place is taken as the appropriate duration impact. In other words, the financial data for each bank are collected for 6 years. The financial data for the year in which the merger occurred is omitted in counting. Only seven public sector banks and two new private sector banks are involved in M&A activities during the financial years from 1991 to 2010. These bidder banks in alphabetical order are as follows: the Bank of Baroda, IDBI Bank, Indian Overseas Bank, Oriental Bank of Commerce, Punjab National Bank, State Bank of India and Union Bank of India in case of public sector bank group and ICICI Bank and HDFC Bank, two banks under the new private sector banks group. The analysis is carried out keeping in view of the importance of individual merger for the acquirer bank. That is to say, each merger is treated as an independent event for its impact on bank's merger analysis. Thus, it is carried out for 1-year merger case or for 2-year merger cases or for 3-year or even 4-year merger cases. There are four banks each with a single merger event, namely Indian Overseas Bank, Oriental Bank of Commerce, State Bank of India and Union Bank of India. The three banks, each with two merger cases, are HDFC Bank, IDBI Bank and Punjab National Bank. Another two banks each with events of three mergers and four cases are Bank of Baroda and ICICI Bank. Detailed information of each of the bank's mergers and acquisitions is provided in Table 3.2.

The financial indicators are the profitability, solvency and efficiency. The average values of the selected financial parameters for the periods $T-3$, $T-2$ and $T-1$ are compared with its average values at $T+1$, $T+2$ and $T+3$ for each bank. In the next step, paired student t-test is performed to check the statistical significant of the two means of pre-merger and post-merger periods.

The formula of paired sample t-test is given by:

$$t = \left\{ \sum_{i=1}^{N} (X_0 - X_1)/N \right\} / \sigma \sqrt{N} \qquad (3.1)$$

where,

X_0 pre-merger performance of the bank (s)
X_1 post-merger performance of the bank (s)
N   number of parameters used in the sample
σ the standard deviation (S.D.) of the distribution of the change in performance of the merging banks.

By using the above-mentioned Formula (3.1), pre-merger and post-merger impact of the individual merging bank is measured on each of the performance indicators.

Pre- and Post-merger Performance of Banks

The results of the descriptive t-test for each of the merging banks are shown in Tables 3.4, 3.5, 3.6, 3.7, 3.8, 3.9, 3.10, 3.11 and 3.12. The tables are sequenced in alphabetical order rather than in chronological order of the years of merging event.

Table 3.4 Descriptive statistics of paired t-test for Bank of Baroda

Financial ratios	Period	Mean	St. Dev.	t-value	Prob.	Remark
Merger Case 1: Bank of Baroda merger, 1999						
ROA	Pre-merger	0.85	0.139	0.478	0.680	Not significant
	Post-merger	0.77	0.302			
ROE	Pre-merger	15.51	1.827	0.518	0.656	Not significant
	Post-merger	14.11	5.324			
CAR	Pre-merger	12.38	0.804	0.225	0.843	Not significant
	Post-merger	12.26	0.815			
Spread	Pre-merger	3.04	0.153	6.091*	0.026	Significant
	Post-merger	2.82	0.214			
OC/TA	Pre-merger	2.34	0.03	0.381	0.740	Not significant
	Post-merger	2.30	0.209			
Profit per employee	Pre-merger	0.84	0.204	−1.550	0.261	Not significant
	Post-merger	1.30	0.670			
Growth rate of assets	Pre-merger	17.87	5.551	4.397	0.142	Not significant
	Post-merger	9.88	2.981			
Merger Case 2: Bank of Baroda merger, 2002						
ROA	Pre-merger	0.70	0.220	−9.330*	0.011	Significant
	Post-merger	1.00	0.229			
ROE	Pre-merger	13.29	4.344	−23.099*	0.002	Significant
	Post-merger	17.24	4.103			
CAR	Pre-merger	12.73	0.603	−0.428	0.710	Not significant
	Post-merger	13.06	0.739			
Spread	Pre-merger	2.97	0.110	0.000	1.000	Not significant
	Post-merger	2.97	0.204			
OC/TA	Pre-merger	2.36	0.165	2.135	0.166	Not significant
	Post-merger	2.12	0.035			
Profit per employee	Pre-merger	0.86	0.244	−11.26*	0.008	Significant
	Post-merger	2.02	0.370			
Growth rate of assets	Pre-merger	10.13	2.936	−0.586	0.663	Not significant
	Post-merger	11.30	0.099			
Merger Case 3: Bank of Baroda merger, 2004						
ROA	Pre-merger	1.02	0.197	2.196	0.159	Not significant
	Post-merger	0.8	0.085			
ROE	Pre-merger	18.11	2.631	4.730*	0.042	Significant
	Post-merger	13.10	1.282			
CAR	Pre-merger	12.63	1.295	−0.157	0.889	Not significant
	Post-merger	12.80	0.933			
Spread	Pre-merger	2.81	0.191	1.090	0.390	Not significant

(continued)

Table 3.4 (continued)

Financial ratios	Period	Mean	St. Dev.	t-value	Prob.	Remark
	Post-merger	2.49	0.310			
OC/TA	Pre-merger	2.16	0.04	2.785	0.108	Not significant
	Post-merger	1.84	0.240			
Profit per employee	Pre-merger	1.77	0.326	−2.969	0.097	Not significant
	Post-merger	2.93	0.922			
Growth rate of assets	Pre-merger	9.57	2.549	−7.436	0.085	Not significant
	Post-merger	25.85	0.547			

*Significant at the 5% level

Bank of Baroda (BOB)

Table 3.4 reports the results of paired t-test of pre- and post-merger period for the Bank of Baroda. There are three cases of merger for the analysis of Bank of Baroda. Out of these three merger cases, two are compulsory mergers and one is voluntary merger of Bareilly Corporation Bank Ltd with Bank of Baroda in 1999. The robustness of results of paired sample t-test was partially valid in the sense that only three performance indicators, namely profitability measures, ROA and ROE, and profit per employee of the bank, are found to be significant at the 5% level. The other performance indicators, namely CAR, Spread, OC/TA and growth rate of assets, have insignificant t-values.

The second merger case relates to compulsory merger of the Benares State Bank Ltd in 2002. Result of the paired t-test shows that only three performance indicators, namely ROA, ROE and profit per employee, are statistically significant at 5% level and other indicators remaining statistically insignificant. The third case of merger of BOB occurred in 2004, a case of compulsory merger of South Gujarat Local Area Bank Ltd where none of the performance indicators except ROE is found statistically significant even though the mean values are somewhat improved in post-merger period for certain indicators.

In short, above three cases of mergers of small banks with large bank like BOB are likely to have very limited impact, and thus, a few of the performance indicators are statistically significant. Consistent improvement in three indicators, namely ROA, ROE and profit per employee, are found to be statistically significant in each case of the mergers while only increase in ROE is found statistically significant in the case of third merger.

HDFC Bank

For the HDFC Bank, two cases of merger both of voluntary type are analysed. The first case is merger of the Times Bank Ltd with it in 2000 and the second one is merger of the Centurion Bank of Punjab Ltd in 2008. Table 3.5 shows the results of paired t-test for both the merger cases. In both the merger cases of the HDFC Bank, even though most of the indicators show improvement in post-merger period, none of the indicators are found statistically significant.

ICICI Bank

Four banks or financial institutions are merged with ICICI Bank all in voluntary merger mode (Table 3.6). The first merger case was south-based Bank of Madura Ltd in 2001 with no significant impact visible on performance of acquiring bank as paired sample t-test shows all indicators statistically significant. The second merger case was that of ICICI Ltd with its subsidiary bank in 2002 and thus called reverse merger. Since this merger took place with a lapse of 1 year, no radical changes are found in the comparison of mean values for two periods. Sample paired t-test shows that the performance indicators ROA and ROE are statistically significant at the 5% level. The third case of acquisition by ICICI Bank was the Maharashtra-based distressed Sangli Bank Ltd in 2007. Contradictory results are found in this case of merger as against the expected results of merger. None of the indicators, except CAR and Spread, are found statistical significant at 5% level. The fourth acquisition case of ICICI Bank was a Rajasthan-based distressed small size entity, the Bank of Rajasthan merged with it in 2010. Except ROA, none of the performance indicators are found statistically significant.

Table 3.5   Descriptive statistics of paired *t*-test for HDFC Bank

Financial ratios	Period	Mean	St. Dev.	*t*-value	Prob.	Remark
Merger Case 1: HDFC Bank merger, 2000						
ROA	Pre-merger	1.99	0.212	4.076	0.055	Not significant
	Post-merger	1.48	0.035			
ROE	Pre-merger	21.35	1.938	0.833	0.492	Not significant
	Post-merger	19.97	1.291			
CAR	Pre-merger	12.66	1.106	1.880	0.200	Not significant
	Post-merger	12.24	1.491			
Spread	Pre-merger	3.21	0.545	0.785	0.514	Not significant
	Post-merger	2.84	0.281			
OC/TA	Pre-merger	1.91	0.397	0.188	0.868	Not significant
	Post-merger	1.86	0.084			
Profit per employee	Pre-merger	9.71	0.217	−0.272	0.811	Not significant
	Post-merger	9.74	0.350			
Growth rate of assets	Pre-merger	110.84	80.787	1.501	0.374	Not significant
	Post-merger	33.48	7.891			
Merger Case 2: HDFC Bank merger, 2008						
ROA	Pre-merger	1.34	0.032	−3.213	0.085	Not significant
	Post-merger	1.63	0.127			
ROE	Pre-merger	18.31	0.993	0.994	0.425	Not significant
	Post-merger	17.24	1.272			
CAR	Pre-merger	12.70	1.144	−4.022	0.057	Not significant
	Post-merger	16.73	0.636			
Spread	Pre-merger	3.73	0.243	−2.222	0.156	Not significant
	Post-merger	4.12	0.111			
OC/TA	Pre-merger	2.60	0.265	0.017	0.988	Not significant
	Post-merger	2.60	0.067			
Profit per employee	Pre-merger	6.16	1.210	−0.749	0.532	Not significant
	Post-merger	7.15	1.077			
Growth rate of assets	Pre-merger	35.05	15.45	0.955	0.515	Not significant
	Post-merger	23.26	2.02			

Since data is limited to till 2012, analysis was carried out for 2 years in each period.

To say in brief, in all the four merger cases, the performances are different. None of the indicators are statistically significant in the first case showing no impact, better performance on ROA and ROE is in

Table 3.6   Descriptive statistics of paired t-test for ICICI Bank

Financial ratios	Period	Mean	St. Dev.	t-value	Prob.	Remark
Merger Case 1: ICICI Bank merger, 2001						
ROA	Pre-merger	0.87	0.045	−2.982	0.096	Not significant
	Post-merger	1.34	0.232			
ROE	Pre-merger	16.53	4.823	−0.703	0.555	Not significant
	Post-merger	19.06	1.783			
CAR	Pre-merger	14.09	4.813	0.960	0.438	Not significant
	Post-merger	11.08	0.710			
Spread	Pre-merger	1.76	0.261	1.638	0.243	Not significant
	Post-merger	1.54	0.186			
OC/TA	Pre-merger	1.39	0.274	−3.690	0.066	Not significant
	Post-merger	1.97	0.085			
Profit per employee	Pre-merger	8.46	1.758	−2.468	0.132	Not significant
	Post-merger	11.33	0.577			
Growth rate of assets	Pre-merger	68.20	6.675	3.270	0.189	Not significant
	Post-merger	25.56	11.766			
Merger Case 2: ICICI Bank merger, 2002						
ROA	Pre-merger	0.79	0.104	−6.414*	0.023	Significant
	Post-merger	1.40	0.164			
ROE	Pre-merger	11.36	4.235	−11.24*	0.008	Significant
	Post-merger	18.04	3.376			
CAR	Pre-merger	14.22	4.697	0.686	0.564	Not significant
	Post-merger	11.83	1.496			
Spread	Pre-merger	1.39	0.752	−0.606	0.606	Not significant
	Post-merger	1.65	0.053			
OC/TA	Pre-merger	1.19	0.553	−2.823	0.106	Not significant
	Post-merger	1.93	0.139			
Profit per employee	Pre-merger	7.87	2.560	−2.411	0.137	Not significant
	Post-merger	11.00	1.00			
Growth rate of assets	Pre-merger	245.49	257.397	1.170	0.450	Not significant
	Post-merger	41.91	11.355			
Merger Case 3: ICICI Bank merger, 2007						
ROA	Pre-merger	1.32	0.261	0.649	0.583	Not significant
	Post-merger	1.15	0.186			
ROE	Pre-merger	15.45	3.007	3.163	0.087	Not significant
	Post-merger	8.46	1.041			
CAR	Pre-merger	12.27	0.934	−4.960*	0.038	Significant
	Post-merger	18.16	2.279			
Spread	Pre-merger	1.67	0.025	−9.341*	0.011	Significant
	Post-merger	2.24	0.083			

(continued)

Table 3.6   (continued)

Financial ratios	Period	Mean	St. Dev.	t-value	Prob.	Remark
OC/TA	Pre-merger	1.97	0.835	3.296	0.081	Not significant
	Post-merger	1.70	0.139			
Profit per employee	Pre-merger	10.00	1.00	0	1	Not significant
	Post-merger	10.00	1.00			
Growth rate of assets	Pre-merger	43.52	9.078	2.757	0.221	Not significant
Merger Case 4: ICICI Bank merger, 2010						
	Post-merger	3.80	11.299			
ROA	Pre-merger	1.06	0.106	−21.8*	0.029	significant
	Post-merger	1.60	1.141			
ROE	Pre-merger	7.87	0.134	−5.012	0.063	Not significant
	Post-merger	12.15	1.344			
CAR	Pre-merger	17.47	2.744	−0.634	0.640	Not significant
	Post-merger	18.63	0.156			
Spread	Pre-merger	2.20	0.007	−0.95	0.516	Not significant
	Post-merger	2.39	0.276			
OC/TA	Pre-merger	1.74	0.177	0.563	0.674	Not significant
	Post-merger	1.65	0.049			
Profit per employee	Pre-merger	10.00	1.414	−1.087	0.473	Not significant
	Post-merger	11.25	0.212			
Growth rate of assets	Pre-merger	-4.66	0.665	−10.247	0.062	Not significant
	Post-merger	0.10	0.007			

*Significant at the 5% level

the second case, deterioration in performance of CAR and Spread is reported in the third case, and higher ROA is realized in the fourth case in post-merger period. Hence, there is no substantial impact of these mergers on the ICICI Bank due to small size banks involved.

IDBI Bank

Two cases of mergers of IDBI Bank are important for analysis, one in 2005 and another in 2006 (Table 3.7). It is a case of voluntary but reverse merger of the IDBI, a long-term development financial institution with its own subsidiary IDBI Bank in 2005. Another case is a

Table 3.7 Descriptive statistics of paired t-test for IDBI Bank

Financial ratios	Period	Mean	St. Dev.	t-value	Prob.	Remark
Merger Case 1: IDBI Bank merger, 2005						
ROA	Pre-merger	0.90	0.12	4.446*	0.047	significant
	Post-merger	0.65	0.023			
ROE	Pre-merger	18.04	11.478	1.332	0.314	Not significant
	Post-merger	8.84	0.495			
CAR	Pre-merger	11.82	3.225	−0.251	0.825	Not significant
	Post-merger	12.42	1.153			
Spread	Pre-merger	1.77	1.337	1.310	0.320	Not significant
	Post-merger	0.65	0.161			
OC/TA	Pre-merger	1.90	0.747	3.108	0.090	Not significant
	Post-merger	0.80	0.173			
Profit per employee	Pre-merger	6.65	1.664	−2.258	0.152	Not significant
	Post-merger	8.57	0.248			
Growth rate of assets	Pre-merger	294.87	326.509	1.167	0.4509	Not significant
	Post-merger	28.89	4.278			
Merger Case 2: IDBI Bank merger, 2006						
ROA	Pre-merger	0.83	0.175	3.381	0.077	Not significant
	Post-merger	0.61	0.071			
ROE	Pre-merger	13.85	11.765	0.603	0.608	Not significant
	Post-merger	9.49	1.007			
CAR	Pre-merger	13.56	2.780	1.106	0.384	Not significant
	Post-merger	11.61	0.322			
Spread	Pre-merger	1.07	1.286	0.286	0.802	Not significant
	Post-merger	0.81	0.310			
OC/TA	Pre-merger	1.23	0.692	1.166	0.364	Not significant
	Post-merger	0.73	0.058			
Profit per employee	Pre-merger	9.17	2.922	0.343	0.764	Not significant
	Post-merger	8.57	0.248			
Growth rate of assets	Pre-merger	267.30	365.495	0.898	0.534	Not significant
	Post-merger	33.70	2.523			

*Significant at the 5% level

compulsory merger of United Western Bank with IDBI Bank in 2006. Paired t-test in case of first merger shows that only ROA is statistically significant because parent IDBI is very large relative to the bank merged with. Thus, no significance impact is witnessed in rest of the performance indicators. Quite similar results are observed in the case of second merger. The mean values of all the performance indicators except CAR are poor in post-merger period. And regarding the *t*-test result, none of the indicators are significant. To sum up, in both the merger cases, the impact on performance of the bank is poor even though operating cost ratio and profit per employee improved for the bank in the case of the voluntary merger.

Indian Overseas Bank (IOB)

One merger case is for from the Oriental Bank of Commerce that occurred in 2007, a case of voluntary merger of Bharat Overseas Bank. Even though it is a voluntary merger, poor performance is observed in most of the performance indicators in post-merger period. Sample paired *t*-test indicated that except Spread, none of the performance indicators showed significant impact (Table 3.8).

Table 3.8   Descriptive statistics of paired *t*-test for Indian Overseas Bank

Financial ratios	Period	Mean	St. Dev.	*t*-value	Prob.	Remark
Merger Case 1: Indian Overseas Bank merger, 2007						
ROA	Pre-merger	1.32	0.04	2.492	0.130	Not significant
	Post-merger	0.80	0.330			
ROE	Pre-merger	27.78	0.486	3.616	0.069	Not significant
	Post-merger	14.81	6.476			
CAR	Pre-merger	13.50	0.614	−0.795	0.510	Not significant
	Post-merger	14.18	0.854			
Spread	Pre-merger	3.72	0.085	10.275*	0.009	Significant
	Post-merger	2.60	0.108			
OC/TA	Pre-merger	2.03	0.307	2.744	0.111	Not significant
	Post-merger	1.64	0.223			
Profit per employee	Pre-merger	3.31	0.694	−0.720	0.546	Not significant
	Post-merger	3.99	1.292			
Growth rate of assets	Pre-merger	27.70	15.39	1.693	0.340	Not significant
	Post-merger	22.33	19.87			

*Significant at the 5% level

Table 3.9 Descriptive statistics of paired t-test for Oriental Bank of Commerce

Financial Ratios	Period	Mean	St. Dev.	t-value	Prob.	Remark
Merger Case 1: Oriental Bank of Commerce merger, 1997						
ROA	Pre-merger	1.53	0.133	2.918	0.100	Not significant
	Post-merger	1.03	0.208			
ROE	Pre-merger	22.23	1.695	2.709	0.114	Not significant
	Post-merger	18.16	3.956			
CAR	Pre-merger	17.26	0.382	8.835	0.071	Not significant
	Post-merger	12.45	0.389			
Spread	Pre-merger	3.83	0.049	11.072*	0.008	Significant
	Post-merger	2.97	0.110			
OC/TA	Pre-merger	2.27	0.189	4.993*	0.038	Significant
	Post-merger	1.88	0.125			
Profit Per employee	Pre-merger	1.19	0.234	−3.055	0.093	Not significant
	Post-merger	1.67	0.208			
Growth rate of Assets	Pre-merger	18.80	12.679	−1.400	0.395	Not significant
	Post-merger	20.48	14.378			
Merger Case 2: Oriental Bank of Commerce merger, 2004						
ROA	Pre-merger	1.33	0.351	0.409	0.722	Not significant
	Post-merger	1.21	0.185			
ROE	Pre-merger	24.47	4.220	3.250	0.083	Not significant
	Post-merger	10.03	3.510			
CAR	Pre-merger	13.17	1.897	0.692	0.561	Not significant
	Post-merger	12.36	0.212			
Spread	Pre-merger	3.38	0.312	2.636	0.119	Not significant
	Post-merger	2.29	0.435			
OC/TA	Pre-merger	1.64	0.07	1.998	0.184	Not significant
	Post-merger	1.39	0.228			
Profit per employee	Pre-merger	3.63	1.365	−3.015	0.095	Not significant
	Post-merger	5.61	0.235			
Growth rate of assets	Pre-merger	13.00	10.823	−1.224	0.436	Not significant
	Post-merger	24.06	1.958			

*Significant at the 5% level

Oriental Bank of Commerce (OBC)

Two merger cases are analysed for the Oriental Bank of Commerce: both are compulsory mergers. Results of the sample paired t-test of the bank for all the performance indicators reported that improvement in spread and OC/TA are found to be significant. No statistical significant is found in case of rest of the five performance measuring variables. For the second merger case, the performance indicators give similar results as that of first merger case. The paired *t*-test result indicated a statistically insignificant change in performance indicators (Table 3.9).

Table 3.10 Descriptive statistics of paired *t*-test for Punjab National Bank

Financial ratios	Period	Mean	St. Dev.	*t*-value	Prob.	Remark
Merger Case 1: Punjab National Bank merger, 1993						
ROA	Pre-merger	0.40	0.20	0.395	0.366	Not significant
	Post-merger	0.24	0.52			
ROE	Pre-merger	20.94	11.61	1.025	0.207	Not significant
	Post-merger	6.48	13.55			
Spread	Pre-merger	3.14	0.40	0.163	0.448	Not significant
	Post-merger	3.06	0.30			
OC/TA	Pre-merger	2.46	0.03	−3.813	0.081	Not significant
	Post-merger	3.07	0.20			
Profit per employee	Pre-merger	0.12	0.06	−0.755	0.529	Not significant
	Post-merger	0.20	0.13			
Growth rate of assets	Pre-merger	5.98	5.04	−1.64	0.174	Not significant
	Post-merger	10.49	1.15			
Merger Case 2: Punjab National Bank merger, 2003						
ROA	Pre-merger	0.83	0.134	−2.341	0.144	Not significant
	Post-merger	1.10	0.070			
ROE	Pre-merger	20.16	2.579	0.802	0.506	Not significant
	Post-merger	17.79	3.164			
CAR	Pre-merger	10.99	0.924	−1.564	0.258	Not significant
	Post-merger	13.01	1.545			
Spread	Pre-merger	3.33	0.256	0.814	0.501	Not significant
	Post-merger	3.26	0.123			
OC/TA	Pre-merger	2.60	0.303	23.568*	0.002	Significant
	Post-merger	2.24	0.309			
Profit per employee	Pre-merger	1.07	0.326	−13.31*	0.006	Significant
	Post-merger	2.53	0.136			
Growth rate of assets	Pre-merger	16.53	2.428	0.924	0.525	Not significant
	Post-merger	13.44	2.305			

*Significant at the 5% level

Punjab National Bank (PNB)

Two merger cases are studied for the Punjab National Bank. Both the cases are compulsory mergers. No statistically significant impact is found in any of the indicators. The performance of the bank in the second merger case is somewhat different. In the second merger case, two parameters, namely OC/TA and Profit per employee, are found to be significant at the 5% level. And the rest of the parameters did not have any significant t-values suggesting no impact (Table 3.10).

State Bank of India (SBI)

One merger case is analysed for the State Bank of India, which occurred in 1996 when a small bank, Kashi Nath Seth Bank Ltd, compulsorily merged with it. There is no sign of impact as the paired sample t-test for all the performance parameters of the SBI was not found significantly different in post-merger period (Table 3.11).

Table 3.11   Descriptive statistics of paired t-test for State Bank of India

Financial ratios	Period	Mean	St. Dev.	t-value	Prob.	Remark
Merger Case 1: State Bank of India merger, 1996						
ROA	Pre-merger	0.473	0.194	−1.021	0.415	Not significant
	Post-merger	0.750	0.290			
ROE	Pre-merger	14.007	3.878	−0.500	0.666	Not significant
	Post-merger	16.547	5.635			
Spread	Pre-merger	3.045	0.379	0.772	0.521	Not significant
	Post-merger	2.793	0.191			
OC/TA	Pre-merger	2.8967	0.232	1.720	0.228	Not significant
	Post-merger	2.5633	0.133			
Profit per employee	Pre-merger	0.263	0.127	−2.678	0.116	Not significant
	Post-merger	0.697	0.236			
Growth rate of assets	Pre-merger	13.902	6.391	−0.883	0.539	Not significant
	Post-merger	20.683	4.466			

Table 3.12 Descriptive statistics of paired *t*-test for Union Bank of India

Financial ratios	Period	Mean	St. Dev.	*t*-value	Prob.	Remark
Merger Case1: Union Bank of India merger, 1999						
ROA	Pre-merger	0.81	0.263	0.247	0.828	Not significant
	Post-merger	0.73	0.340			
ROE	Pre-merger	14.34	3.915	−0.270	0.813	Not significant
	Post-merger	16.06	7.502			
CAR	Pre-merger	10.49	0.386	−1.393	0.293	Not significant
	Post-merger	11.45	0.841			
Spread	Pre-merger	3.08	0.383	0.339	0.769	Not significant
	Post-merger	3.02	0.101			
OC/TA	Pre-merger	2.63	0.131	3.292	0.081	Not significant
	Post-merger	2.26	0.323			
Profit per employee	Pre-merger	0.67	0.251	−1.672	0.343	Not significant
	Post-merger	1.69	0.658			
Growth rate of assets	Pre-merger	12.69	1.455	−0.472	0.719	Not significant
	Post-merger	13.04	2.517			

Union Bank of India (UBI)

One case for a merger is recorded here, as Sikkim Bank compulsorily merged with Union Bank of India in 1999. Because of very small size of bank acquired, none of the performance parameters are found significant for the Union Bank of India (Table 3.12).

Reasons for Statistical Insignificant of Ratios

Profitability Ratios

From the individual table for each of the merged banks, it is observed that the profitability measures ROA and ROE are improved for some of the merged cases of banks in post-merger period. However, mean values of these ratios did not improve for all banks. The squeeze on profitability has been driven from expenditure side like increase in the interest costs of deposits, growing functional diversification of banks and rapid growth in the wages and salary of staff and accelerated promotions. An increase in profitability ratios of acquiring banks is adjusted enough to offset the losses of banks acquired. In addition, in majority of merger cases, each of the banks merged is too small to make impact on big size bank merged with.

Solvency Ratio

All the merged banks fulfilled the regulatory requirement CRAR of 9% level. This signified that the merged banks successfully managed to meet the increased requirement under the new regulatory framework. In other words, banks could absorb the operating losses of merged entities easily and ultimately squeeze of the profitability of banks. However, the average CRAR for some banks declined in the post-merger period, and these banks needed recapitalization with fresh funds in order to cope with new environment.

Insignificant coefficients of the profitability parameters and solvency ratios impacted on the growth performance of the assets of the banking firms. For example, the growth rate of the total assets is declined after mergers for one of the merging banks (PNB).

Other Ratios

Non-performing assets (NPAs) have been the major track with varying importance for each bank's performance. Besides, slow adoption of technology across the banking functions and branches has delayed the accrual of benefits of big size. Business restructuring and manpower restructuring imposed the additional cost in some of the banks covered here. Thus, given all these capital intensive advances associated with modernization of banks in post-reform era, it is not certain to have noticeable positive impact on performance of banks involved in mergers.

Table 3.13 Summary of the descriptive statistics of statistically significant ratios

Acquiring bank	ROA	ROE	CAR	Spread	OC/TA	Profit per employee	Asset growth rate
Compulsory merger cases							
BOB (case2)	Significant	Significant	X	X	X	Significant	X
BOB (case3)	X	Significant	X	X	X	X	X
OBC (case1)	X	X	X	Significant	Significant	X	X
PNB (case2)	X	X	X	X	Significant	Significant	X
Voluntary merger cases							
BOB (case1)	X	X	X	Significant	X	X	X
ICICI (case2)	Significant	Significant	X	X	X	X	X
ICICI (case3)	X	X	Significant	Significant	X	X	X
ICICI (case4)	Significant	X	X	X	X	X	X
IDBI (case1)	Significant	X	X	X	X	X	X
IOB	X	X	X	Significant	X	X	X

Source Tables 3.4, 3.5, 3.6, 3.7, 3.8, 3.9, 3.10, 3.11 and 3.12

Conclusion

Table 3.13 provides bank-wise statistically significant mean difference of each performance indicator—pre- and post-merger from 1991–2010.

In all the nine merging banks with total 18 cases of mergers, there was no consistency in trend as there appear to be different performance in various cases of mergers. Table 3.13 shows the summary statistics of statistical significant ratios for the merging banks. Regarding indicator ROA, it is found statistical significant in one merger case of the Bank of Baroda and two merger cases of ICICI Bank. Regarding the second indicator, ROE, statistical significant is found for Bank of Baroda and ICICI Bank only. ROE is found significant in two cases of mergers for BOB and one merger case for ICICI Bank. Regarding the CAR and profit per employee indicators, statistical significant is recorded for three cases only, i.e. ICICI Bank, Bank of Baroda and Punjab National Bank. In the case of indicator Spread, statistical significant ratios are observed for more number of banks. These banks are Bank of Baroda, ICICI Bank, Indian Overseas Bank and Oriental Bank of Commerce. For the ratio OC/TA, only two banks show statistically significant values. These banks are Oriental Bank of Commerce and Punjab National Bank.

In brief, different indicators show statistical significant impact for each of the merger cases. For example, spread shows the maximum number of statistical significant, covering four out of the nine merging banks. Other indicators have a limited significance. These statistically significant performance indicators are ROA and ROE in the case of BOB and ICICI Bank, respectively. Though mergers and acquisitions may be theoretically sound but its impact on profitability, capital and growth rate is not significant as expected. Generally, the strategy of M&A focuses on long-term gains and not in short-term objectives. Hence, the null hypothesis that there is no significant improvement after merger is accepted in majority of the merged cases with few exceptions as reported in summary table above. That is, the null hypothesis is rejected only in few cases (Table 3.13).

Further, when results are classified as compulsory mergers cases and voluntary mergers cases separately, there is no difference as more or less equal number of significant ratios is seen for both categories. This indicates that in Indian banking sector merging banks seem to be of very small relative to the size of bank merged with so as to make impact insignificant irrespective of type such as compulsory and voluntary cases. Even when looked at performance of control period (normal years without M&A transactions) of a bank, results of this study remain unchanged.

In conclusion, the strategy of mergers and acquisitions may be good for restructuring in terms of number of banks but to consolidate the banks for efficiency reason is doubtful. The future banking policy must take note of this empirical reality and long-drawn experience of M&As during past 2 decades.

References

Akhavein, J.D., Allen N. Berger, and David B. Humphrey. 1997. The Effects of Megamergers on Efficiency and Prices: Evidence from a Bank Profit Function. *Review of Industrial Organization* 12 (1): 95–139.

Alhadeff, C.P., and D.A. Alhadeff. 1955. Recent Bank Mergers. *The Quarterly Journal of Economics* 69 (4): 503–532.

Asquith, K.P., and E.H. Kim. 1982. The Impact of Merger Bids on the Participating Firm's Security Holders. *The Journal of Finance* 37 (5): 1209–1228.

Ayadi, Rym, and G. Pujals. 2005. *Banking Mergers and Acquisitions in the EU: Overview, Assessment and Prospects*, No. 2005/3 in SUERF Studies, The European Money and Finance Forum.

Berger, Allen N., and David B. Humphrey. 1994. Bank Scale Economies, Mergers, Concentration, and Efficiency: The US Experience. In *Finance and Economics Discussion Series*, 94–23, Board of Governors of the Federal Reserve System (US).

Bishnoi, T.R., and R.R. Rajamohan. 2004. Mergers, Acquisitions and Takeovers in India—An Analysis of Effects on Corporate Sector. In *Competiveness of Indian Industry—Empirical Studies*, ed. P. Verma and T.R. Bishnoi. New Delhi: Wisdom Publications.

Cheng, David C., Benton E. Gup and Larry D. Wall. 1989. Financial Determinants of Bank Takeovers: Note. *Journal of Money, Credit and Banking* 21 (4): 524–536.

Focarelli, D., F. Panetta, and C. Salleo. 2002. Why Do Banks Merge? *Journal of Money, Credit and Banking* 34 (4): 1047–1066.

Grossman, S.J., and O.D. Hart. 1981. The Allocational Role of Takeover Bids in a Situation of Asymmetric Information. *Journal of Finance* 36 (2): 253–270.

Hannan, T.H., and S.A. Rhoades. 1987. Acquisition Targets and Motives: The Case of the Banking Industry. *Review of Economics and Statistics* 69 (1): 67–74.

Hay, D.A., and D.J. Morris. 1991. *Industrial Economics and Organization: Theory and Evidence*, 2nd ed. Oxford: Oxford University Press.

Hunter, William C., and Larry O. Wall. 1989. Bank Merger Motivations: A Review of the Evidence and an Examination of Key Target Bank Characteristics. *Economic Review* (September/October): 2–19.

Jensen, M.C., and R.S. Ruback. 1983. The Market for Corporate Control: The Scientific Evidence. *Journal of Financial Economics* 11 (1–4): 5–50.

Kalhofer, C., and A. Badreldin. 2010. The Effect of Mergers and Acquisitions on Bank Performance in Egypt. *The Journal of Economic Policy and Research* 6 (1): 74–85.

Killian, J. McCarthy, and W. Dolfsma. 2013. *Understanding Mergers and Acquisitions in the 21st Century: A Multidisciplinary Approach*. Basingstoke: Palgrave Macmillan.

Levy, H., and M. Sarnat. 1970. International Diversification of Investment Portfolios. *American Economic Review* 60 (4): 668–675.

Lewellen, W. 1971. A Pure Financial Rational for the Conglomerate Merger. *The Journal of Finance* 26 (2): 521–537.

Lintner, J. 1971. Expectations, Mergers and Equilibrium in Purely Competitive Securities Markets. *American Economic Review* 61 (2): 101–111.

Manne, H.G. 1965. Mergers and the Market for Corporate Control. *Journal of Political Economy* 73 (2): 110–120.

Marris, R. 1964. *The Economic Theory of Managerial Capitalism*. London: Macmillan.

Mueller, D.C. 1980. *The Determinants and Effects of Mergers: An International Comparison*. Cambridge, MA: Oelgeschlager, Gunn and Hain.

Palepu, K. 1986. Predicting Takeover Targets: A Methodology and Empirical Analysis. *Journal of Accounting and Economics* 8 (1): 3–35.

Peristiani, S. 1997. Do Mergers Improve the X-Efficiency of U.S. Banks? Evidence from the 1980s. *Journal of Money, Credit and Banking* 29 (3): 326–337.

Phillips, D., and C. Pavel. 1986. Interstate Banking Game Plans: Implications for the Midwest. *Economic Perspectives*. Federal Reserve Bank of Chicago, (March/April): 23–39.

Piper, T.R., and S.J. Weiss. 1974. The Profitability of Multibank Holding Company Acquisitions. *The Journal of Finance* 29 (1): 163–174.

Rezaee, Zabihollah. 2001. *Financial Institutions, Valuations, Mergers, and Acquisitions: The Fair Value Approach*, 2nd ed. Newyork: Wiley

Rhoades, S.A. 1993. Efficiency Effects of Horizontal (In-Market) Bank Mergers. *Journal of Banking & Finance* 17 (2–3): 411–422.

Rhoades, S.A. 1987. The Operating Performance of Acquired Firms in Banking. In *Issues after a Century of Federal Competition Policy*, ed. R.L. Wills, J.A. Casewell, and J.D. Culbertson, 277–292. Lexington, MA: Lexington Books.

Rhoades, S.A., and A.J. Yeats. 1974. Growth, Consolidation and Mergers in Banking. *The Journal of Finance* 29 (5): 1397–1405.

Rose, Peter S. 1988. *Bank Mergers in a Deregulated Environment: Scrutinizing the Promises, Avoiding the Pitfalls*. Rolling Meadows, IL: Bank Administration Institute.

Shaffer, S. 1993. A Test of Competition in Canadian Banking. *Journal of Money, Credit and Banking* 25 (1): 49–61.

4

Concentration and Competition

Introduction

This chapter analyses the degree of competition and concentration in Indian banking system with particular focus on public sector banks having more than 70% of the total shares of deposits and advances of scheduled commercial banks. One of the objectives of financial reforms, focusing mainly banking sector, was to promote competition and efficiency. Privatization of public sector banks, issue of new bank licenses and M&As were attempted to further this above objective. Both the structural and non-structural methods are used in measurement of concentration and competition. This chapter begins with an overview of banking concentration at global level followed by empirical evidences in select studies on diverse aspects of market structure from 1991 to 2013. It gives a brief review of the vast literature on competition and concentration in banking systems of various countries or group of countries surveyed at regional and global levels over the period. Data, methods of measurement and interpretation of empirical results are given at the end. The last section gives a conclusion.

© The Author(s) 2017
T.R. Bishnoi and S. Devi, *Banking Reforms in India*, Palgrave Macmillan Studies in Banking and Financial Institutions, DOI 10.1007/978-3-319-55663-5_4

Since 1991, efficiency-induced structural changes became inevitable in the Indian banking. These changes, in sequence of broad financial reforms, occurred gradually due to many factors—prudential regulation and transparency, deregulation of interest rates and privatization of state-owned banks, M&As along with entry of new domestic private- and foreign-owned banks, enforcing banks to adopt international service benchmarks as competitive practices, etc. Historically, RBI's regulation policy intended to consolidate banking system by M&As to eliminate or rehabilitate the existing weak banks. Thus, there was a spate of M&As. Since Independence, consolidation by M&As remained in vogue, either voluntarily or compulsory to cleanse sick units among banks under close supervision of Reserve Bank of India. In recent 2 decades, it quickened involving more than 20 cases including couple of big size banks such as ICICI Bank and IDBI Bank through reverse merger of parent firms that were important development financial institutions so far. Entry of new private sector bank was banned for long period till 1993 when the RBI issued new bank licenses. So, there are multiple objectives for permitting the entry of new banks: promotion of competition, advanced technology and financial innovations, financial inclusion, restructuring banking system, etc. Basel Norms of prudential regulation proved to be a game-changer where banks' net worth and assets quality were linked with risk management. The three-phase Basel norms were implemented as prudential regulation in response to globalization of financial markets and also deal with challenges of post-World Trade Organization (WTO) agreement. Generally, consolidation is considered as an antidote to bank failures as it is expected to contribute to bank efficiency and strengthening of the banking system as a whole. Indian firms' 'Going Global' slogan also strongly influenced consolidation process of the banks as size became important, though with enhanced concentration for stability in the financial markets. The significance of bank concentration for banking stability is known from the fact the analysis of different crisis episodes revealed that crises are less likely in more concentrated banking systems.

Enhancing competition in the banking sector has been an important objective of financial sector reforms so as to achieve the overall efficiency and stability of the financial system. Objectives of greater competition are to increase efficiency, productivity, innovations and eventually financial stability. Competition is an essential ingredient of financial sector development strategy. The degree of competition is an important aspect of financial sector functioning and economic growth (Claessens and Laeven 2004). After the initiation of financial sector reforms, competition among banks, non-banks and other financial institutions has increased in India. Its impact has been felt in terms of cost-based pricing of services, narrower spreads and improvement in quality of services with the increased use of better technology and introduction of innovative new products and services in the market. Competition among commercial banks has also increased with the entry of new private sector banks and the permission granted to foreign banks to increase their number of branches in the nineties. For the domestic Public Sector Banks (PSBs), competition expected to increase with the relaxation of many guidelines and principles, which allow them to shift their portfolios for optimizing the ultimate objectives. Increased bank competition raises the level of income and reduces the severity of business cycles (Smith 1998). Competition does not mean the physical presence of banks but simply that they can handle the entire market freely. Competition does not necessarily require many financial institutions because a concentrated system can be competitive if it is contestable (Claessens and Klingebiel 2001). Intense competition lowers the probability of a systematic banking crisis in a country and thus tends to be good for public welfare as banks operate with a thin profit margin. Besides, strong legal and institutional framework, good governance and transparency are equally essential for competition and consolidation. Poor disclosures and compliance with RBI directives and guidelines, and lack of transparency can lead to information asymmetry, thereby increasing risk and uncertainty to stakeholders. These risks may be operational risk, contagion risk and systematic risk which increase the chance of financial fragility and adverse effects on fiscal and monetary policy (Beck et al. 2003).

Market concentration is a standard yardstick of competitiveness and efficiency of the firms in the industry. In the recent years, competition in the banking sector tends to rise and consequently it appears that the market structure of the banking sector tends to change. In other words, the number of banks has become reasonably large but the dominance still lies in the hands of a few large PSB. Such banks occupied a large share of deposits and advances, leading the entire market system. Price-based or non-price-based factors are very moderately operating leading to low competition among banking firms. Technology is regarded as one of the most important factors that pushed up competition among banks. For example, increasing use of ATMs, Internet and mobile banking is the solid indication of technology penetration. Banks, therefore, have been introducing innovative products and services for seeking newer sources of income, diversifying into non-traditional activities and economizing on capital. Banks can now spread their coverage to different income earners with different types of business of home, car and consumer loans. To gain the competitive strength, size also matters in order to reap the benefits of economies of scale. So, it is often argued that M&As that have taken place with accelerated pace during past two decades were driven by competitive pressures generated among firms. The competition would thus depend on the degree of concentration, entry barriers, the range and heterogeneity of products, price differentiation allowed, the outreach of branch network and the use of technology.

Here competition in banking sector does not imply microscopic type. It is rather a competition among few big banks with numerous medium and small size banking entities. The policy imperative assumed to attain a proper balance between working concentration and healthy competition in the banking system.

There was a series of reforms in Indian banking system to bring structural changes in the post-reform period. All these changes are expected to have positive impact on the overall competition of the banking sector. The process of consolidation leads to enhanced concentration—with fair competition among the banks. The *k*-firm concentration ratios, Herfindahl-Hirschman Index (HHI), Theil's Entropy, Lerner Index, etc., are some of the popular yardsticks of measuring bank concentration and competition.

Bank Concentration at global Level: It is relevant to look at the trend in banking concentration at global economy. Table 4.1 gives the concentration ratio of three largest firms in total assets in several countries. A

Table 4.1 Trend in banking concentration ratio across countries

Country	1991	1998	2006	2013
Advanced economies				
Singapore	0.86	0.85	0.96	0.84
Germany	0.55	0.67	0.62	0.60
Spain	0.71	0.76	0.40	0.93
France	0.60	0.55	0.23	0.31
Australia	0.89	0.58	0.62	–
Canada	0.71	0.47	0.66	0.61
United Kingdom	0.56	0.61	0.46	0.45
The Netherlands	0.55	0.83	0.80	0.96
Korea, Rep.	0.58	0.86	1.00	–
Japan	0.32	0.32	0.88	0.95
Italy	0.69	0.56	0.39	0.25
USA	0.20	0.22	0.33	0.35
Emerging market economies				
South Africa	0.99	0.80	0.99	0.98
Israel	0.85	0.74	0.77	–
China	0.91	0.56	0.36	0.39
Turkey	0.83	0.58	0.92	0.91
Indonesia	0.72	0.40	0.28	0.30
Philippines	0.83	0.75	0.72	0.75
Brazil	0.94	0.40	0.62	0.71
Malaysia	0.42	0.30	0.76	0.71
Thailand	0.56	0.50	0.99	0.97
Argentina	0.76	0.32	0.50	0.66
India	0.46	0.35	0.25	0.28
Russian Federation	0.99	0.72	0.24	0.08

Source Reserve Bank of India. 2006-2008. Report on Currency and Finance, Volume 1, Mumbai
The World Bank: Global Financial Development Database

cross-country analysis indicates that concentration ratios in total assets declined between 1991 and 2013 in various countries which included among others China, Indonesia, India, etc. In some advanced countries such as USA, Japan, Germany, the Netherlands and Spain, it increased over the period although the concentration ratio in USA was low. The concentration ratio in Indian banking system (0.28) was far lower relative to that of other emerging nations except Russian Federation (0.08) in 2013. In India, the largest three firms share about 25–30% of the total market shares. Concentration ratios suggest heterogeneous banking structure in advanced and emerging market economies with higher monopoly element in majority of countries. Case of perfect competition is a rare phenomenon in the real instance with the presence of high oligopoly element or monopolistic competition in USA, Italy, France, India, China, Indonesia, etc. Studies in the bank competition and concentration in past two decades also support this conclusion as most of the market structures are found to be monopolistic with certain exceptions—some cases of monopoly and very few monopolistic competition markets. The values of HHI also support the pattern of concentration ratios. In 2004, the lowest concentration in terms of HHI is for USA followed by Germany and highest being in Spain among the advanced economies. India has the lowest HHI values in the sample of emerging nations, indicating a greater degree of banking competition (Table 4.2).

Table 4.3 highlights the scenario of banking structure covered in select studied in some of countries. The monopolistic competition was the distinct market feature during the 1990s and in subsequent decades as noted by different studies for cross section of countries over a period of time. In general, in majority of these countries, banking market is best described as monopolistic competition with the exception being Japan and Italy.

Table 4.2 Herfindahl-Hirschman Index across countries

Country	1998	2004
Advanced economies		
USA	117	157
Germany	245	283
United Kingdom	339	493
Italy	489	542
France	399	682
Spain	854	1188
Emerging market economies		
India	720	541[e]
Malaysia	1317	1334
Chile	974	1462[c]
Mexico	1542[a]	1529[d]
South Africa	1310[b]	1840[e]
Brazil	2164[a]	3352

Note [a]for 2000; [b]for 2001; [c]for 2002; [d]for 2005 and [e]for 2006
Source RBI: Report on Currency and Finance, 2008

Table 4.3 Studies on *H*-statistic of select countries

Study	Country	Period	*H*-statistic
Shaffer (1982)	New York	1979	Monopolistic competition
Nathan and Neave (1989)	Canada	1982–1984	(1982)—Perfect competition; (1983–1984)—Monopolistic competition
Molyneux et al. (1994)	France, Germany, Italy, Spain and UK	1986–1989	Monopoly—Italy; Monopolistic competition—other countries
Molyneux et al. (1996)	Japan	1986–1988	Monopoly
Bikker and Groeneveld (1998)	15 EU Countries	1989–1996	Monopolistic competition
Bikker and Haaf (2002)	23 OECD Countries	1988–1998	Monopolistic competition
Gelos and Roldos (2004)	Argentina, Brazil, Chile, Czech Republic, Mexico, Hungary, Poland, and Turkey	1994–1999	Monopolistic competition
Claessens and Laeven (2004)	50 countries (both developed and developing)	1994–1901	Monopolistic competition
Prasad and Ghosh (2005)	India	1996–1904	Monopolistic competition

Empirical Studies

There is ample number of studies conducted over the period that comprises literatures on banking competition and concentration across the countries. Many studies attempted to measure competition over time using both structural and non-structural models. Notwithstanding the studies yielding varied conclusions with regard to competitive behaviour of banking firms for past decades using different methods, there is a need to look at this unsettled issue in the context of reforms unshackling potential competition in India. Studies surveyed below are inconclusive in view of their heterogeneous results with clear exposition of various degrees of firm concentration governed by the conditions of market structures. The literature on the measurement of competition may be divided into two main streams—the structural and the non-structural methods. Under the structural approach, measurement of competition encompasses the Structure-Conduct-Performance (SCP) paradigm and the efficiency hypothesis with roots in the Industrial Organization Theory. The SCP paradigm asserts that firms are able to earn higher profits in concentrated markets because they can resort to oligopolistic behaviour and collusive arrangements. Structure and performance are positively related because firms in higher concentrated market are supposed to have collusive behaviour and greater market power, resulting in better market performance and increasing profit (Goldberg and Rai 1996). The commonly used methods are the HHI, k-firm concentration ratios and the other structure-conduct-performance models. In the SCP paradigm, as stated above, the structure of the financial market determines the conduct of its participant banking firms and affects their performance. 'Structure of the financial market' means the concentration in supply side with considerable degree of product differentiation and market entry barriers. Here market structure implied size distribution of participating banks in the industry assuming that these distribution parameters are quite stable over time and affect the conduct of constituent firms. 'Conduct' refers to the strategic behaviour of firms in terms of making loans and investment, price of product and service, degree of innovation, advertisement and collusion. 'Performance' refers to the efficiency and profitability of firms and this relates to price margin, allocation efficiency and credit risk management. In the SCP model, basic indicator of market power is the HHI, which measures the degree of market concentration. It assumes that market structure affects banks' behaviour within regulatory framework, which in turn determines their performance. The idea is that banks with larger market shares may have more market power and use it to its advantage as a smaller number of big banks make collusion more likely. To test the SCP hypothesis, performance (profit) is explained by market structure (as measured by the HHI). The advantage of the SCP paradigm is that it provides a very clear structure-based analytical framework deriving performance of firms from conduct governed by the

degree of market competition. On the other hand, the efficient structure hypothesis states that the market behaviour of firm largely depends
on the operational efficiency of the firm. The efficient firm may have
some competitive advantages; hence, it can increase its size and market
share and realize better performance.

In view of the theoretical and empirical deficiencies of the structural models described above, the non-structural models of competitive
behaviour have been developed, namely the Iwata model, the Bresnahan
model and the Panzar and Rosse (P-R) model, which test competition
and market power in the absence of structural measures.

These studies are organized in the sequence of structural and non-
structural methods which is also a historical order in their development
and use.

Panzar and Rosse (1987) propose an approach based on the so-called
H-statistic, which is the sum of the elasticities of the reduced-form
revenues with respect to the input prices. This H-statistic ranges
from $-\infty$ to 1. An H-value equal to or smaller than zero indicates
monopoly or perfect collusion, whereas a value between zero and one
provides evidence of a range of oligopolistic or monopolistic competition. A value of one indicates perfect competition. This approach was
applied by Bikker and Haaf (2002) to study monopolistic competition
in OECD countries during 1988–1998; Gunalp and Celik (2006)
in Turkish banking industry, Claessens and Laeven (2004) for cross-
country studies, etc., to mention a few in order to test the degree of
competition.

Panzar and Rosse (1987) is one of the non-structural models for
the measurement of competition. It is an extended version of the
Iwata model (Iwata 1974) and Bresnahan model (Bresnahan 1982;
Lau 1982). They focused on the competitive conduct of firms without employing explicit information about the structure of the market.
These models belong to the New Empirical Industrial Organization
approaches. The basic premise of non-structural approach is that the
firms within an industry behave differently depending on the market
structure in which they operate (Baumol 1982). This approach has also
been applied to all EU countries by Bikker and Haaf (2002) and to the
Turkish banking industry by Gunalp and Celik (2006).

Bresnahan (1982) and Lau (1982) analyse bank behaviour on an aggregate level and estimate the banks' average conjectural variation. These analyses are based on the proposition that perceived MC curve equals MR curve with high conjectural variation implying that a bank is highly aware of its interdependence with other firms in terms of output and prices (via the demand equation).

These studies focused on the degree of competition among firms with a single product. In such case, banks were viewed as producing a single product, e.g. loans by using deposits as inputs. Bresnahan model was fitted in a general equilibrium model where the profit-maximizing firms would select their prices and quantities at the level; i.e. MC equals the perceived MR. The degree of competition was estimated on the basis of firms' reactions to changes in the slope of the demand function. Actually the responses were quite few from the side of competitive firms, except from a monopolist.

Applicability of this test is limited because banks produce multiple products in real sense. With this background, Suominen (1994) extended Bresnahan's study in the case of two products for Finnish banking. Deposits and loans were the two main banks' outputs used. Two tests were conducted for measuring the degree of competition in banks. In both the tests, methods of Least Squares estimator (OLS, 2SLS and 3SLS) were applied. The first test was performed using the two-product model with monthly data for the period (September 86–December 89). The second one was tested using the one-product model with annual data over the period 1960–1984. The two-product test gave evidence that some monopoly power was present in the pricing of banking services in the late 1980s. The two-product and one-product test results indicate that competition became less intense after deregulation. One factor behind this rather surprising result could be the enormous growth in demand for banking products in the late 1980s: in 1985–1990, the demand for loans and deposit services rose from 8 to 18%.

In another analysis of structural models, Shaffer (1993) examined the degree of market power practiced in the Canadian banking industry over the period 1965–1989 using a nonlinear simultaneous-equation specification that identifies the oligopoly solution concept. Labour, deposits and the physical capital were defined as the input variables. The quantity of output was measured as the dollar value of assets and the price of output as the interest rate earned on assets. Empirical findings revealed the presence of perfect competition and strongly rejected the hypothesis of joint monopoly. In other words, the estimated parameter was indistinguishable from zero, implying consistency with perfect competition.

Bikker and Haaf (2002) assessed the degree of competition and concentration of banks in 23 industrialized countries inside and outside Europe using the Panzar-Rosse H-statistic and Bresnahan model. The estimated H-statistic provides strong evidence of the presence of monopolistic competition of the banking markets in the industrialized world. However, in some countries, perfect competition has been found among large banks. Competition is stronger among large banks and weaker among small banks while medium size banks take an intermediate position. Competition seems to be somewhat stronger in Europe than in countries such as the USA, Canada and Japan. The k-bank concentration ratios and the Herfindahl Index confirms that a few large (cartel) banks can restrict competition and so rest of the competitors are unable to engender competition, supporting the conventional view that concentration impairs competitiveness.

Classens and Laeven (2004) estimated competitiveness indicators for a large section of countries by using the Panzar and Rosse (P-R) Methodology. A panel data from BANKSCOPE for the year 1994–2001 were collected, covering 50 cross sections of countries. All banks—commercial banks, saving banks, co-operative banks and BHCs—were included in the sample. They estimated the H-statistic on the basis of four models and taking average of the estimated four as a measure of the competitiveness of various banking markets. The H-statistic varied generally between 0.60 and 0.80, suggesting that monopolistic competition is the best description of the degree of competition. They found positive results for greater foreign bank presence. They also found some evidence that entry restrictions on commercial banks can reduce competition. There was no evidence that banking system's concentration was negatively associated with competitiveness. On the contrary, they found some evidence that more concentrated banking systems were more competitive. Their findings confirmed that contestability rather than structure is more important for competition.

Very few studies on this aspect of Indian financial services were done so far. Prasad and Ghosh (2005) examined the degree of competition in the Indian banking system, employing the P-R methodology. It covered 27 state-owned banks, 29 private sector banks, 23 private domestic banks and 14 major foreign banks for the period from 1996 to 2004, divided into two subperiods: 1996–1999 and 2000–2004. Employing the P-R test, they fit the model using interest revenue and total revenue as dependent variables. The control variables are introduced to take into account bank-specific and firm-level risks. The results indicated monopolistic competition structure of banks across time periods and across bank groups, with a more robust H-statistic for the second subperiod and for the private and foreign banks.

Based on the total assets data for the period from 1998–1999 to 2008–2009, Sharma and Bal (2010) examined the nature and extent of changes in the market concentration and their impact on competition among the Indian banks. It covered total assets of 75 scheduled commercial banks in the initial period of study that gradually decreased to 61 banks in its terminal period. The study employs different types of concentration ratios including the k-concentration ratio, HHI, country concentration of industries, Entropy and Gini Index. The empirical results reflected a greater degree of banking competition in Indian banks in initial year as shown by decrease in the concentration ratios based on HHI and k-bank concentration. Further, the Gini Index as a relative measure of concentration also decreased during the time period of study, suggesting a decrease in inequality among Indian commercial banks. In sum, the analysis found strong evidence of changing market structure as decreasing concentration ratios over the years reflected greater degree of competition in Indian banking.

Using P-R H-statistic, Misra (2011) analysed the degree of competition in the Indian banking sector after the financial sector reforms. The study period was spread over 1997–2008 with two-panel data sets of each 6 years, i.e. (1997–2002) and (2003–2008). Total revenue as a percentage of total assets was taken as a dependent variable. The independent variables were employee expenses, administrative expenses and funds expenses. Empirical results indicated no change in competition in Indian banking with the P-R *H*-values for the two subperiods were almost equal at 0.549 and 0.551, respectively. The result rejected the monopoly and perfect competitions as P-R *H*-value is neither zero nor one, indicating the presence of monopoly power in banking industry.

In view of above studies covering a limited reform period of a decade, it is worth noting marked gap made of uncovered years from 1991 to 2004 and post 2009 to 2015. Our study covers a quarter century of reform period from 1991 to 2015. Unlike above ones based on either one method, it is based on both the structural and the non-structural approaches to take into account the compatibility and discrepancy of both the methods of measuring market power and competition.

Methodological Approach and Theoretical Model

For measurement of concentration and competition in banking industry, more than one approach is available in literature. Our study employs both—the structural models (formal) and the non-structural models based on panel data.

Under the structural approach, the degree of concentration and competition among the firms is measured using the conventional method of *k*-firm concentration ratios {CR(*n*)} and HHI. The concentration ratios are calculated for five performance variables of the banks such as total assets, total deposits, total income, total advances and total net worth. Similarly, the HHI is estimated for the entire period mentioned.

The popular non-structural P-R model is employed to find out the competitive behaviour of banks. The structural equation of this basic model is that the elasticity of factor inputs determines interest revenue of the firm. Thus, dependent variable, the ratio of interest income to total assets, is explained through regression in terms of different factor inputs and control variables. The factor inputs are interest expended to total deposits, provisions of wages and salaries to total assets and other operating costs to total assets as the input prices. And three control variables in the structural equation are: size variable denoted by total assets, ratio of equity to total assets and loans to total assets ratio. The H-statistic is estimated for the entire period as well as for two constituent subperiods.

Data covers a period of about a quarter of century, namely from 1991–1992 to 2014–2015, subdivided into two different subperiods from 1991–1992 to 2000–2001 (10 years) in the first subperiod (first phase of banking reforms) and the rest of the 14 years from 2001–2002 to 2014–2015 in the second subperiod (second and third phases of reforms). All these data are compiled from different reports of the Reserve Bank of India for the various years. In all, there are 28 PSBs in 1991–1992, which reduced due to mergers to 26 banks in 2014–2015. State Bank of Saurashtra and State Bank of Indore were merged with State Bank of India in 2008 and 2010, respectively. Further, the New Bank of India was included only for 2 years—1992 and 1993. In the year 2004–2005, IDBI was added to the list of PSB covered.

Structural Measures of Concentration Ratio and Herfindahl-Hirschman Index

According to the theory of firm, four factors determine the market structure: number of independent firms, seller concentration, product differentiation and entry barriers in industry. For example, monopolistic competition tends to have a large number of firms with few being dominant ones, low or non-existent market concentration, slightly differentiated products or close substitutes and free or very easy entry. Oligopoly seems to have few firms with medium or high concentration, homogeneous or close substitute products and very difficult new entry due to high barriers. As seen above, most of the research works depended on sole concentration ratio that is one of the four factors distinguishing market structure of banking industry and thus gives a partial view of market structure. In India, number of commercial banks is limited to or less than 90, offering close substitute services/products to very large number of clients exceeding 120 crores.

Among these banks, five big banks accounted for about 2/3 or more of total bank deposits wherein SBI group staking share of one-third of deposits. High entry barrier renders new bank set-up difficult that includes license, minimum paid-up capital of Rs. 500 crores or more, control of balance sheet, management quality and other aspects of operation.

Here the concentration ratio as a measure of competition is worked out and its values are presented in the following section.

The k-bank concentration ratio is a discrete measure of concentration index, which is simple and can be calculated even the entire data set is not available. Simplicity and limited data requirement make the k-concentration ratio one of the most frequently used measures of concentration in industry. The importance of concentration ratios arises from their ability to capture structural features of a market. It is a measure of the relative share controlled by a given number of firms in an industry. Thus, concentration ratio is calculated from the market shares of the firms in the respective industry. The most common concentration ratios are the CR_4 (four largest firm) and the CR_5 (five largest firms). In the present study, these values are computed for each of the analysis periods. The concentration ratio is defined as the percentage of market share held by the largest firms (m) in an industry.

It takes the form:

$$CR_m = \sum_{i=1}^{m} s_i \qquad (4.1)$$

Therefore it can be expressed as:

$$CR_m = s_1 + s_2 + s_3 + \cdots + s_m,$$

where s_i is the market share and m defines the ith firm.

Concentration ratio ranges from a low of 0% to a high of 100%. At the low end, a 0% concentration ratio indicates an extremely competitive market. At the high end, a 100% concentration ratio means an extremely concentrated oligopoly or even monopoly.

On the basis of market share, it is possible to classify the degree of concentration in an industry. For example, the three largest firms' market share can demonstrate the degree of competition in the following ways:

Market share from 0 to <50% indicates nil concentration; from 50 to <60%, low concentration; from 60 to <75%, medium concentration; and from 75% and above, high concentration. Concentration indices are useful in that they give an easily computable and interpretable indication of competition in the industry.

The HHI is the second most popular summary measure of market concentration. The HHI measures the size of firms in relation to the industry and indicates the degree of competition among them. It is a commonly accepted measure of market concentration. In the United States, the HHI plays a significant role in the enforcement process of anti-trust laws in banking. Since 1982, the US Department of Justice has based its merger guidelines on the HHI.

The HHI is calculated by squaring the market share of each firm competing in the market and then summing the resulting numbers (where the market shares are expressed in fractions). Increases in the Herfindahl-Hirschman Index generally indicate a decrease in competition and an increase of market power, whereas decreases indicate the opposite.

The HHI is expressed as:

$$H = \sum_{i=1}^{N} s_i^2 \qquad (4.2)$$

where s_i is the market share of firm i in the market and N is the number of firms.

HHI ranges in fraction from zero to one (0 to 1). That is, when market share is close to one (1), it is monopoly with 100% market share and value of zero (0) indicates perfect competition when there are large numbers of firms with no one firm having substantial market share. Between these two extreme indices lies medium or low competition. In other words, the HHI ranges from $1/N$ to one, where N is the number of firms in the market. Equivalently, if per cent is used as whole numbers, the index can range up to 100², or 10,000. Thus, the HHI number can range from close to zero to 10,000.

These are the most popular tools used in structural methods for measuring concentration and degree of competition of the firms in an industry used by SCP hypothesis. Despite the wide use and popularity of the structure-conduct-models, non-structural method of measuring competition and concentration has been developed because of certain drawbacks against the SCP models. The P-R model (1987) is considered as an improvement over the SCP model. The P-R model measures the degree of competition based on the elasticities of revenue with respect to factor input prices.

Non-structural Method of the Panzar-Rosse Model

Panzar and Rosse model measures the competitive behaviour of banks on the basis of comparative static properties of reduced-form revenue equations based on cross-sectional data. This model stems from a general equilibrium market model and is one of the most widely used techniques to study competitive conditions in the banking. The basic premise behind the model is that firms employ different pricing strategies in response to changes in factor input prices depending on the competitive behaviour of market participants. Thus, competition is measured by the extent to which changes in input prices are reflected in firms' equilibrium. As the P-R model follows the log-linear form, the sum of factor price elasticities is termed as 'H-statistic'. In other words, the (P-R) H-statistic measures the sum of elasticities of the total revenue of the bank with respect to the bank's input prices. The H-statistic gives the overall level of competition prevailing in the market under consideration—namely monopoly or perfect collusion or monopolistic competition or perfect competition/contestable market. Under perfect competition, an increase in input prices raises both marginal costs and total revenues by the same amount, and hence, the H-statistic tends to be 1. Under monopoly, an increase in input prices results in a rise in marginal costs, a fall in output and revenues, leading to an H-statistic less than or equal to 0. When H-statistic is between 0 and 1, the market system operates under monopolistic competition. In the 'intermediate' case of monopolistic competition, the H-statistic assumes a value between 0 and 1, with an increase in input prices leading to a less than proportional increase in revenues, as the demand for bank products facing individual banks is inelastic. Under monopolistic competition where firms are competitive enough to imitate each of the other's products and with possibility of entry of new firms, there is an increase in competition, and the revenues would increase less than proportionally, as the demand for banking products facing individual bank is less than perfectly elastic. However, it is possible for H-statistic to be greater than 1 in some oligopolistic markets. This comparative static analysis requires the estimation of a reduced-form revenue function. The H-statistic is interpreted as follows.

$H < 0$ indicates a monopoly;
$H = 1$ indicates perfect competition; and
$0 < H < 1$ indicates monopolistic competition.

The reduced-form revenue model thus takes the form:

$$\ln(\text{IR}_{it}) = \alpha_i + \beta_1\ln(\text{Funds}_{it}) + \beta_2\ln(\text{Labour}_{it}) + \beta_3\ln(\text{Other Costs}_{it})$$
$$+ \gamma_1\ln(\text{Size}_{it}) + \gamma_2\ln(\text{Loan}_{it}) + \gamma_3\ln\left(\text{Equity}_{it}\right) + \varepsilon_i \quad (4.3)$$

where

ln denotes the natural logarithmic operator,
i denotes banks and t denotes years,
IR is the ratio of total interest revenue to total assets,
Funds is the ratio of total interest expenses to total deposits,
Labour is the ratio of personal/staff expenses to total assets,
Other costs are the ratio of other operating and administrative expenses to total assets,
Size is denoted by total assets,
Loans are the ratio of net loans to total assets,
Equity is the ratio of net worth to total assets,
ε is the stochastic error term that captures time-varying and bank-specific random components.

In the above reduced-form structural equation, the first three independent variables are the factor input prices for interest rates on deposits, wages and salaries paid to employees and cost of other administrative expenses, respectively. Other independent variables included in the model are the bank-specific control variables taken to capture effects of size, capacity differences and the risk factor involved. In the notation of above Eq. (4.3), the H-statistic is given by $(\beta_1 + \beta_2 + \beta_3)$. The value of H-statistic depends on the competitive environment and corresponding behaviours of banks. Under perfect competition, the value of H-statistic is 1 defines that a 1.0% change in cost will lead to a 1.0% change in revenues. Under the monopoly market structure, the value of H-statistic is 0 because in monopoly market, increase in factor inputs' cost increases the marginal cost, reduces the outputs and ultimately decrease in revenue. The value of H between 0 and 1 indicates the monopolistic competition in the market; the higher value indicates higher degree of competition.

Analysis of Results

k-Firm Concentration Ratios and Herfindahl-Hirschman Index Values

This section presents analysis of k-firm concentration ratios and the HHI values for most of the variables, namely banking variables—total assets, total deposits, total income, total advances and net worth—for the period 1991–1992 to 2014–2015. Table 4.4 produces the results of four-bank and five-bank concentration ratios in terms of the above variables. The State Bank of India (SBI) claimed the highest share of each variable among the all 28 PSB throughout the period followed by Bank of Baroda, Bank of India, Punjab National Bank and Canara Bank.

On the basis of the total assets, CR_4 was 53% in 1991–1992, which gradually declined to 42% in 2007–2008 to reverse thereafter to touch 46% in 2014–2015. During intervening years, there were slight fluctuations in the values of CR_4 due to variations in credit off-take and macroeconomic conditions. A similar pattern is discernible in terms of

Table 4.4 Concentration ratios of four largest firm (CR_4) and five largest firms (CR_5) for various banking parameters

Year	Total assets		Total deposi		Total income		Total advances		Net worth	
	CR_4	CR_5	CR_4	CR_5	CR_4	CR_5	CR_4	CR_5	CR_4	CR_5
1991–1992	0.53	0.58	0.49	0.55	0.52	0.58	0.53	0.58	0.44	0.50
1992–1993	0.50	0.56	0.47	0.54	0.51	0.58	0.52	0.57	0.43	0.49
1993–1994	0.50	0.56	0.47	0.54	0.50	0.56	0.51	0.57	0.45	0.52
1994–1995	0.48	0.54	0.46	0.52	0.50	0.56	0.49	0.55	0.41	0.47
1995–1996	0.48	0.54	0.46	0.53	0.50	0.56	0.50	0.56	0.39	0.45
1996–1997	0.48	0.54	0.46	0.53	0.49	0.55	0.51	0.57	0.43	0.49
1997–1998	0.48	0.55	0.47	0.53	0.48	0.55	0.51	0.57	0.43	0.49
1998–1999	0.49	0.55	0.47	0.54	0.49	0.55	0.50	0.56	0.45	0.51
1999–2000	0.48	0.54	0.47	0.53	0.48	0.54	0.49	0.55	0.45	0.51
2000–2001	0.49	0.55	0.48	0.54	0.48	0.54	0.49	0.55	0.45	0.51
2001–2002	0.49	0.55	0.48	0.54	0.48	0.54	0.47	0.54	0.46	0.52
2002–2003	0.48	0.54	0.47	0.53	0.48	0.53	0.48	0.54	0.47	0.53
2003–2004	0.47	0.53	0.46	0.52	0.47	0.53	0.47	0.53	0.46	0.52
2004–2005	0.45	0.50	0.45	0.51	0.46	0.51	0.44	0.50	0.44	0.50
2005–2006	0.44	0.50	0.44	0.50	0.45	0.51	0.43	0.49	0.45	0.51
2006–2007	0.43	0.48	0.42	0.48	0.43	0.48	0.43	0.49	0.45	0.51
2007–2008	0.42	0.48	0.41	0.47	0.43	0.48	0.42	0.48	0.47	0.53
2008–2009	0.44	0.50	0.43	0.49	0.44	0.49	0.44	0.50	0.48	0.53
2009–2010	0.43	0.49	0.41	0.48	0.43	0.49	0.43	0.49	0.47	0.53
2010–2011	0.44	0.50	0.42	0.49	0.43	0.49	0.44	0.50	0.44	0.50
2011–2012	0.43	0.50	0.43	0.49	0.43	0.49	0.44	0.50	0.46	0.51
2012–2013	0.44	0.50	0.43	0.49	0.42	0.48	0.44	0.50	0.46	0.52
2013–2014	0.45	0.51	0.44	0.50	0.42	0.48	0.46	0.52	0.47	0.54
2014–2015	0.46	0.52	0.45	0.51	0.43	0.49	0.46	0.52	0.48	0.54
Average (%)	0.47	0.53	0.45	0.51	0.46	0.52	0.47	0.53	0.45	0.51

Source Calculated by authors based on the formula given in (4.1)

CR_5 with the respective figures of 58% in 1991–1992, 48% in 2007–2008 and 52% in 2014–2015. Average of the four-firm and five-firm concentration ratios is 47 and 53%, respectively, for the entire period. Regarding other remaining banking variables, concentration ratios appeared to follow the same trend as that of total assets and total deposits over the period.

In net worth, banks show relatively the least concentration because of government's uniform norms of bank capitalization. The CR_4 was range-bound between the lowest of 44% in 1991–1992 and the highest of 48% in 2014–2015. Same pattern is also visible in terms of CR_5. Average of the CR_4 and CR_5 of the banks is 45 and 51%, respectively. For all the different variables, about half of (45–50%) the market share remained under the control of big four/five banks. Thus, it indicates that the Indian banks are oligopolistic in nature as a few PSB dominated as revealed by the share of various bank-specific variables. However, conversely, the market share of these large banking firms declined gradually over the period, allowing an increase in competition among them. Mean of CR_4 and CR_5 in all variables is lower in later period than those of initial period, indicating a decline in market power of big banks with rise in competition.

The values of Herfindahl Index of selected banking variables fluctuated to decline slightly in close range (0.04–0.05 points) (Table 4.5). HHI values for most of the variables, namely total assets, income, advances slightly declined from 0.13 in 1991–1992 to 0.09 in 2014–2015. In the case of total deposits and net worth, the value of HHI declined marginally from 0.10 to 0.08 for the same years and that of net worth increased in reverse order. Average of HHI values of each of the five variables was either 0.09 or 0.10 with no significant departures in values of two subperiods. This shows the continuance of PSB's oligopoly market structure in post-reform period as revealed by this method.

From the marginal declining of mean HHI values of each variable, it is understood that competition level among banks recorded the absence of substantial change. Oligopoly character of Indian banking based on CR_4 and CR_5 is well supported by the trend of HHI values.

The Panzar-Rosse Model: Regression Results

This section gives the regression results of fixed effect model applied to 28 PSB that produces H-statistic values for the entire period 1991–1992 to 2014–2015 and also for two different subperiods—the period from 1991–1992 to 2000–2001 and second subperiod from 2001–2002 to 2014–2015 (Table 4.6). The estimated coefficients of cost of funds, cost of labour and cost of other operating expenses are found statistically significant at the 5% level for the entire period from 1991–1992

Table 4.5 HHI values of various banking parameters

Year	Total assets	Total deposits	Total income	Total advances	Net worth
1991–1992	0.13	0.10	0.13	0.13	0.08
1992–1993	0.12	0.10	0.12	0.12	0.08
1993–1994	0.12	0.10	0.11	0.11	0.09
1994–1995	0.11	0.09	0.11	0.11	0.08
1995–1996	0.11	0.09	0.11	0.11	0.07
1996–1997	0.11	0.09	0.11	0.11	0.09
1997–1998	0.11	0.09	0.11	0.11	0.09
1998–1999	0.11	0.10	0.11	0.11	0.10
1999–2000	0.11	0.10	0.11	0.11	0.10
2000–2001	0.12	0.11	0.11	0.11	0.10
2001–2002	0.12	0.11	0.11	0.10	0.10
2002–2003	0.11	0.10	0.11	0.10	0.10
2003–2004	0.10	0.10	0.10	0.09	0.10
2004–2005	0.10	0.09	0.10	0.09	0.09
2005–2006	0.09	0.09	0.10	0.09	0.09
2006–2007	0.08	0.08	0.08	0.08	0.09
2007–2008	0.09	0.08	0.08	0.08	0.11
2008–2009	0.09	0.09	0.09	0.09	0.11
2009–2010	0.09	0.08	0.09	0.09	0.10
2010–2011	0.09	0.08	0.09	0.09	0.08
2011–2012	0.08	0.08	0.08	0.08	0.09
2012–2013	0.08	0.08	0.08	0.09	0.09
2013–2014	0.08	0.08	0.08	0.09	0.10
2014–2015	0.09	0.08	0.09	0.09	0.10
Average (1992–2004)	0.11	0.10	0.11	0.11	0.09
Average (2005–2015)	0.09	0.08	0.09	0.09	0.10
Average (1992–2015)	0.10	0.09	0.10	0.10	0.09

Source Calculated by authors based on the formula given in (4.2)

to 2014–2015. Among the factor inputs, the cost of funds (0.444) appeared to be major explanatory variable followed by the cost of labour (0.194) and other operating costs (0.097) for interest revenue. Hence the H-statistic of 0.735, significantly different from both 0 and 1, implying that banking market structure is far from monopoly and perfect competition and substantiates the view that Indian banks operate under oligopoly. This is in contrast to the conclusion of Prasad and Ghosh (2005)

Table 4.6 Regression results of the Panzar-Rosse model

	Coefficients	S.E.	t-values	P-value
(a) Estimates for the period: 1991–1992 and 2014–2015				
Cost of funds	0.444[a]	0.015	29.16	0.000
Cost of labour	0.194[a]	0.014	13.92	0.000
Cost of other operating cost	0.097[a]	0.020	4.82	0.000
Size	0.037[a]	0.007	5.10	0.000
Equity	−0.059[a]	0.009	−6.40	0.000
Loans	0.030	0.026	1.14	0.254
H-statistic	0.735			
No. of observations	647			
R-square	0.768			
F-statistic (P-value)	338.13 (0.0000)			
Wald test for $H = 1$: F-statistic (P-value) = 217.91(0.0000)				
Wald test for $H = 0$: F-statistic (P-value) = 225.75(0.0000)				
(b) Estimates for the first subperiod 1991–1992 to 2000–2001				
Cost of funds	0.441[a]	0.048	9.31	0.000
Cost of labour	0.086[a]	0.021	4.03	0.000
Cost of other operating cost	0.033	0.035	0.96	0.338
Size	0.029[a]	0.012	2.43	0.016
Equity	−0.026[a]	0.011	−2.38	0.018
Loans	0.163[a]	0.044	3.68	0.000
H-statistic	0.560			
No. of observations	270			
R-square	0.511			
F-statistic (P-value)	41.26 (0.0000)			
Wald test for $H = 1$: F-statistic (P-value) = 166.25(0.0000)				
Wald test for $H = 0$: F-statistic (P-value) = 6.44 (0.0003)				
(c) Estimates for the second subperiod 2001–2002 to 2014–2015				
Cost of funds	0.403[a]	0.021	19.20	0.000
Cost of labour	0.251[a]	0.021	11.86	0.000
Cost of other operating cost	0.073[a]	0.029	2.53	0.012
Size	0.084[a]	0.011	7.70	0.000
Equity	−0.053[a]	0.021	−2.53	0.012
Loans	−0.059	0.041	−1.46	0.145
H-statistic	0.727			
No. of observations	377			
R-square	0.655			
F-statistic (P-value)	108.45 (0.0000)			
Wald test for $H = 1$: F-statistic (P-value) = 84.69(0.0000)				
Wald test for $H = 0$: F-statistic (P-value) = 137.79(0.0000)				

Note [a]denotes significant at the 5% level

with an H-statistic value of 0.41 for the period 1996–2004. Further the value of H-statistic is closer to the value 1, which indicates insignificant competition among the firms. In other words, the high value of H-statistic of 0.73 indicates inelastic demand curve that implies an increase in input prices leads to a less than proportionate increase in revenues. The results for two different subperiods are approximately similar to the above one, but the value of H-statistic in the first subperiod is lower than that of the second subperiod. Among the control variables, only size and equity are significant with the negative sign for the equity variable. In the first subperiod, estimated coefficients of cost of funds and cost of labours are found statistically significant at the 5% level with the values of 0.441 and 0.086, respectively. This means that the cost of funds fairly explains the H-statistic and its value for this period is 0.560. All the three factor input prices are found statistically significant in the second subperiod. The estimated coefficient for cost of funds is 0.403; for the cost of labour is 0.25; and for the other operating cost is 0.073. The H-statistic (0.727) in the second subperiod is higher than the value (0.560) in first subperiod. The estimated coefficients of the explanatory variables size, equity and loans are found significant in each of the two subperiods except for loans variable in the second subperiod. The result of the fixed effect model is robust in each of the periods as shown by the significant P-values of the F-statistic. The Wald tests for perfect competition ($H = 1$) and for monopoly ($H = 0$) reject the null hypotheses to confirm the presence of oligopoly in Indian banking system.

Price and Non-price Competition

In oligopoly, banks determine prices and rates by observing actions of rival firms or follow strategy of price leadership on the basis of cost efficiency. Price competition includes certain rates and user charges such as deposit rates, loan rates, base rate, prime lending rates, charges on issuing bank draft, check book, fees levied on exchange currencies, money transfer, issue of credit cards, loans processing for firms and retailers—project loans, car/vehicle loans, housing, etc.—and how banks fixed their prices, etc. (Table 4.7). Though the bank service user charges are

Table 4.7 Price and non-price competition of the banks: 2014–2015

(A) Price competition
   1. Deposit rates (1–3 years)
   2. Loan rates (retail and corporate)
   3. Base rates/PLR
   4. Fees for credit cards, commission, exchange and brokerage as per cent of
      total income
(B) Non-price competition
   1. Advertisement budget
   2. Customer education/financial literacy

fixed by individual bank according to their own cost of funds, borrowers group (wholesale or retail) within the RBI guidelines but these are kept synchronized with leading banks such as SBI. Non-price competition includes range of the products and services, conduct of financial literacy programmes for excluded sections of society, the budget for advertisement and other awareness campaigns to increase the use and accessibility of credit facilities for different groups of the society. RBI has issued guidelines occasionally for bank charges to prevent exploitative user levies.

Table 4.8 reports the statistics of price and non-price competition variables for each of the banking services for the financial year 2014–2015. Since trend of base rate and loan rate is same, it is considered later here. Average base rate of the PSB is 9.66% with movement in close range about mean value. Neither much variations are seen in deposits rate with an average of 7.41%, the least value of 6.75% of the United Bank of India and the highest of 7.75% of the State Bank of Hyderabad. All the banks offered an average of above 7% deposit rate during the financial year 2014–2015. For those banks paying different rates of interest for 1–2 years maturity and for 2–3 years maturity, the average deposit rate is taken. All the banks have a base rate ranging from a minimum of 9.45% to a maximum of 9.75%. The choice of the deposit maturity period of 1–3 years is due to the fact that it commands a share of 27% in total deposits—the highest among all maturities for the scheduled commercial banks. The other deposit maturities ranging from 1–14 days and over 5 years with corresponding 3 and 19% of

Table **4.8**   Bank-wise base rate (loans), deposit rate (1–3 years), fees and commission and expenses on advertisement: 2014–2015 (%)

Sr. No.	Name of the bank	Base rate (Loans)	Deposit rate (1–3 years)	Commission, exchange and brokerage as per cent of total income	Advertisement expenses as per cent of operating expenses
1	Allahabad Bank	9.70	7.30[a]	4.46	0.74
2	Andhra Bank	9.75	7.50	1.90	0.56
3	Bank of Baroda	9.65	7.30	3.13	0.94
4	Bank of India	9.70	7.30	3.38	1.36
5	Bank of Maharashtra	9.70	7.55[a]	4.34	0.73
6	Canara Bank	9.65	7.55	1.92	0.60
7	Central Bank of India	9.70	7.60	3.10	0.46
8	Corporation Bank	9.65	7.50	2.13	0.15
9	Dena Bank	9.70	7.55[a]	1.84	0.86
10	IDBI Bank	9.75	7.60[a]	6.02	1.03
11	Indian Bank	9.65	7.25	1.57	0.31
12	Indian Overseas Bank	9.70	7.15[a]	3.84	0.25
13	Oriental Bank of Commerce	9.70	7.35[a]	4.12	0.80
14	Punjab and Sind Bank	9.75	7.40[a]	0.85	0.17
15	Punjab National Bank	9.60	7.35[a]	5.26	0.35
16	Syndicate Bank	9.70	7.30	3.72	0.77
17	UCO Bank	9.70	7.50	1.24	1.27
18	Union Bank of India	9.65	7.55	1.10	1.03
19	United Bank of India	9.65	6.75	1.70	0.31
20	Vijaya Bank	9.45	7.25	0.88	0.54
21	State Bank of Bikaner and Jaipur	9.55	7.25	6.22	0.92
22	State Bank of Hyderabad	9.65	7.75	5.15	0.61
23	State Bank of India	9.30	7.40[a]	7.53	0.74
24	State Bank of Mysore	9.65	7.55[a]	5.89	0.59
25	State Bank of Patiala	9.65	7.45[a]	5.55	1.18
26	State Bank of Travancore	9.95	7.60[a]	5.01	0.45
	Public Sector Banks	9.66	7.41	3.53	0.68

Note [a]Denotes average taken for different deposit rates charged by banks in each period
Source Reserve Bank of India: Statistical Tables Relating to Banks in India 2014–15

total deposits are without stable and consistent trend. Another source of competition among the firms is the commissions and exchange fees charged in delivering services to customers. All the banks earned an average income of 3.53% from the fees and commission charges. Eight PSBs earned income from such user charges above 5% in 2014–2015; another 8 banks earned between 3 and 5%; and the remaining banks earned less than 3%. Looking at the non-price competition, it appears that the amount of advertisement budget is very small which accounts to a minimum of 0.15% to a maximum of 1.36%, with an average of 0.68% for all banks. By comparing the price and non-price elements, it is obviously clear that not much competition is visible in these indicators for several reasons such as consortium lending, directed priority sector credit targets, government interference, corporate borrowers' connections with bureaucracy and political leadership. Indian Banks Association's direct role in wage setting with service conditions, or fixing certain interest rates/prices, and RBI's regulation and supervision reduced incentives and competency of management to compete (Joshi and Little 1996). PSBs are controlled by strong trade union making them inflexible organizations. Another non-price competition to mention is the financial literacy campaign and financial inclusion plans adopted by each of the banks under government policy imperatives to extend the accessibility of financial services in the economy and use of institutional finance at larger scale across sectors.

Conclusion

The results are summarized on degree of concentration and competition in the commercial banks for the period from 1991–1992 to 2014–2015. How the market concentration does affect the conduct of banks and degree of competition? The literature on the measurement of competition can be divided into two major strands: (i) structural models and (ii) non-structural models. Both the structural and non-structural approaches were used in measuring bank competition for simple reason to find out if any variation or conformity in the results produced different methods. Under the structural approach, the k-firm concentration ratios and HHI are used. The concentration ratios indicate that an average of 45–47% of the market share, expressed in terms of five banking variables, is dominated by four largest firms and 51–53% by five largest firms in the industry. However, their market share declined gradually over the period, owing to rising competition among them. The results of the HHI values also support the above conclusion based on concentration ratios. The mean HHI value of total assets, total income and total advances is on an average 0.10% over the entire period from 1991–1992 to 2014–2015 and that of total deposits and net worth 0.09%. The results of HHI for the variables show low competition suggesting implications for efficiency.

Regarding the type of relationship between market structure and banks' behaviour, the non-structural P-R model gives a clear picture of the degree of competition for period 1991–1992 to 2014–2015 and the two subperiods: 1991–1992 to 2000–2001 and 2001–2002 to 2014–2015, in the banking industry. The model tested competition using interest revenue as dependent variables with the cost of funds, labour and the other operating and administrative expenses, all factor inputs as independent explanatory variables and the estimated coefficients of these parameters producing the H-statistic. The model also includes three other control variables—size variable denoted by total assets, equity by ratio of net worth to total assets and the ratio of loans to total assets. The results found oligopoly behaviour of banks across time periods, with a more robust H-statistic for the second subperiod. The cost of funds, i.e. the ratio of interest cost to total deposits, turned out to be the significant indicator along with other factor inputs which also possess the expected positive sign.

This is followed by the cost of labour and cost of other operating expenses, respectively, which are also statistically significant at the 5% level in each of the analysis periods.

From our analysis, it is fair to conclude that the banking industry in India is more akin to an oligopoly type of framework, a rare feature of banking structure in developed countries and other emerging markets. Oligopoly banking characterizes by high interest spread (so-called scarcity rent) that is typically 100% in the case of Indian banks. High entry barriers another important feature of oligopolistic system, not market structure, determine competition in India, like most banking markets. Entry of foreign banks in greater number would have made a qualititative diffference in competition, profitability and service bench marks in domestic banking sector (Claessens et al. 2001). Cross-country comparison of monopolistic competitive banking systems with that oligopoly Indian banking system particularly the PSB carries a greater systematic risk than probable crisis in the banking systems of other countries.

References

Baumol, W. 1982. Contestable Markets: An Uprising in the Theory of Industry. *American Economic Review* 72 (1): 1–15.

Beck, T., A. Demirguc-Kunt, and R. Levine. 2003. Bank Concentration and Crises. *NBER Working Paper Series*, (Working Paper 9921, August).

Bikker, J.A., and K. Haaf. 2002. Competition, Concentration and Their Relationship: An Empirical Analysis of the Banking Industry. *Journal of Banking & Finance* 26 (11): 2191–2214.

Bikker, J.A., and J.M. Groeneveld. 1998. Competition and Concentration in the EU Banking Industry. Research Series Supervision No. 8, 25 June 1998, *De Nederlandsche Bank*.

Bresnahan, T.F. 1982. The Oligopoly Solution Concept is Identified. *Economic Letters* 10 (1–2): 87–92.

Claessens, S., and D. Klingebiel. 2001. Competition and Scope of Activities in Financial Services. *The World Bank Research Observer* 16 (1): 19–40.

Claessens, S., and L. Laeven. 2004. What Drives Bank Competition? Some International Evidence. *Journal of Money, Credit and Banking* 36 (3): 563–568.

Claessens, S., A. Demirguc-Kunt, and H. Huizinga. 2001. How Does Foreign Entry Affect the Domestic Banking Market? *Journal of Banking & Finance* 25 (5): 891–911.

Gelos, G.R., and J. Roldos. 2004. Consolidation and Market Structure in Emerging Market Banking Systems. *Emerging Markets Review* 5 (1): 39–59.

Goldberg, L.G., and A. Rai. 1996. The Structure-Performance Relationship for European Banking. *Journal of Banking & Finance* 20 (4): 745–771.

Gunalp, B., and T. Celik. 2006. Competition in the Turkish Banking Industry. *Applied Economics* 38 (11): 1335–1342.

Iwata, G. 1974. Measurement of Conjectural Variations in. *Econometrica* 42 (5): 947–966.

Joshi, Vijay, and I.M.D. Little. 1996. *India's Economic Reforms 1991–2001*. New Delhi: Oxford University Press.

Lau, L.J. 1982. On Identifying the Degree of Competitiveness from Industry Price and Output Data. *Economic Letters* 10 (1–2): 93–99.

Misra, A.K. 2011. Competition in Banking: The Indian Experience. *International Conference on Economics and Finance Research*, IPEDR Vol. 4, Singapore: IACSIT Press.

Molyneux, P., D.M. Lloyd-Williams, and J. Thorton. 1994. Competitive Conditions in European Banking. *Journal of Banking & Finance* 18 (3): 445–459.

Molyneux, P., J. Thornton, and D.M. Lloyd-Williams. 1996. Competition and Market Contestability in Japanese Commercial Banking. *Journal of Economics and Business* 48 (1): 33–45.

Nathan, A., and E.H. Neave. 1989. Competition and Contestability in Canada's Financial System: Empirical Results. *Canadian Journal of Economics* 22 (2): 576–594.

Panzar, J.C., and J.N. Rosse. 1987. Testing for Monopoly Equilibrium. *Journal of Industrial Economics* 25 (4): 443–456.

Prasad, A., and Saibal Ghosh. 2005. Competition in Indian Banking, IMF Working Paper, WP/05/141.

Reserve Bank of India. 2006–2008. Report on Currency and Finance, Volume 1, Mumbai.

Reserve Bank of India: Statistical Tables Relating to Banks in India. 2014–2015.

Shaffer, S. 1982. Competition, Conduct and Demand Elasticity. *Economic Letters, Federal Reserve Bank of New York* 10 (1–2): 167–171.

Shaffer, S. 1993. A Test of Competition in Canadian Banking. *Journal of Money, Credit and Banking* 25 (1): 49–61.

Sharma, M.K., and H.K. Bal. 2010. Bank Market Concentration: A Case Study of India. *International Review of Business Research Papers* 6 (6): 95–107.

Smith, R.T. 1998. Banking Competition and Macroeconomic Performance. *Journal of Money, Credit and Banking* 30 (4): 793–815.

Suominen, M. 1994. Measuring Competition in Banking: A Two-Product Model. *The Scandinavian Journal of Economics* 96 (1): 95–110.

The World Bank. 2014. Global Financial Development Database. USA: Washington.

5

Cost Efficiency and Productivity

Introduction

The theory of economies of large scale is generally discussed in the context of the optimum size of the firm. According to the theory, average cost is high for a small volume of output; it decreases as output increases until the most efficient scale (optimum size) of production is reached and rises again as output increases beyond that level. Theoretically, it is stated that the long-run cost function is U-shaped. The curve suggests that when output is small, the average cost is high and it continues to decrease as output increases, till it reaches its minimum. The level of output at this stage is called 'minimum cost efficient'. In other words, the firm experiences economies of scale in such conditions. Beyond this stage of production, the average cost is higher than the minimum and it increases as output increases. Under such conditions, the firm encounters diseconomies of scale. Consequently, firms tend to limit their size of operation around the minimum cost-efficient output level, where they would have availed of the maximum advantage of the scale economies. With the reforms, there is a structural and operational change in the functioning of the entire banking system and it is meaningful to

© The Author(s) 2017
T.R. Bishnoi and S. Devi, *Banking Reforms in India*, Palgrave Macmillan Studies in Banking and Financial Institutions, DOI 10.1007/978-3-319-55663-5_5

evaluate the cost-size relationships of the banks. The present study attempts to analyse the cost analysis of banking industry with special focus on optimum size of a bank. It studies the cost structure, economies/diseconomies as well as the optimum size of public sector banks for the period from 1991–1992 to 2014–2015. It also examines the relation between size of bank output and cost components (i.e. interest cost; wages and salaries; depreciation on banks' property; and general cost) to identify the sources of economies/diseconomies of scale. It also tries to find out the minimum efficient size of the firm for each of the specified periods. The below-mentioned two hypotheses are examined in this study:

1. Large banks are expected to be more efficient than small bank at a point of time.
2. Large banks are expected to show improved performance over a period of time as compared to small banks.

These hypotheses are examined with reference to economies of scale and optimum size of the public sector banks for the period from 1991–1992 to 2014–2015.

Empirical Studies

A comprehensive survey of studies on scale economies in US banking is done by Benston et al. (1982) and concluded with the evidence of economies of scale. Rangarajan and Mampilly (1972) demonstrated with empirical evidence of the familiar U-shaped average cost curve for Indian banks. These studies share a significant contribution in the framework of scale economies in banking industry. Unlike the other industries, the major issues in banking industry is in defining bank's output and its relevant cost function as banks produce heterogeneous products and services. As is well known, one of the main problems to solve before estimating the form of banks' cost function is to define bank outputs and to choose measures for them. Since financial institutions produce multiple products in terms of services rather than easily identifiable physical products, it is not clear how to define and measure output. Benston (1965, 1972) and Bell and Murphy (1968) measured total output in terms of number of deposit accounts and loans produced. Greenbaum (1967) estimated real value of output, i.e. gross bank income in the analysis of commercial banks. In the Indian context, Rangarajan and Mampilly (1972) used total deposits as the measure of output in the analysis of cost and size relationship of banks. In a study of Canadian banks, Allen and Liu (2007) used the intermediation approach to output, taking different forms of loans as a measure of output.

Todhanakasem et al. (1986) estimated the economies of scale in US banking for the period from 1978 to 1980, using a risk-adjusted profit function with the assumption that it has several advantages over the cost-function approach. The results indicated larger economies of scale for branch banks than for unit banks with the average values of 1.05 and 1.45, respectively. In some of the studies, all the variants of total cost are not included in the analysis of cost. Clark and Speaker (1994) used operating cost plus interest costs as a measure of total cost and provided evidence on the extent of economies of scale and scope economies of the banking industry in Chicago. Empirical results indicated that large and statistically significant economies of scale existed for all size classifications. For the smallest size, the estimated overall economies of scale was 0.85 and for the largest firms with value of 0.93. Apergis and Rezitis (2004) investigated the cost structure of the Greek banking industry for the period 1982–1997. The significant feature of this study was that it is based on three types of outputs—loans, investment assets and deposits. Empirical results showed that the Greek banking industry exhibited the presence of economies of scale with the value of scale economies in each year and in the whole time period was significantly greater than zero. Using translog cost functions, Allen and Liu (2007) measured the economies of scale of Canada's six largest banks and their cost efficiency for the period from 1983 to 2003. The results found scale economies with values greater than 1 for each model which were statistically significant. Further, the results showed that banks have experienced technological progress as explained by the trend variable and that regulatory changes have helped to reduce the production cost of banks. In a recent study, Stimpert and Laux (2011) examined the relationships among size, costs and profitability in the US banking industry. Regardless of the size measure employed, the increasing size was associated with higher costs that increase at an increasing rate, inevitably resulting in diseconomies of scale of the firms.

If the industry is subject to economies of scale, larger institutions would be more efficient and could provide services at lower cost, ceteris paribus (Benston 1972). Research has established the existence of scale economies, but many of these studies suggest that, in a wide range of industries, minimum efficient scale, necessary to operate at the lowest point on the average cost curve, occurs at relatively modest levels of output (Scherer 1980). The empirical literature on bank scale economies generally concludes that the average cost curve is relatively flat, with some evidence of scale inefficiencies for both the smallest and the largest banks (Clark 1996). Conceptually, economies of scale permit larger firms to produce their products and provide their services at lower average costs per unit than smaller firms (Shepherd 1979).

Statistical Cost Function

In most of the cost-size relationship studies as indicated above, the amount of total deposits is taken as a measure of output. In a similar way, we also employ total deposits as the output variable. Costs are defined to include both the interest costs and the operating costs. Operating costs comprise all expenses related to the use of physical and labour factor inputs. The cost-output relationship is also carried out for specified cost items of the total operating cost variable. These are wages and salaries, general expenses, and depreciation and repairs. Interest costs comprise interests paid to all depositors and to other creditors of the bank. Since more than 70% of the total cost is accounted for by the interest cost for each bank group in the year 1991–1992 and around 80% in 2014–2015 and therefore interest cost is also taken as a measure of cost.

The nature of relationship between cost and size will be subject to the empirical verification in terms of the estimated values of marginal cost (b), mean average cost $(\overline{AC})$ and mean elasticity of output (Total Deposits) with respect to specified cost items and total cost, i.e. the value of e.

Data and variables: The size of the banks is measured on the basis of deposits held and total costs measured by the total expenses incurred by each of the banks for each specific period. The total cost composed of various cost items—interest cost, wages and salaries to employees, depreciation on banks' property and general cost. The banks are classified into two groups—the large banks group which consists of the 14 banks that nationalized in 1969 and the small banks group of 12 banks. These 12 banks are the sum of 7 SBI associates and 5 other banks that nationalized in 1980. The New Bank of India is dropped from the data as it is merged with the Punjab National Bank in 1993. The rationale of combining the small banks and subsidiaries is that with reforms the banks were made independent and given autonomy to take decision in its functioning and hence, combining will not have adverse effect on the performance analysis of the banks group. The State Bank of India being very large bank is excluded from the analysis as its comparison with other banks will distort picture and is insignificant under the analysis. The economies of scale (deposit elasticities of total cost) relating to 26 public sector banks (excluding the SBI) are estimated for the selected years, namely 1991–1992, 1995–1996, 1999–2000, 2004–2005, 2009–2010 and 2014–2015. The rationale for the choice of the year 1991–1992 is that it is the immediate year of the initiation of financial sector reforms and choice for 1999–2000 is that it is also the immediate year after the second stage reforms stated in 1998. Evaluation of the performance of the public sector banks is pertinent and meaningful for such specific years. The justification for the choice of other years is based on a gap of 4 or 5 years in the period and finally for the year 2014–2015 is the latest complete data available for the analysis.

Statistical cost analysis: Assuming the linear cost-size relationship, the below-mentioned cost function is adopted from Sandesara (1979).

The cost function can be written as:

$$\text{TC} = a + bX, \tag{5.1}$$

where,

TC   total costs,
X total deposits
a intercept, and
b marginal cost

A linear cost function implies a constant marginal cost and falling average cost curve if the intercept term is positive. To measure the extent of these economies, output (deposits) elasticities of total cost would be computed at their mean value by the formula:

$$e = b\frac{\overline{X}}{\overline{TC}}, \qquad (5.2)$$

where

e elasticity
$\overline{X}$ mean output (deposits) and
$\overline{TC}$ mean total cost

Similarly, the mean average cost would be worked out by the formula:

$$\overline{AC} = \frac{a}{\overline{X}} + b \qquad (5.3)$$

where,

$\overline{AC}$ mean average cost

The same formula would be used to work out the cost elasticity and $\overline{AC}$ for the cost components.

Analysis of Results

Cost function of the linear form mentioned in Eq. (5.1) is applied for each bank group in each of the selected financial years to check out the scale operation. The analysis of economies of scale for each of the bank groups and all banks together is carried out for 6 different years. Regression of the above Eq. (5.1) is performed for specified cost items on the total output (Total Deposits) for the selected years, 1991–1992, 1995–1996, 1999–2000, 2004–2005, 2009–2010 and 2014–2015, separately for each bank group and also all banks together. The regression results are reported here.

Before proceeding with the regression analysis, an overview of the data on the average size of banks, aggregate deposits in each bank group are analysed. Value of average size of each bank group and aggregate deposits is given for each year of analysis.

Average Size and Size Range

The average size of total deposits of the small banks group was Rs. 2589 crores in 1991–1992. The corresponding values for the large banks group and all banks together in group are Rs. 10,178 crores and Rs. 6675 crores, respectively, in 1991–1992. There is an increase in the average size in terms of total deposits for the small banks group in each period, by more than two times. The average size of the total deposits of small banks group was Rs. 123,568 crores for 2014–2015, which is more than 40 times than that in 1991–1992. Further data of the large banks group show that the change in the average deposits was also visible but small banks group has more significant changes than its counterpart (Table 5.1).

Marginal Cost and Mean Average Cost

All the estimated values of marginal cost (**b**) are found to be statistically significant in all the cases of cost variables at the 1% level, and a few of them are at the 5% level for each year of analysis. For an exception only for three years, 1999–2000, 2004–2005 and 2014–2015 in which cost of wages and salaries for the small banks is found statistically insignificant.

Total Cost: The marginal cost (**b**) of the large banks (0.107) is found higher than that of the small banks (0.089) in 1991–1992. The higher marginal cost (**b**) for large banks as against the small banks continues in periods 1995–1996, 1999–2000 and 2004–2005. But the marginal

Table 5.1 Size range and average size by bank group for selected years: 1991–1992 to 2014–2015 (Rs. Crores)

Bank group	Minimum	Maximum	Aggregate deposits	Average size	Maximum Minimum
1991–1992					
Small banks (12)	1266	3861	31,070	2589	3.05
Large banks (14)	3374	19,210	142,491	10,178	5.69
All banks (26)	1266	19,210	173,561	6675	15.17
1995–1996					
Small banks (12)	2465	8711	64,071	5339	3.53
Large banks (14)	5971	28,370	230,353	16,454	4.75
All banks (26)	2465	28,370	294,425	11,324	11.51
1999–2000					
Small banks (12)	5096	22,095	132,409	11,034	4.34
Large banks (14)	13,287	51,308	408,083	29,149	3.86
All banks (26)	5096	51,308	540,492	20,788	10.07
2004–2005					
Small banks (12)	9051	47,850	277,463	23,122	5.29
Large banks (14)	20,897	103,167	773,366	55,240	4.94
All banks (26)	9051	103,167	1,050,828	40,417	11.40
2009–2010					
Small banks (11)	30,625	120,258	1,475,629	113,510	3.93
Large banks (14)	51,344	249,330	2,014,501	143,893	4.86
All banks (25)	30,625	249,330	2,720,236	108,809	8.14
2014–2015					
Small banks (10)	66,064	204,010	1,235,677	123,568	3.09
Large banks (14)	108,818	617,560	4,122,423	294,459	5.68
All banks (24)	66,064	617,560	5,358,100	223,254	9.35

Source RBI: Statistical tables relating to banks in India, various issues

costs of large banks (0.065 and 0.067) tend to be lower than that of small banks (0.070 and 0.085) in the years 2009–2010 and 2014–2015, respectively. However, in terms of the mean average cost $(\overline{AC})$ the large banks have lower magnitudes than the small banks in all the years except for the year 2004–2005.

We now proceed for explanations of the total cost items used in the analysis—they are interest cost, wages and salaries, depreciation on banks' property and general expenses.

1. Interest cost: The marginal cost (**b**) of the large banks (0.053) was found lower than that of the small banks (0.074) for 2014–2015.

The marginal interest cost (**b**) of the deposits for the large banks appeared to be lower than that of the small banks for all the years except in 1991–1992 and 2004–2005. In terms of the mean average cost ($\overline{AC}$), large banks were found with lower values than the small banks in each of the years selected.

2. Wages and Salaries: The marginal cost (**b**) of the large banks (0.008) was found higher as against the small banks (0.004) in 2014–2015. For all the other years too, the marginal cost (**b**) for large banks was higher than that of the small banks. The mean average cost ($\overline{AC}$) of both the large banks (0.010) and small banks (0.010) is same in 2014–2015. But for the years 2009–2010, 2004–2005 and 1999–2000, the mean average cost ($\overline{AC}$) of the large banks was found higher than that of the small banks. However, the large banks do perform better in mean average cost ($\overline{AC}$) as against the small banks in the rest of the years 1991–1992 and 1995–1996.

3. Depreciation: Both the large banks and small banks were found with same magnitudes of the marginal depreciation cost (**b**) in all the selected years except in 1999–2000, in which the large banks (0.001) have lower marginal cost (**b**) than that of the small banks (0.002). When the marginal costs (**b**) are compared, the large banks showed relatively better performance than the small banks. The mean average cost $\overline{AC}$ for the large banks (0.001) was found higher than that of small banks (0.0009) in 2014–2015, whereas for the period 1999–2000 the large banks (0.001) have lower mean average cost $\overline{AC}$ than the small banks (0.002). In all of the other years, both the large banks and small banks have equal values of mean average cost $\overline{AC}$.

4. General Expenses: The value of **bs** is same for the large banks in 2009–2010 and 2014–2015, i.e. 0.005. In other years, the large banks have either lower magnitudes of **bs** than that of the small banks or vice versa. The mean average cost $\overline{AC}$ of the large banks (0.005) is lower than that of the small banks (0.007) in 2014–2015. In other years, the large banks have lower mean average cost $\overline{AC}$ than that of the small banks except for the period 1999–2000, in which both the banks have equal values of mean average cost $\overline{AC}$ (of 0.007 each).

Briefly, it is observed that the large banks were more efficient than the small banks on both variants of cost, namely marginal cost and average cost. As we discussed in detail, the value of marginal cost of the large banks was lower than that of the small banks in the later years 2009–2010 and 2014–2015. No doubt, the large banks did have higher marginal cost (**b**) for the years from 1991–1992 to 2004–2005. In the subsequent years, the large banks perform better than their counterparts. This is supported by the lower mean average cost $\overline{AC}$ for the large banks as against the small banks in all the years with an exception in 2004–2005. Cost item-wise, the marginal cost and mean average cost of the large banks were found to be lower than those of the small banks for most of the years.

The details of cost item-wise, marginal cost and mean average cost nature of the banks are shown in Table 5.2.

Economies of Scale

The values of 'e' in the range of 1.05 or 0.95 may be treated as close to 1. And the value of 'e' less than 0.95 or more than 1.05 exhibited economies of scale or diseconomies of scale. The computed values of the mean elasticity of specified cost items with respect to the total deposits for each bank group and all banks together are given in Table 5.2 for selected years.

The mean elasticity of total cost with respect to output (e) was less than 1 for the large banks ($e = 0.824$) and for the small banks ($e = 0.903$) in 2014–2015. The large banks (0.967), however, operated at cost-efficient scale with an 'e' value of 1 as against the small banks (0.749) operating with economies of scale in the year 2004–2005. In the remaining years, both the bank groups fall under the zone of scale of economies. The mean elasticity with respect to the variants of total cost items is found to be close to 1 for the large banks and small banks. For the large banks, these are the unitary elasticity of interest cost ($e = 0.980$) for the 1991–1992; general cost items ($e = 1.039$) for 1995–1996; wages and salaries ($e = 0.998$) for 2004–2005; again wages and salaries ($e = 0.957$); and general cost items ($e = 0.982$) for

Table 5.2 Regression results of specified cost items on total deposit, mean elasticity and scale position for the selected years: 1991–1992 to 2014–2015

Bank group/cost items	Marginal cost (b)	Mean average cost ($\overline{AC}$)	Mean elasticity of cost with respect to total deposits (e)	R-square (R^2)	Scale position
(1)	(2)	(3)	(4)	(5)	(6)
1991–1992					
Large banks (14)					
Interest cost	0.084* (13.790)	0.086	0.980	0.94	Minimum $\overline{AC}$
Wages and salaries	0.015* (9.402)	0.021	0.704	0.88	Economies
Depreciation and repairs	0.001* (4.948)	0.001	1.217	0.67	Diseconomies
General expenses	0.007* (9.977)	0.008	0.809	0.89	Economies
Total costs	0.107* (20.015)	0.117	0.919	0.97	Economies
Small banks(12)					
Interest cost	0.066* (6.005)	0.082	0.806	0.78	Economies
Wages and salaries	0.014* (3.178)	0.025	0.551	0.50	Economies
Depreciation and repairs	0.001** (2.214)	0.001	1.072	0.33	Diseconomies
General expenses	0.009* (7.203)	0.011	0.865	0.84	Economies

(continued)

Table 5.2 (continued)

Bank group/cost items	Marginal cost (b)	Mean average cost ($\overline{AC}$)	Mean elasticity of cost with respect to total deposits (e)	R-square (R^2)	Scale position
(1)	(2)	(3)	(4)	(5)	(6)
Total costs	0.089* (5.985)	0.118	0.751	0.78	Economies
All banks (26)					
Interest cost	0.085* (27.207)	0.085	1.000	0.97	Minimum $\overline{AC}$
Wages and salaries	0.017* (17.892)	0.022	0.771	0.93	Economies
Depreciation and repairs	0.001* (10.088)	0.001	1.188	0.81	Diseconomies
General expenses	0.008* (20.212)	0.009	0.892	0.95	Economies
Total costs	0.111* (37.272)	0.117	0.950	0.98	Minimum $\overline{AC}$
1995–1996					
Large banks (14)					
Interest cost	0.072* (15.331)	0.076	0.941	0.95	Economies
Wages and salaries	0.02* (7.655)	0.027	0.757	0.83	Economies
Depreciation and repairs	0.001* (7.544)	0.001	1.089	0.83	Diseconomies
General expenses	0.009* (12.833)	0.008	1.039	0.94	Minimum $\overline{AC}$

(continued)

Table 5.2 (continued)

Bank group/cost items	Marginal cost (b)	Mean average cost ($\overline{AC}$)	Mean elasticity of cost with respect to total deposits (e)	R-square (R^2)	Scale position
(1)	(2)	(3)	(4)	(5)	(6)
Total costs	0.102* (20.331)	0.112	0.907	0.97	Economies
Small banks (12)					
Interest cost	0.073* (8.757)	0.080	0.914	0.89	Economies
Wages and salaries	0.018** (2.671)	0.028	0.679	0.44	Economies
Depreciation and repairs	0.001* (4.456)	0.001	0.895	0.67	Economies
General expenses	0.007* (8.803)	0.009	0.732	0.89	Economies
Total costs	0.092* (7.629)	0.117	0.786	0.85	Economies
All banks (26)					
Interest cost	0.074* (29.505)	0.078	0.958	0.97	Minimum $\overline{AC}$
Wages and salaries	0.023* (14.464)	0.027	0.870	0.90	Economies
Depreciation and repairs	0.001* (11.717)	0.001	1.040	0.85	Minimum $\overline{AC}$
General expenses	0.009* (22.905)	0.009	1.016	0.96	Minimum $\overline{AC}$
Total costs	0.106* (36.822)	0.114	0.934	0.98	Economies

(continued)

Table 5.2 (continued)

Bank group/cost items	Marginal cost (b)	Mean average cost ($\overline{AC}$)	Mean elasticity of cost with respect to total deposits (e)	R-square (R^2)	Scale position
(1)	(2)	(3)	(4)	(5)	(6)
1999–2000					
Large banks (14)					
Interest cost	0.068* (36.954)	0.073	0.928	0.99	Economies
Wages and salaries	0.019* (8.863)	0.023	0.838	0.87	Economies
Depreciation and repairs	0.001* (6.789)	0.001	0.897	0.79	Economies
General expenses	0.007* (18.892)	0.007	1.069	0.97	Diseconomies
Total costs	0.095* (33.689)	0.103	0.917	0.99	Economies
Small banks (12)					
Interest cost	0.078* (19.205)	0.077	1.012	0.97	Minimum $\overline{AC}$
Wages and salaries	0.004 (1.515)	0.020	0.201	0.19	Economies
Depreciation and repairs	0.002* (5.937)	0.002	1.382	0.78	Diseconomies
General expenses	0.006* (10.025)	0.007	0.823	0.91	Economies
Total costs	0.09* (19.447)	0.105	0.852	0.97	Economies

(continued)

Table 5.2 (continued)

Bank group/cost items	Marginal cost (b)	Mean average cost ($\overline{AC}$)	Mean elasticity of cost with respect to total deposits (e)	R-square (R^2)	Scale position
(1)	(2)	(3)	(4)	(5)	(6)
All banks (26)					
Interest cost	0.07* (58.242)	0.074	0.943	0.99	Economies
Wages and salaries	0.021* (13.900)	0.022	0.955	0.89	Minimum $\overline{AC}$
Depreciation and repairs	0.001* (9.539)	0.001	0.836	0.79	Economies
General expenses	0.006* (30.030)	0.006	0.892	0.97	Economies
Total costs	0.098* (55.416)	0.104	0.941	0.99	Economies
2004–2005					
Large banks (14)					
Interest cost	0.043* (32.136)	0.045	0.942	0.99	Economies
Wages and salaries	0.018* (7.474)	0.018	0.998	0.82	Minimum $\overline{AC}$
Depreciation and repairs	0.002* (8.509)	0.002	1.731	0.86	Diseconomies
General expenses	0.006* (10.975)	0.006	0.940	0.91	Economies
Total costs	0.069* (28.273)	0.071	0.969	0.96	Minimum $\overline{AC}$

(continued)

Table 5.2 (continued)

Bank group/cost items	Marginal cost (b)	Mean average cost ($\overline{AC}$)	Mean elasticity of cost with respect to total deposits (e)	R-square (R^2)	Scale position
(1)	(2)	(3)	(4)	(5)	(6)
Small banks (12)					
Interest cost	0.04* (20.420)	0.046	0.886	0.98	Economies
Wages and salaries	0.004 (1.414)	0.015	0.267	0.17	Economies
Depreciation and repairs	0.002* (5.632)	0.002	1.029	0.76	Minimum $\overline{AC}$
General expenses	0.007* (5.671)	0.008	0.953	0.76	Minimum $\overline{AC}$
Total costs	0.052* (14.613)	0.069	0.749	0.96	Economies
All banks (26)					
Interest cost	0.044* (51.685)	0.045	0.967	0.99	Minimum $\overline{AC}$
Wages and salaries	0.018* (11.462)	0.017	1.045	0.85	Diseconomies
Depreciation and repairs	0.001* (7.874)	0.001	0.733	0.72	Economies
General expenses	0.006* (16.885)	0.007	0.904	0.92	Economies
Total costs	0.069* (39.966)	0.070	0.975	0.99	Minimum $\overline{AC}$

(continued)

Table 5.2 (continued)

Bank group/cost items	Marginal cost (b)	Mean average cost ($\overline{AC}$)	Mean elasticity of cost with respect to total deposits (e)	R-square (R^2)	Scale position
(1)	(2)	(3)	(4)	(5)	(6)
2009–2010					
Large banks (14)					
Interest cost	0.049* (16.226)	0.055	0.901	0.96	Economies
Wages and salaries	0.01* (8.573)	0.010	0.957	0.86	Minimum $\overline{AC}$
Depreciation and repairs	0.001* (4.600)	0.001	1.279	0.64	Diseconomies
General expenses	0.005* (12.772)	0.005	0.982	0.93	Minimum $\overline{AC}$
Total costs	0.065* (19.636)	0.071	0.919	0.97	Economies
Small banks(12)					
Interest cost	0.058* (15.667)	0.059	0.974	0.97	Minimum $\overline{AC}$
Wages and salaries	0.006* (5.079)	0.009	0.646	0.74	Economies
Depreciation and repairs	0.001* (3.582)	0.001	1.187	0.59	Diseconomies
General expenses	0.005* (6.715)	0.006	0.906	0.83	Economies
Total costs	0.07* (20.123)	0.075	0.931	0.98	Economies

(continued)

Table 5.2 (continued)

Bank group/cost items	Marginal cost (b)	Mean average cost ($\overline{AC}$)	Mean elasticity of cost with respect to total deposits (e)	R-square (R^2)	Scale position
(1)	(2)	(3)	(4)	(5)	(6)
All banks (26)					
Interest cost	0.05* (27.385)	0.056	0.897	0.97	Economies
Wages and salaries	0.01* (14.338)	0.010	0.985	0.90	Cost efficient
Depreciation and repairs	0.001* (8.085)	0.001	1.254	0.74	Diseconomies
General expenses	0.005* (19.338)	0.005	0.961	0.94	Minimum $\overline{AC}$
Total costs	0.066* (34.163)	0.072	0.918	0.98	Economies
2014–2015					
Large banks (14)					
Interest cost	0.053 (11.053)	0.065	0.819	0.911	Economies
Wages and salaries	0.009 (5.560)	0.010	0.866	0.720	Economies
Depreciation and repairs	0.001 (7.459)	0.001	1.438	0.823	Diseconomies
General expenses	0.005 (16.312)	0.005	0.907	0.957	Economies
Total costs	0.067 (11.425)	0.081	0.824	0.916	Economies

(continued)

Table 5.2 (continued)

Bank group/cost items	Marginal cost (b)	Mean average cost ($\overline{AC}$)	Mean elasticity of cost with respect to total deposits (e)	R-square (R^2)	Scale position
(1)	(2)	(3)	(4)	(5)	(6)
Small banks (12)					
Interest cost	0.074 (24.124)	0.077	0.968	0.986	Minimum $\overline{AC}$
Wages and salaries	0.004 (2.231)	0.010	0.390	0.384	Economies
Depreciation and repairs	0.001 (4.874)	0.001	1.462	0.748	Diseconomies
General expenses	0.006 (7.072)	0.007	0.898	0.862	Economies
Total costs	0.085 (31.032)	0.094	0.903	0.992	Economies
All banks (26)					
Interest cost	0.054 (18.107)	0.067	0.801	0.937	Economies
Wages and salaries	0.009 (9.018)	0.010	0.869	0.787	Economies
Depreciation and repairs	0.001 (12.046)	0.001	1.443	0.868	Diseconomies
General expenses	0.005 (22.709)	0.006	0.865	0.957	Economies
Total costs	0.069 (19.012)	0.084	0.819	0.943	Economies

Note t-values in the parentheses, * significant at the 5% level, ** significant at 1% level
The value (s) of marginal cost is the estimated regression coefficient and the value of mean average cost is worked out by using Formula (5.1)

2009–2010. As against this, mean elasticity of the variants of total cost for the small banks is found to be close to 1 in the case of interest cost ($e = 1.012$) in 1999–2000; both in depreciation ($e = 1.029$) and in general cost items ($e = 0.953$) in 2004–2005; again in interest cost ($e = 0.974$) for 2009–2010; and lastly ($e = 0.968$) in 2014–2015. In the other cost items, both the banks groups have operated either on economies or diseconomies of scale.

Sources of Economies and Diseconomies of Scale

As we mentioned above, the mean elasticity of cost with respect to deposits (e) which is less than 1 indicates economies of scale and more than 1 suggests diseconomies of scale. No cases of diseconomies of scale are found in the elasticity of total cost with respect to output for the large banks, small banks and also in all banks together. However, in terms of the variants of the total cost, scale diseconomies were found in some of the cost items for each bank group and all banks together in select years. For example, in the case of all 26 public sector banks in 2014–2015, the diseconomies originating in depreciation are wiped out by the economies of scale observed in other cost item, the highest economies being in interest cost. Similarly, to counterbalance such diseconomies, the economies are available in interest cost and depreciation for large banks; and in all cost items for small banks in the period.

Now, detailed analysis throws some observations on the extent and sources of economies of scale/diseconomies of scale for each banks group. With regard to the interest cost, the magnitude of economies available to large banks ($e = 0.819$) seems to be higher than the same to the small banks ($e = 0.968$) in 2014–2015. With respect to the wages and salaries, large banks ($e = 0.866$) showed lower economies than the small banks ($e = 0.390$) in 2014–2015. However, in terms of depreciation cost item, both the large banks ($e = 1.438$) and the small banks ($e = 1.462$) experienced diseconomies of scale. Lastly, in terms of the general cost, the 'e' for the large banks (0.907) is lower than that of small banks (0.898) in 2014–2015.

The sources of economies or diseconomies of scale and their magnitudes vary among the groups of banks in each selected years. The interest cost became a source of economies of scale for the large banks for the years from 1995–1996 to 2014–2015 and for the small banks group in 1991–1992, 1995–1996 and 2004–2005. Comparing the magnitudes of economies available, the large banks have lower values of 'e' than that of small banks in years 1991–1992; 1995–1996; and 2004–2005. However, in the remaining three years, the large banks have higher values of elasticity of interest cost (e) than same of the small banks. In wages and salaries, the large banks realized economies all the time except in the 2 years, 2004–2005 and 2009–2010, when these banks were working at the cost-efficient scale. For the small banks, wages and salaries turned out to be a source of economies of scale in the entire period. And the values of mean elasticity of small banks are higher than those of the large banks over these years. Regarding the depreciation cost item, economies of scale is observed in 1999–2000 for large banks and for small banks in 1995–1996. The comparison of the magnitudes of elasticity values (e) of depreciation cost for both the bank groups showed that whenever there are economies in large banks, the small banks are in the zone of diseconomies or vice versa. As far as the general cost item is concerned, the large banks realized economies of scale in 1991–1992, 2004–2005 and 2014–2015; seen operating at the minimum efficient scale in 1995–1996 and 2009–2010. For the small banks, the general cost items indicated economies of scale in each of the years except in 2004–2005 (at MES). The values of mean elasticity of the large banks (0.809 and 0.940) were higher than corresponding values of 0.865 and 0.943 obtained for the small banks in 1991–1992 and 2004–2005. For the years 2009–2010 and 2014–2015, the mean elasticity values of the large banks were lower than those of the small banks; and in the other 2 years, both groups are at the minimum efficient scale.

As against these economies, the very same cost items become sources of diseconomies during some other years. For instance, depreciation has been the source of diseconomies of scale for the large banks all the time in 1991–1992, 1995–1996, 2004–2005, 2009–2010 and

Table 5.3 Sources of economies and diseconomies of scale: 1991–1992 to 2014–2015

Bank group/year	Sources of		
	Economies of scale		Diseconomies of scale
(1)	(2)		(3)
Large banks (14)			
1991–1992	Wages and salaries; General expenses		Depreciation
1994–1995	Interest cost; Wages and salaries		Depreciation
1999–2000	Interest cost; Wages and salaries; Depreciation		General expenses
2004–2005	Interest cost; General expenses		Depreciation
2009–2010	Interest cost		Depreciation
2014–2015	Interest cost; Wages and salaries; General expenses;		Depreciation
Small banks (12)			
1991–1992	Interest cost; Wages and salaries; General expenses		Depreciation
1994–1995	Interest cost; Wages and salaries; Depreciation; General expenses		–
1999–2000	Wages and salaries; General expenses		Depreciation
2004–2005	Interest cost; Wages and salaries		–
2009–2010	Wages and salaries; General expenses		Depreciation
2014–2015	Wages and salaries; General expenses		Depreciation
All banks (26)			
1991–1992	Wages and salaries; General expenses		Depreciation
1994–1995	Wages and salaries		–
1999–2000	Interest cost; Depreciation; General expenses		–
2004–2005	Depreciation; General expenses		Wages and Salaries
2009–2010	Interest cost		Depreciation
2014–2015	Interest cost; Wages and salaries; General expenses		Depreciation

Source Calculated by authors based on Table 5.2

lastly for 2014–2015 and for the small banks for the most of the time in 1991–1992, 1999–2000, 2009–2010 and 2014–2015. The overall performance of the large banks group is fairly cost efficient in terms of aggregate total cost, operating either at the economies of scale in some years or at minimum efficient scale in other years. And no cases of diseconomies of scale are found in the aggregate total cost item for the large banks as the diseconomies in depreciation are balanced out with the economies and cost-efficient scale associated with other cost items. The performance of the small banks group is also good as there are economies of scale in terms of aggregate total cost item in each of the years chosen. In short, comparative performance of small banks group and large banks group reveals cost-efficient scale for both of them with some exceptions that being the diseconomies of scale in depreciation cost for each group.

For all banks together, the scale performance is significantly notable. There are economies of scale and cost-efficient scale in each of the cost items for each year studied except three cases of diseconomies of scale that are found in the depreciation cost item, which are in 1991–1992 ($e = 1.188$), 2009–2010 ($e = 1.254$) and in 2014–2015 ($e = 1.443$), respectively. To sum up, the operation of the public sector banks is fairly cost efficient with some exceptions of diseconomies of scale arising from depreciation cost (Table 5.3).

Minimum Efficient Size

The minimum efficient size (MES) in total output (total deposits) is defined as the level of output at which fall in average total cost ($\overline{AC}$) over a given interval of output was found for the first time to be less than one per cent. The minimum efficient size or output works out to be at the output level of Rs. 700 crores in 1991–1992. For the financial year 1995–1996, the minimum efficient output level is obtained at Rs. 1000 crores and then at Rs. 1200 crores in the financial year 1999–2000. In the financial year 2004–2005, the minimum efficient scale output of the banks is Rs. 3000 crores. In the case of the financial years 2009–2010 and 2014–2015, the minimum efficient scale is estimated at Rs. 9000 crores and Rs. 19,000 crores, respectively. It is evident from Table 5.1 that MES was attained in all public sector banks in each of the years selected (Table 5.4).

Table 5.4 Average total cost by level of total deposits (Output) and minimum efficient size/output (MES): 1991–1992 to 2014–2015

Total output (Rs. in crore)	Average total cost	Fall in AC (%)	Total output (Rs. in crore)	Average total cost	Fall in AC (%)
(1)	(2)	(3)	(1)	(2)	(3)
1991–1992			*2004–2005*		
200	20.124		1000	6.16	
300	13.786	6.338	2000	3.42	2.73
400	10.617	3.169	3000	2.51	0.91
500	8.716	1.901	4000	2.06	0.46
600	7.448	1.268	5000	1.78	0.27
700	6.543	0.905	6000	1.60	0.18
800	5.864	0.679	7000	1.47	0.13
900	5.335	0.528	8000	1.37	0.10
1000	4.913	0.423	9000	1.30	0.08
1400	3.826	1.087	10,000	1.24	0.06
MES	700		MES	3000	
1995–1996			*2009–2010*		
700	13.25		1000	65.83	
800	11.73	1.524	2000	33.24	32.58
900	10.543	1.185	3000	22.38	10.86
1000	9.595	0.948	4000	16.95	5.43
1100	8.819	0.776	5000	13.69	3.26
1200	8.172	0.647	6000	11.52	2.17
1300	7.625	0.547	7000	9.97	1.55
1400	7.156	0.469	8000	8.81	1.16
1500	6.750	0.406	9000	7.90	0.91
1600	6.394	0.356	10,000	7.18	0.72
MES	1000		MES	9000	
1999–2000			*2014–2015*		
700	18.78		9000	37.10	
800	16.55	2.22	10,000	33.40	3.58
900	14.82	1.73	11,000	30.37	2.93
1000	13.44	1.38	12,000	27.84	2.44
1100	12.31	1.13	13,000	25.71	2.14
1200	11.36	0.94	14,000	23.88	1.83
1300	10.56	0.80	15,000	22.29	1.59
1400	9.88	0.68	16,000	20.90	1.39
1500	9.29	0.59	17,000	19.67	1.23
1600	8.77	0.52	18,000	18.59	1.09
MES	1200		19,000	17.61	0.97
			20,000	16.77	0.85
			MES	19,000	

Note The values of AC in column (2) is worked out by using Eq. (5.3) with the values of bs as given in Table 5.2 and the value of total output is given above in column (1) year-wise

Source Calculated by Authors based on Table 5.2

Improvement in Cost Efficiency

As to test the second hypothesis, we have analysed whether the large banks have increased their efficiency more than the small banks between 1991–1992 and 1999–2000, 1999–2000 and 2014–2015, and 1991–1992 and 2014–2015. The improvement in efficiency is indicated by either reducing diseconomies of scale, if existed in some cost items, or increasing the scale economies in other cost items. To say, a smaller increase or larger decline in mean elasticity of cost of the large banks relative to that of the small banks indicates better performance of the former group over the period. Any increase (decrease) in elasticity coefficient (e) shows the decline (increase) in the extent of economies available to the banks in case of the elasticity coefficient is less than 1 in the initial year, and the increase (decline) in the extent of diseconomies if the value of the coefficient is more than 1.

From Table 5.5, it is observed that the mean elasticity of total cost of the large banks and small banks showed insignificant changes in 2014–2015 over 1991–1992. Both the bank groups continue to operate in scale economies despite diseconomies associated with depreciation cost item between the periods from 1991–1992 to 2014–2015.

When we look at the relative performance of the large banks and the small banks for the period from 1991–1992 to 1999–2000 and the period from 1999–2000 to 2014–2015 separately, it is clear that the large banks recorded better position than the small banks did in both the periods. For the years from 1991–1992 to 1999–2000, both the bank groups did not record any variation in their elasticity of total cost and continued to generate scale economies. In the years from 1999–2000 to 2014–2015, the large banks perform better than the small banks as there was a decline in the elasticity of total cost by 0.02 points as against the marginal increase in the elasticity of the small banks by 0.07 points. The favourable factors that shaped performance for the large banks in this period are: decline in the elasticities of interest cost by 0.01 points, and wages and salaries by 0.31 points. And for the small banks, the facts that bring adverse change in elasticity are its increase in interest cost (0.01), wages and salaries (0.32), depreciation (0.37) and general expenses (0.04) points. The details of increase or decrease in

Table 5.5 Change in marginal cost, mean average cost each for a deposit of per Rs. 100 and in mean elasticity of cost by bank group: 1991–1992 to 2014–2015

Bank group/cost item	Marginal cost (b)			Mean average cost ($\overline{AC}$)		
	1991 to 1999	1999 to 2014	1991 to 2014	1991 to 1999	1999 to 2014	1991 to 2014
(1)	(2)	(3)	(4)	(5)	(6)	(7)
Large banks (14)						
Interest cost	-1.60	-1.50	-3.10	-1.29	-0.80	-2.09
Wages and salaries	0.40	-1.00	-0.60	0.13	-1.21	-1.08
Depreciation	0.00	0.00	0.00	-0.04	0.04	0.00
General expenses	0.00	-0.20	-0.20	-0.14	-0.13	-0.27
Total costs	-1.20	-2.80	-4.00	-1.33	-2.21	-3.54
Small banks (12)						
Interest cost	1.20	-0.40	0.80	-0.46	-0.04	-0.50
Wages and salaries	-1.00	0.00	-1.00	-0.59	-0.94	-1.52
Depreciation	0.10	-0.10	0.00	0.03	-0.08	-0.05
General expenses	-0.30	0.00	-0.30	-0.38	-0.01	-0.39
Total costs	0.10	-0.50	-0.40	-1.30	-1.07	-2.37
All banks(26)						
Interest cost	-1.50	-1.60	-3.10	-1.05	-0.75	-1.79
Wages and salaries	0.40	-1.20	-0.80	0.08	-1.22	-1.14
Depreciation	0.00	0.00	0.00	-0.05	0.05	0.00
General expenses	-0.20	-0.10	-0.30	-0.29	-0.05	-0.34
Total costs	-1.30	-2.90	-4.20	-1.27	-2.01	-3.28

(continued)

Table 5.5 (continued)

Bank group/cost item	Marginal cost (b)			Mean average cost ($\overline{AC}$)		
	1991 to 1999	1999 to 2014	1991 to 2014	1991 to 1999	1999 to 2014	1991 to 2014
(1)	(2)	(3)	(4)	(5)	(6)	(7)
Large banks (14)						
Interest cost				Minimum $\overline{AC}$	Economies	Economies
Wages and salaries				Economies	Economies	Economies
Depreciation				Diseconomies	Economies	Diseconomies
General expenses				Economies	Diseconomies	Economies
Total costs				Economies	Economies	Economies
Small banks (12)						
Interest cost				Economies	Minimum $\overline{AC}$	Minimum $\overline{AC}$
Wages and salaries				Economies	Economies	Economies
Depreciation				Diseconomies	Diseconomies	Diseconomies
General expenses				Economies	Economies	Economies
Total costs				Economies	Economies	Economies
All banks(26)						
Interest cost				Economies	Economies	Economies
Wages and salaries				Economies	Minimum $\overline{AC}$	Economies
Depreciation				Diseconomies	Economies	Diseconomies
General expenses				Economies	Economies	Economies
Total costs				Minimum $\overline{AC}$	Economies	Economies

Bank group/cost item	Mean elasticity of cost (e)			Position of 'e' in the year		
	1991 to 1999	1999 to 2014	1991 to 2014	1991	1999	2014
(1)	(8)	(9)	(10)	(11)	(12)	(13)
Large banks (14)						
Interest cost	−0.05	0.04	−0.01	Minimum $\overline{AC}$	Economies	Economies
Wages and salaries	0.13	−0.45	−0.31	Economies	Economies	Economies
Depreciation	−0.32	0.56	0.24	Diseconomies	Economies	Diseconomies
General expenses	0.26	−0.17	0.09	Economies	Diseconomies	Economies
Total costs	0.00	−0.01	−0.02	Economies	Economies	Economies
Small banks (12)						
Interest cost	0.21	−0.19	0.01	Economies	Minimum $\overline{AC}$	Minimum $\overline{AC}$
Wages and salaries	−0.35	0.67	0.32	Economies	Economies	Economies
Depreciation	0.31	0.06	0.37	Diseconomies	Diseconomies	Diseconomies
General expenses	−0.04	0.08	0.04	Economies	Economies	Economies
Total costs	0.10	−0.03	0.07	Economies	Economies	Economies
All banks(26)						
Interest cost	−0.06	−0.14	−0.20	Economies	Economies	Economies
Wages and salaries	0.18	−0.09	0.10	Economies	Minimum $\overline{AC}$	Economies
Depreciation	−0.35	0.61	0.25	Diseconomies	Economies	Diseconomies
General expenses	0.00	−0.03	−0.03	Economies	Economies	Economies
Total costs	−0.01	−0.12	−0.13	Minimum $\overline{AC}$	Economies	Economies

Source Calculated by authors based on Table 5.2

marginal cost, mean average cost and elasticity for different bank groups can be seen.

The large banks vis-à-vis the small banks showed greater improvement in terms of attaining cost-efficient scale by maintaining economies of scale over the entire period of analysis. Its attributes are either reducing diseconomies of scale if at all existed in some cost items or increasing the magnitude of economies available in other cost items between 1991–1992 and 2014–2015 (Table 5.5).

Productivity

In order to validate evidences on cost efficiency, analysis of productive efficiency of public sector banks was necessary here. Profitability alone is not the most appropriate criterion to gauge the performance of banks; other activities can better be measured in terms of efficiency in relation to given technology in the banking industry. One significant aspect of performance evaluation of banking reforms is productive efficiency of the banks in terms of technical and scale efficiency.

Empirical Studies on Productivity

Many studies (Divatia and Venkatachalam 1978; Ravindranath 1979; Varde and Singh 1983) attempted to measure productivity in Indian banks but were more concerned with techniques of productivity analysis in public sector banks. Deshpande (1981) concluded that productivity of public sector banks was higher than that of small private sector banks when evaluated for the period from 1974 to 1978–1979. However, profitability and productivity both of scheduled commercial banks showed a considerable decline during 1970–1975, the period of fast branch expansion (Angadi and Devaraj 1983). One of the basic reasons cited for deceleration in this productivity was rapid expansion in rural and semi-urban offices of Indian scheduled commercial banks in the initial period of bank nationalization, without corresponding growth in business of these offices. Most of the earlier studies of estimating bank efficiency focused particularly on accounting ratios or based on specific production or cost function. But more statistical and mathematical tools were added for measurement of efficiency and productivity of banks over the period.

Efficiency of banks across different ownerships was evaluated in the context of deregulation; public sector banks performed significantly better vis-a-vis private sector banks and foreign banks in terms of revenue maximization and relative cost efficiency (Ram Mohan and Ray 2004; Bhattacharyya et al. 1997; Sensarma 2005; Keshari and Paul 1994). In a more diverse way, Das and Kumbhakar (2012) evaluated efficiency and total factor productivity of Indian banks using panel data for period 1996–2005, the period of deregulation. Their research work differed from earlier analyses of efficiency and productivity in the sense that it incorporated quality attribute variables of certain bank-specific parameters such as categories of deposits and loans, number of accounts served, quality of loan portfolio, classes of employees and location of branches. An important evidence worth to reckon was efficiency gains in response to deregulation in banking system. Banks had improved the extent of efficiency from 61% in 1996 to 72% in 2005 and also productivity gains of public sector banks exceeded that of private banks. A comparative analysis of performance of foreign versus domestic banks revealed that latter attained slightly higher level of efficiency in resource utilization than the former due to the consequence of their particular operational characteristics and strategies and preferential treatment rendered to them by the government of India (Keshari and Paul 1994). From the cross section of studies regarding efficiency and productivity, it was observed that the performance of public sector banks group stood in better position than private banks and foreign domestic banks group.

Wheelock and Wilson (1999) studied efficiency and change in productivity of US commercial banks during the period between 1984 and 1993 and found that productivity declined on average but not to the extent of fall in efficiency and along with that there was decline in technical efficiency by banks of all sizes despite technological progress enjoyed by banks in all size categories over the period. It indicated that minority of the banks in each size category were pushing the technology forward while the majority of banks failed to keep up with the technological change. Alam (2001) quantified the productivity, efficiency and technological changes for large US commercial banks during the 1980s using the Malmquist productivity index. All types of banks made tremendous gains in productivity and technological advances between 1983 and 1984. The average bank did not move closer to the frontier; the measured changes in productivity were due to shifts in technology rather than changes in efficiency. And one of the reasons that explained lack of dramatic increases of efficiency was that by the 1980s banks already faced significant competition from other financial institutions. Most of the productivity and efficiency analysis of banks adopted the Data Envelopment Analysis to make out the impact of privatization, liberalization and other restructuring strategies adopted over the period. Here also efficiency of banks is analysed as a part of the cost efficiency (economies of scale) estimated above in this chapter. Here manpower productivity ratios and the Malmquist total factor productivity index were estimated to see the extent of productive efficiency in public sector banks.

Trends in Manpower Productivity

Manpower productivity of banks was analysed with respect to four different ratios, namely ratio of total working funds to pay out, net profit per employee, deposits per employee and wages per employee. As described in this chapter on profitability, the proportion of expenses incurred on payments for wages and salaries came down from 19% in 1991–1992 to 13% in 2014–2015. This is an indication of a gradual shift of manpower- to technology-based services, gradually replacing the conventional labour-intensive technology to technocentric or more capital-intensive technology in the production process. However, the role of manpower and its productivity is significant in determining total output. The first ratio indicates the amount of total bank assets dealt per rupee of manpower expenditure in a year. It shows the extent of manpower utilization in banks; higher the ratio suggests higher productivity of banks in terms of total assets and vice versa. Net profit per employee showed the net productive efficiency of human capital

Table 5.6 Manpower productivity of public sector banks, 1991–1992 to 2014–2015

Period	Total assets to payout (in Rupees Million)	Profit per employee (in Rupees Million)	Deposits per employee (in Rupees Million)	Wages per employee (in Rupees Million)
1991–1992	10.14	0.01	2.52	0.06
1995–1996	10.83	−0.02	4.40	0.12
2000–2001	11.22	0.05	10.81	0.26
2005–2006	16.72	0.26	23.85	0.36
2010–2011	16.42	0.67	63.61	0.73
2014–2015	13.40	0.43	86.85	0.90

Source RBI: Statistical tables relating to banks in India

employed by banks to generate surplus. Like assets, deposits are significant in determining the productivity of banks, accounting more than 90% of total liabilities in banks' balance sheet and also in servicing cost of financial intermediation. The ratio of deposit to total employee evaluates performance of an average employee in resource mobilization from the deposit market. The last ratio of wages per employee indicates price of labour or marginal labour productivity on the assumption of perfect labour market. We have reported these ratios for the period from 1991–1992 to 2014–2015 (Table 5.6).

As far as the first ratio of total assets to payout is concerned; the productivity of public sector banks increased by 10.14 for a rupee spent in 1991–1992, and this ratio improved gradually to 10.83 in 1995–1996 and 16.72 in 2005–2006. This increase in the ratio is positive and significant. Then aggregate value of total assets increased in successive years, but the rise in total expenses was much higher than increase in total assets. Total assets of public sector banks more than doubled in 2010–2011 from its value in 2005–2006, and much more in 2014–2015. Simultaneously, the increase in total expenses was more than that of total assets, thereby leading to a fall in the ratio to 13.40 per rupee spent in 2014–2015.

For the second ratio, ratio of net profit to total number of employees appeared to be very low indicating burden of policy constraints carried over till a decade ago. Then ratio showed a sign of improvement in successive period to touch 0.67 in 2010–2011 followed by slight decline to

0.43 in 2014–2015 on account of higher provisioning made for NPAs. Deposit per employee increased continuously in each of the periods reported. And for the last ratio, wages per employee, the amount paid increased over the period because of wage revision approved under wage accord. These ratios showed an overview of an increasing trend in manpower productivity of public sector banks after reforms were introduced.

It turns now to estimates of productive efficiency of these banks based on Data Envelopment Analysis (DEA) given below.

Analytical Framework and Results

Data and Methodology

The term productivity can be expressed as the ratio of total output to input or factors of production. Efficiency measures the relative performance of firms in an industry, with the existing technology. Efficiency and productivity change of firms can be measured using either parametric approach or non-parametric approach. One specific feature of econometric approach is that it requires specification of production function, cost function, revenue function or profit function and assumptions of the error term. However, the non-parametric approach does not require specifications of error terms and can be computed by constructing index numbers based on the non-parametric techniques. Here it measured efficiency of banks based on the non-parametric approach which is widely used and accepted method in productivity literature. One of the issues in banking is definition of bank outputs and inputs. By taking into consideration the virtues and shortcomings of each approach in measuring outputs and inputs, it employed value added approach in defining outputs and inputs of banks. This study employed two outputs and two inputs, namely total deposits and total income as outputs; interest expenses plus operating expenses as inputs.

The Malmquist Total Factor Productivity Index

The method of Data Envelopment Analysis (DEA) was employed to measure productive efficiency. This method aims to measure how efficiently a decision-making unit uses the available resources to generate a set of outputs (Charnes et al. 1978). One advantage of using this method against the parametric approach is that it deals with multiple inputs and outputs, which also does not require specification of functional form or assumptions about the error term. Moreover, it is assumed that all the banks share a common production function, given its multi-product services and definitions about inputs or outputs. And this method has the benefit to identify the sources of productivity growth as total technical efficiency (TE) that can be decomposed into two parts—pure technical efficiency (PTE) and scale efficiency (SE). Based on the DEA, the Malmquist total factor productivity index (MPI) was used to measure productivity and efficiency of banks during the period. Using DEA, the Malmquist indices were compared based on annual time series data for the period from 1991–1992 to 2014–2015.

The Malmquist productivity index is explained using the output-oriented distance function and assume output quantities to be proportionally expanded without altering the input quantities used (Fare et al. 1994). The method of Data Envelopment Analysis postulates the use of linear programming methods to construct a non-parametric frontier technology for each decision-making unit. For a given production process which employs input vector X^t to produce output vector Y^t, the output set is defined as:

$$S^t\left(X^t\right) = \left\{Y^t : X^t \text{can produce by } Y^t\right\}, \tag{5.4}$$

Introducing the one specified by Reddy (2006), the output distance function based on the output set is as:

$$D^t\left(X^t, Y^t\right) = \min\{\lambda : (Y^t/\lambda) \in S^t\left(X^t\right)\}$$
$$= \{\max\{\lambda : (\lambda/Y^t) \in S^t\left(X^t\right)\}\]^{-1} \tag{5.5}$$

Equation (5.5) is the distance function and it computes the output distance function using the Data Envelopment Analysis, its value ranges from 0 to 1, the higher its value, closer to the production frontier. Following the output-based Malmquist productivity change index specified by Fare et al. (1994) is given below as:

$$M^t\left(X^t, Y^t, X^{t+1}, Y^{t+1}\right) = \left[\frac{D^t(X^{t+1}, Y^{t+1})}{D^t(X^t, Y^t)} \times \frac{D^{t+1}(X^{t+1}, Y^{t+1})}{D^{t+1}(X^t, Y^t)}\right]^{1/2}$$

$$= \frac{D^{t+1}(X^{t+1}, Y^{t+1})}{D^t(X^t, Y^t)}\left[\frac{D^t(X^{t+1}, Y^{t+1})}{D^{t+1}(X^{t+1}, Y^{t+1})} \times \frac{D^t(X^t, Y^t)}{D^{t+1}(X^t, Y^t)}\right]^{1/2} \quad (5.6)$$

This indicates the productivity of production point (X^{t+1}, Y^{t+1}) in relation to production point at (X^t, Y^t). The ratio outside the bracket in Eq. (5.6) is the change in technical efficiency between time t and $t + 1$. The other ratios within the bracket of Eq. (5.6) are the geometric mean of the two productivity indices and it denotes the shift in production technique between time periods t and $t + 1$. Score values greater than one indicate positive total factor productivity growth from period t to $t + 1$.

$$\text{Technical Efficiency Change (TEC)} = \frac{D^{t+1}(X^{t+1}, Y^{t+1})}{D^t(X^t, Y^t)} \quad (5.7)$$

$$\text{Technical Change (TCH)} = \left[\frac{D^t(X^{t+1}, Y^{t+1})}{D^{t+1}(X^{t+1}, Y^{t+1})} \times \frac{D^t(X^t, Y^t)}{D^{t+1}(X^t, Y^t)}\right]^{1/2} \quad (5.8)$$

Technical efficiency change given in Eq. (5.7) can be further decomposed into two components—pure technical efficiency change (PEC) and scale efficiency change (SEC) (Fare et al. 1994). Thus, Eq. (5.7) can be decomposed as:

$$\text{Pure efficiency change (PEC)} = \frac{D_f^{t+1}(X^{t+1}, Y^{t+1})}{D_f^t(X^t, Y^t)} \quad (5.9)$$

and

$$\text{Scale efficiency change (SEC)} = \left[\frac{D^{t+1}(X^{t+1},\, Y^{t+1})}{D^t(X^t,\, Y^t)} \times \frac{D^t_f(X^t,\, Y^t)}{D^{t+1}_f(X^{t+1},\, Y^{t+1})} \right] \quad (5.10)$$

Equation (5.9) denotes the pure efficiency change, subject to a distance function (D_f) with variable returns to scale, between time period t and $t + 1$.

The scale efficiency change component given in Eq. (5.10) is the geometric mean of two scale efficiency measures, at time periods t and $t + 1$. It can be estimated by ratio of TEC to PEC, i.e.

$$\text{SEC} = \text{TEC/PEC} \quad (5.11)$$

From Eqs. (5.9), (5.10) and (5.11), decomposition of the MPI can be defined as:

$$M^t\left(X^t,\, Y^t,\, X^{t+1},\, Y^{t+1} \right) = \text{TCH} \times \text{TEC}$$
$$= \text{TCH} \times \text{PEC} \times \text{SEC} \quad (5.12)$$

The value of product of the index components of TCH, PEC and SCH gives the final MPI. If it is equal to one, then it indicates that performance of the banks is not changed—a value greater than one indicates improvement and less than one means a decline.

This study employs two DEA models to compute the MPI for the banks. For a firm m, the objective function is given as:

$$\left\{ D^u(X^v,\, Y^v) \right\}^{-1} = \max Q_m$$

subject to

$$X^v_{mi} - \sum_{n=1}^{N} S_{mn} X^u_{ni} \geq 0,\ i = 1, \ldots, I$$

$$-Q_m Y^v_{mj} + \sum_{n=1}^{N} S_{mn} Y^u_{nj} \geq 0,\ j = 1, \ldots, J$$

$$S_{mn} \geq 0,\ n = 1, \ldots, N, \quad (5.13)$$

Q_m unrestricted in sign
and

$$\left\{ D_r^u (X^u, Y^u) \right\}^{-1} = \max Q_m$$

subject to

$$X_{mi}^u - \sum_{n=1}^{N} S_{mn} X_{ni}^u \geq 0, \, i = 1, \ldots, I$$

$$-Q_m Y_{mj}^u + \sum_{n=1}^{N} S_{mn} Y_{nj}^u \geq 0, \, j = 1, \ldots, J$$

$$\sum_{n=1}^{N} P_{mn=1}$$

$$S_{mn} \geq 0, \, n = 1, \ldots, N \qquad (5.14)$$

Q_m unrestricted in sign
   where the subscript u denotes t time period and v for $t + 1$ period;

m indicates a specific bank;
I is the number of inputs;
J is the number of outputs;
N is the number of banks represented

The output-oriented Malmquist indices of productivity change were computed using the Data Envelopment Analysis. Details of these results are provided in Table 5.7, where the mean estimates (geometric means) of Malmquist indices of total factor productivity growth (TFPG), its decomposition into efficiency change (ECH) and technical efficiency change (TEC) included. Further, ECH is decomposed into pure efficiency change (PEC) and scale efficiency change (SEC). The results of total factor productivity growth showed that out of twenty-four public sector banks, 22 banks have positive growth. The total factor productivity growth was high for UCO Bank, United Bank of India and Bank of Baroda, (all in large bank group) and Vijaya Bank (in small banks group) as compared to other banks. On the other hand, State Bank of Hyderabad and State Bank of Patiala in the small banks group have a negative growth in total factor productivity. The results also indicated that mean total factor productivity showed a positive growth for each bank group: large banks group (1.329); small banks group (1.190); and all banks together (1.258) during the period under consideration.

The decomposition of total factor productivity growth into technical change and efficiency change indicated positive growth in mean value for each bank group and all the banks together. Mean efficiency change is 1.059 for large banks group; 1.035 for small banks group; and 1.045 for all banks together. Seven out of 24 banks have negative growth in efficiency change. Out of these seven banks, three were from the small banks group, namely Oriental Bank of Commerce, State Bank of Hyderabad and State Bank of Patiala. The other four banks with negative change in production efficiency were in large banks group—Bank of India, Canara Bank, Indian Bank and Union Bank.

The mean of overall technical efficiency is 1.203 for all banks together, 1.148 for small banks group and 1.257 for large banks group. Four out of the total 24 banks have negative technical efficiency growth. All of these banks were in small banks group, namely State Bank of Bikaner and Jaipur, State Bank of Hyderabad, State Bank of Mysore and lastly State Bank of Patiala. Mean scores of technical efficiency change were higher than efficiency change for each of the bank groups and all banks together.

Components of the efficiency change indicated that all the banks together have positive mean scale efficiency of 1.006 and pure technical efficiency change of 1.039. The large banks group also had positive growth in both these scores. However, for the small banks group, the scale efficiency has a negative change of 0.988 (Table 5.7).

Table 5.7 Changes in total factor productivity and its components: 1991–1992 to 2014–2015

Name of the bank	TFPG	Components of TFPG		Components of TEC	
		TCH	TEC	PEC	SEC
Allahabad Bank	1.286	1.175	1.095	1.058	1.035
Andhra Bank	1.329	1.217	1.092	1.070	1.021
Bank of Baroda	1.453	1.453	1.000	1.000	1.000
Bank of India	1.299	1.406	0.924	0.979	0.943
Bank of Maharashtra	1.266	1.060	1.194	1.165	1.025
Canara Bank	1.197	1.236	0.968	1.000	0.968
Central Bank of India	1.139	1.124	1.014	0.908	1.116
Corporation Bank	1.353	1.353	1.000	1.000	1.000
Dena Bank	1.322	1.264	1.046	1.101	0.950
Indian Bank	1.295	1.362	0.951	0.957	0.994
Indian Overseas Bank	1.387	1.285	1.079	1.074	1.005
Oriental Bank of Commerce	1.184	1.262	0.938	0.938	1.000
Punjab and Sind Bank	1.395	1.341	1.040	1.214	0.857
Punjab National Bank	1.229	1.130	1.088	1.000	1.088
Syndicate Bank	1.438	1.307	1.100	1.026	1.072
UCO Bank	1.710	1.444	1.184	1.140	1.038
Union Bank of India	1.114	1.130	0.986	0.935	1.054
United Bank of India	1.470	1.224	1.200	1.193	1.006
Vijaya Bank	1.536	1.254	1.225	1.277	0.960
State Bank of Bikaner and Jaipur	1.056	0.974	1.084	1.107	0.979
State Bank of Hyderabad	0.978	0.996	0.982	0.978	1.005
State Bank of Mysore	1.042	0.988	1.055	1.000	1.055
State Bank of Patiala	0.895	0.998	0.897	0.910	0.986
State Bank of Travancore	1.134	1.097	1.034	1.015	1.019
Mean (All Banks)	1.258	1.203	1.045	1.039	1.006
Mean (Small Banks)	1.190	1.148	1.035	1.051	0.988
Mean (Large Banks)	1.329	1.257	1.059	1.038	1.021

Source Calculated by authors using Eq. (5.6)

Table 5.8 reports the distribution of banks by total factor productivity change over the period. It is observed that half of all the 24 banks have total factor productivity change between 1.26 and 1.50 score values. And only 2 banks were found with total factor productivity change of more than 1.50. In terms of efficiency change, there was equal distribution between 1.00 to 1.25 and 1.26 to 1.50 ranges. For the technical efficiency change, the distribution is different as 17 banks have technical

Table 5.8 Distribution of banks by total factor productivity change

Levels	TFPG	TCH	TEC	PEC	SEC
Less than 1.00	2	4	7	7	8
1.00–1.25	8	10	17	17	16
1.26–1.50	12	10	0	0	0
More than 1.50	2	0	0	0	0

Source Calculated by authors based on Table 5.7

efficiency change within the range from 1.00 to 1.25, and the rest were having less than 1.00 efficiency score. There was no change in the pattern of components of the technical efficiency change.

Conclusion

The analysis of cost-output relation in the Indian public sector banks is important for the post-reform period. This analysis intends to make an up-to-date study of cost-size relationship of Indian banking industry. An average size of the large banks was 2 times that of the small banks in 2014–2015. The marginal costs of large banks (0.065 and 0.067) tend to be lower than that of small banks (0.070 and 0.085) in the years 2009–2010 and 2014–2015, respectively. In the other years, the small banks have lower marginal cost than that of the large banks. However, in terms of the mean average cost ($\overline{AC}$) the large banks have lower values than those of the small banks in all the years except for the year 2004–2005. MES is estimated at the deposits of Rs. 700 crores in 1991–1992, Rs. 1000 crores in 1995–1996, Rs. 1200 crores in 1999–2000, Rs. 3000 crores in 2004–2005, Rs. 9000 crores in 2009–2010 and Rs. 19,000 crores in 2014–2015. This MES was attained by all the public sector banks in each of the years selected.

The large banks operated at a scale reaping economies in all the years, the exception being year 2004–2005 achieving a position of the minimum $\overline{AC}$. For the small banks, there are economies of scale in all the selected years. Both the bank groups did not show diseconomies with respect to total cost even though there are diseconomies associated with other individual cost items. In terms of sources of efficiency or inefficiency, the large banks were able to enjoy economies in some major costs of wages and salaries in four out of the six selected years; general cost (in 1991–1992 and 2004–2005); interest cost in five out of the 6 years; and depreciation only in 1999–2000. Diseconomies of the large banks are found in depreciation in most of the years and for the general costs in 1999–2000. For the small banks, the constant sources of economies are wages and salaries; general cost in five out of the six years; and lastly, interest cost in four out of 6 years. It is worth noting that there were diseconomies of scale in depreciation cost for the small banks.

In terms of increase in efficiency with respect to economies of scale, the large banks showed greater improvement in both the periods of 1991–1992 to 1999–2000 and 1999–2000 to 2014–2015 but relatively the performance of small banks was not so for the same period.

Although there were evidences of superior performance by the large banks as compared to small ones on most of the indicators of cost efficiency in this period, the former were enjoying economies of scale with size lower than MES from 1995–1996 onwards, suggesting a potential benefit from further expansion in size. This implies that growth in banks generates positive effect on cost efficiency particularly in the case of interest cost and wages and salaries; both accounted for about 90% of total cost in Indian public sector banks. Growth in bank size tends to alter the composition of deposits (ratio of interest bearing to non-interest bearing) and staffing pattern (ratio of subordinates to officers), thereby saving in expenditures on interest and wages. Technological progression, provision of research and development, risk prevention, control and management become feasibly affordable with enlargement of bank size. Outsourcing of banking functions without additional risk as found in current practices is more advantageous in medium size bank or large one. Small banks enjoyed such advantages are limited.

This also makes a favourable case for bank takeovers (M&A) for attaining faster inorganic growth for medium size banks, as bigger size banks tend to have cost advantage over the small ones as findings of this research suggest. It would be significantly important to enlarge the small banks' size by either acquiring weak small banks with losses or small banks merging with large banks–private or public sector banks. However, it is important to mention that past mergers and acquisitions of banks in India since 1991 did not improve profitability in all cases (Bishnoi and Sofia 2015). But there may be other gains associated with size growth, as earning cost economies or postponing diseconomies of scale, and these necessarily need not result in higher profits. Profit is a function of both the price and cost per unit of output, and cost efficiency alone does not guarantee for higher profitability in the absence of efficient price of product.

Manpower productivity ratios indicated positive change as expected; cost ratio decelerated and other ratios improved to suggest productivity gains from 1991–1992 to 2014–2015. Twenty-two of 24 public sector banks have positive total factor productivity growth in 1991–1992 to 2014–2015. Half of all the 24 banks have total factor productivity change between 1.26 and 1.50 score values. And only 2 banks were found with total factor productivity change of more than 1.50.

References

Alam, Ila M.S. 2001. Nonparametric Approach for Assessing Productivity Dynamics of Large U.S. Banks. *Journal of Money, Credit and Banking* 33 (1): 121–139.

Allen, J., and Y. Liu. 2007. Efficiency and Economies of Large Canadian Banks. *Canadian Journal of Economics* 40 (1): 225–244.

Angadi, V.B., and V.J. Devaraj. 1983. Productivity and Profitability of Banks in India. *Economic and Political Weekly* 18 (48): M160–M170.

Apergis, N., and A. Rezitis. 2004. Cost Structure, Technological Change, and Productivity Growth in the Greek Banking Sector. *International Advances in Economic Research* 10 (1): 1–15.

Bell, F.W., and N.B. Murphy. 1968. Economies of Scale and Division of Labor in Commercial Banking. *Southern Economic Journal* 35 (2): 131–139.

Benston, G.J. 1965. Branch Banking and Economies of Scale. *The Journal of Finance* 20 (2): 312–331.

Benston, G.J. 1972. Economies of Scale of Financial Institutions. *Journal of Money, Credit and Banking* 4 (2): 312–341.

Benston, G.J., G.J. Hanweck, and D.B. Humphrey. 1982. Scale Economies in Banking—A Restructuring and Reassessment. *Journal of Money, Credit and Banking* 14 (4): 435–456.

Bhattacharyya, A., C.A.K. Lovell, and Pankaj Sahay. 1997. The Impact of Liberalization on the Productive of Indian Commercial Banks. *European Journal of Operational Research* 98 (2): 332–345.

Bishnoi, T.R., and Sofia Devi. 2015. Mergers and Acquisitions of Banks in Post-Reform India. *Economic and Political Weekly* 50 (37): 50–58.

Charnes, A., W.W. Cooper, and E. Rhodes. 1978. Measuring the Efficiency of Decision Making Units. *European Journal of Operations Research* 2 (6): 429–444.

Clark, J.A. 1996. Economic Cost, Scale Efficiency, and Competitive Viability in Banking. *Journal of Money, Credit and Banking* 28 (3): 342–364.

Clark, J.A., and P.J. Speaker. 1994. Economies of Scale and Scope in Banking: Evidence from a Generalized Translog. *Quarterly Journal of Business and Economics* 33 (2): 3–25.

Das, A., and S.C. Kumbhakar. 2012. Productivity and Dynamics in Indian Banking: An Input Distance Function Approach Incorporating Quality of Inputs and Outputs. *Journal of Applied Econometrics* 27 (2): 205–234.

Deshpande, M.A. 1981. Profitability and Productivity in Commercial Banks. In *On Bankers and Economists*, ed. N.K. Thingalaya. New Delhi: MacMillan India Ltd.

Divatia, V.V., and T.R. Venkatachalam. 1978. Operational Efficiency and Profitability of Public Sector Banks. (R.B.S Occasional Papers, June): 1–16.

Fare, R., S. Grosskopf, M. Norris, and Z. Zhang. 1994. Productivity Growth, Technical Progress and Efficiency Change in Industrialized Countries. *American Economic Review* 84 (1): 66–83.

Greenbaum, S.I. 1967. Competition and Efficiency in the Banking System— Empirical and Research and its Policy Implications. *The Journal of Political Economy* 75 (4): 461–479.

Keshari, P.K., and M.T. Paul. 1994. Relative Efficiency of Foreign and Domestic Banks Author. *Economic and Political Weekly* 29 (9): M31–M36.

Ram, Mohan T.T., and S.C. Ray. 2004. Comparing Performance of Public and Private Sector Banks: A Revenue Maximisation Efficiency Approach. *Economic and Political Weekly* 39 (12): 1271–1272, 1274–1276.

Rangarajan, C., and P. Mampilly. 1972. Economies of Scale in Banking. *Reserve Bank of India, Technical Studies Prepared for the Banking Commission* I: 244–68.

Ravindranath, K.V. 1979. Operational Efficiency and Profitability of Public Sector Banks: A Comment. *Pigmy Economic Review*, (April): 3–7.

Reddy, A.A. 2006. Productivity Growth in Regional Rural Banks. *Economic and Political Weekly* 41 (11): 1079–1086.

Sandesara, J.C. 1979. Economies of Scale in Indian Manufacturing Industry, (Mimeo). Department of Economics, University of Bombay, Chap. II.

Scherer, F.M. 1980. *Industrial Market Structure and Economic Performance*, 2nd ed. Chicago: Rand McNally.

Sensarma, R. 2005. Cost and Profit of Indian banks during 1986–2003. *Economic and Political Weekly* 40 (12): 1198–1200.

Shepherd, W.G. 1979. *The Economics of Industrial Organization*. Englewood Cliffs, NJ: Prentice-Hall.

Stimpert, J.L., and J.A. Laux. 2011. Does Size Matter? Economies of Scale in the Banking Industry. *Journal of Business & Economics Research* 9 (3): 47–56.

Todhanakasem, W., M.J. Lynge, W.J. Primeaux, and P. Newbold. 1986. Economies of Scale and Organizational Efficiency in Banking. *Managerial and Decision Economics* 7 (4): 255–261.

Varde, V.S., and S.P. Singh. 1983. Profitability of Commercial Banks (Section-B, Chapter I), 35–41. Bombay: NIBM.

Wheelock, D.C., and P.W. Wilson. 1999. Technical Progress, Inefficiency and Productivity change in U.S. Banking, 1984–1993. *Journal of Money, Credit and Banking* 31 (2): 212–234.

6

Profitability

Introduction

Public sector firms in India were not emphasizing the objectives of profitability in initial phases as primary focus remained in promoting social and economic welfare of the public. So was the case of public sector banks with social orientation in branch expansion and use of bank funds for more than 3 decades since the nationalization of banks in 1969. This was to align the banking policy with other welfare-enhancing macropolicy measures. However, in long-term profitability objective cannot be substituted by any other goals for the reason of survival and growth particularly in globalized banking environment, and thus, the banking reforms have rightly stressed market orientation and importance of profitability for financial health and viability while moderating earlier stance of social banking objectives. Since government banks were marginally privatized over a decade and now public listed firms, it is, therefore, capable of raising capital from private and institutional investors including Foreign Institutional Investors (FIIs) and also enjoys operational autonomy and commercial freedom in their banking activities. Thus, profit

© The Author(s) 2017
T.R. Bishnoi and S. Devi, *Banking Reforms in India*, Palgrave Macmillan Studies in Banking and Financial Institutions, DOI 10.1007/978-3-319-55663-5_6

maximization objective is pursued by banks for their healthy growth and competitiveness and it is opportune to examine this aspect here.

In this chapter, profitability of public sector banks is analysed for the period from 1991–1992 to 2014–2015. Introduction section is followed by bank profitability measured by three parameters, namely return on assets (ROA), return on equity (ROE) and profit margin (PM).

1. Return on assets: It is a measure of performance which measures profit of a firm in relation to its total assets. It reflects ability of a bank's management to generate profits from bank's assets. It shows profits earned per rupee of assets and indicates how effectively bank's assets are managed to generate revenues. It is defined as the ratio of profit after tax to total assets of a firm for a given time period. It is expressed as:

$$ROA = Profit\ after\ tax/Total\ assets$$

2. Return on equity: ROE measures the rate of return on shareholders' equity. It is a measure of efficiency. It indicates how well a firm manages its investment funds to generate earnings growth. It is defined as the ratio of profit after tax to average value of net worth. However, this ratio alone cannot be used to judge the financial performance without considering other profitability ratios mentioned above. It is expressed as

$$ROE = Profit\ after\ tax/Net\ worth\ (capital + reserves)$$

3. Profit margin: This ratio is a good index of operating efficiency. It shows PM of banks' operations. It is defined as the ratio of net profit as percentage to total income of bank. It measures how much out of every rupee of income a firm actually keeps in earnings. A high PM indicates a more profitable and that has control over its costs of production. It is expressed as:

$$Profit\ Margin = Net\ Profit/Total\ Income$$

The term profit is an accounting concept which is defined as a difference between total earnings from all earning assets and expenditure on managing entire asset-liabilities portfolio. And profitability is a relative concept which describes the relationship of absolute quantity of profit with various other parameters. Profits and profitability are significant for the banks to support and compensate for any loan losses, exchange rate variations, shortage of liquidity, inadequate capital and reserves, etc., and so improving profits and profitability is important to generate internal capital (Verghese 1983). Various factors determine the profitability of banks. Profitability of banks is governed by endogenous variables (such as changes in monetary policy—both qualitative and quantitative credit controls—priority sector lending schemes, variation in interest rates on deposits and advances and taxes on interest income), exogenous factors (management of banks' resources, containing the expenditures, timely recovery of loans, etc.) as well as other structural factors to the system (Angadi and Devaraj 1983). The definition of profitability and its determinants varies from bank-specific variables to financial structure variables to legal and institutional variables to macro-economic variables and so on.

Empirical Studies

Banks' profitability performance is affected largely by four factors—volume of business, gross margin, manpower expenses and branch expansion (Singh 1974). Interest rate change is the most important factor determining profitability of banks during the post-nationalization and pre-deregulation period (Verghese 1983). The trend has changed after adoption of the liberalization policies. Banks have gained considerable commercial freedom within the broad regulatory framework. The profitability of public sector banks was very low before reforms due to social banking as the main objective of banks and was to lay down for social banking. The performance of PSBs improved during post-liberalization period from 1991–1992 to 1999–2000 in absolute and relative terms (Ram Mohan 2002). The study was based on the performance of PSBs by taking a number of indicators, viz., net profits, net interest margin, intermediation cost and non-performing assets. However, the PSBs witnessed a decline in their profitability during the period from

1997–1998 to 2000–2001, mainly due to continuous decline in net interest margin (Chaudhuri 2002).

In a different analytical framework, Batra (1996) analysed profitability of the Indian scheduled commercial banks using a profit function that is a hybrid of Cobb-Douglas and translog covering pre- and post-nationalization periods (1955–1987). Profitability is measured by ratio of profits to total current operating expenses and ratio of gross profits to working funds. The explanatory variables employed were the gross rate of loans and investments, average total wages, policy variables, prices paid on deposits and borrowings, and branch variable in order to capture the economic feasibility of banking. Empirical results indicated significance of loans and investments in banks assets' portfolio and also of policy variables (SLR and CRR) in operational efficiency. And cost on deposits was significant (negative), showing an increase in total deposits. It is associated with higher costs in terms of rates of interests and also shifting maturity pattern for longer term deposits. Further, branching variable has limited role in explaining profitability.

Koeva (2003) examined the behaviour of determinants of bank intermediation costs and profitability of all commercial banks in India for the period from 1991–1992 to 2000–2001. Banks with higher administrative costs were found to have significantly higher spreads and lower profitability. Banks with higher level of NPAs were found to have significantly lower profitability. However, in some specifications, larger share of investment in government securities was associated with higher spreads. Banks with higher share of current deposits have significantly lower bank spreads and higher profitability. Branches as a variable did not have significant impact on the profitability but number of branches was found to have a positive and significant impact on the net interest margin. The empirical results also indicated that ownership type has a significant effect on some of the performance indicators. Foreign banks and private sector banks were found to perform better than the nationalized banks, no doubt for the State Bank and its associates. Industry concentration as measured by the Herfindahl index declined during the decade. Competition increased during financial liberalization with correspondingly lower profitability of Indian banks.

Ghosh (2009) investigates the performance of Indian commercial banks during the post-reform period 1992–2004. The results indicate high levels of efficiency in costs and lower levels in profits, reflecting the importance of inefficiencies in revenue side of banking activity. Decomposition of profit efficiency shows that a large portion of outlay is due to allocative inefficiency.

A recent study by Rakhe (2010) compared financial performance of foreign banks with other bank groups covering 59 banks in India for the period from 2000 to 2009. Net profit to total asset ratio was taken as the dependent variable. The results found that efficiency of fund management (the amount of interest expenses required for generating one rupee interest income) has determined profits to a large extent followed by generation of other income. The performance of foreign banks is found to be comparatively better than domestically owned banks in terms of cost efficiency, fund management and other income diversification.

In a different perspective, Haslem (1968) measured profitability of banks using different effects—management effects, size effects, location effects and time effects. And each variable significantly affected relative profitability and majority of operating relationships that determine profitability.

Grifell and Lovell (1999) estimated sources of change in profits of Spanish commercial banks, which covered roughly two-thirds of all commercial banks during the period 1987–1994. The study considers the linkage between productivity change and profit change. The change in profit is decomposed into three different sources—productivity change effect (which includes a technical change effect and an operating efficiency effect), activity effect (which includes a product mix effect, a resource mix effect and a scale effect) and price effect. The combined productivity and activity effect, which arguably reflects factors largely under the control of bank management, made a positive contribution to profit change in all 7 years. However, negative price effect offsets positive combined productivity and activity effect during the entire sample period.

Using bank-level data of 80 countries, Demirguc-Kunt and Huizinga (1999) analysed the determinants of profitability and net interest margin for the period from 1988 to 1995. Profitability was measured by the ratio of profit before tax to total assets and various bank characteristic variables, macroeconomic variables as well as institutional and legal variables taken as explanatory variables. Empirical findings found a positive relationship between profitability and capitalization of banks, whereas there was a negative relation between reserves and profitability. Larger bank asset to GDP ratio and lower market concentration ratio were associated with lower margins and profits. Foreign banks as compared to domestic banks were found with higher margins and profits in developing countries, while the reverse held in the case of developed countries. And institutional factors have more pronounced effects on interest margins and profitability in developing countries than in developed countries. Also, there was evidence that the corporate tax burden was fully passed on to bank customers.

Goddard et al. (2004) investigated profitability of major banking sectors of six European countries based on cross-sectional, pooled cross-sectional time series and dynamic panel models for the period 1992–1998. ROA is taken as a measure of profitability, which is determined by total assets (size variable), off-site balance sheet (OBS) business as a proportion assets plus OBS business (to capture the non-interest income and fee-generating services from various contingent liabilities), the ratio of capital to total assets (as a measure of risk) and dummy variables for ownership (commercial bank or savings or cooperative banks). Despite the growth in competition in European financial markets, there was significant persistence of profit from 1 year to the next. While some evidence of a significant size-profitability relation was found in some of the estimations, overall the evidence for any consistent or systematic relationship was relatively weak. The relationship between the importance of off-balance-sheet business in a bank's portfolio and profitability is positive for the UK, but either neutral or negative for the elsewhere. However, positive relationship was found between the ratio of capital to assets and profitability, which contradicts the theoretical relationship between risk and return. There is a little evidence of any systematic relationship between ownership type and profitability.

Loukoianova (2008) analyses the efficiency and profitability of Japanese banks from 2000–2006 using nonparametric approach to analyse banks' cost and revenue efficiency. Results show that performance of Japanese banks has steadily improved since 2001, but there are significant differences within the banking sector, with regional banks being less cost and revenue efficient relative to both City and Trust banks. While Japanese bank profitability is low compared to that in other advanced countries, there is considerable potential for efficiency gains, particularly through increased cost-sharing arrangements among regional banks, consolidation of regional banks with major or other regional banks and the creation of bank consortia to pool resources for asset and risk management.

From the literatures, it is evident that many studies incorporate bank-specific variables and macroeconomic indicators in explaining profitability of banks. This study differs from the earlier studies on the choice of indicators of profitability, namely ROA, ROE and PM. It also used bank-specific variables such as cost efficiency, credit quality, credit risk and interest income ratio to explain profitability. This analysis is compatible with the one used by Koeva (2003) that analyses profitability of Indian commercial banks for the period from 1991–1992 to 2000–2001 with slight differences in the selection of explanatory variables and profitability indicators taken.

Profitability

Structure of Operating Income and Expenditure

An overview of cost and income structure will reveal the nature of profits and losses in working of banks. Tables 6.1 and 6.2 give information on operating income and expenditures by bank group for the selected years.

Operating Income: From Table 6.1, we see that the contribution of total income earned through interest income is higher than income from other sources for each bank group. On an average, almost 90% of the income earnings are through interest income for each bank group. In 1991–1992, State Bank and its associated banks group have 87.69% of total income by interest earnings, 90.29% for the nationalized banks

Table 6.1 Composition of operating income: 1991–1992 and 2014–2015 (%)

Sr. No.	Item	SBI and associates		Nationalized banks		Public sector banks	
		1991–1992	2014–2015	1991–1992	2014–2015	1991–1992	2014–2015
I.	Interest earned	87.69	87.98	90.29	90.80	89.28	89.94
	Interest/Discount earned on advances/bills	53.34	65.89	55.01	67.28	54.36	66.86
	Income on investments	19.71	20.51	25.29	21.50	23.12	21.20
	Interest on balances with RBI and other inter-bank funds	10.92	0.40	9.48	1.42	10.04	1.11
	Others	3.72	1.17	0.50	0.60	1.76	0.77
II.	Other income	12.31	12.02	9.71	9.20	10.72	10.06
	Commission, exchange and brokerage	8.09	7.05	5.20	3.11	6.33	4.32
	Net profit (loss) on revaluation of investment, sale of assets, sale of investments and exchange transactions	3.99	3.03	3.52	3.61	3.71	3.43
	Miscellaneous income	0.23	1.95	0.99	2.47	0.69	2.31
	Total income (I + II)	(100.00)	(100.00)	(100.00)	(100.00)	(100.00)	(100.00)
	Rs. million	134,288	2,297,027	210,180	5,219,423	344,467	7,516,450

Source RBI: Statistical tables relating to banks in India, relevant issues

Table 6.2 Composition of total cost: 1991–1992 and 2014–2015 (%)

Sr No.	Item	SBI and its associates		Nationalized banks		Public sector banks	
		1991–1992	2014–2015	1991–1992	2014–2015	1991–1992	2014–2015
III.	Interest expended	72.08	73.16	73.01	80.52	72.73	78.35
	Interest on deposits	54.50	66.92	61.32	74.42	58.90	72.20
	Interest on RBI/inter-bank borrowings	14.58	2.75	7.47	2.11	9.99	2.30
	Others	3.00	3.49	4.31	3.99	3.84	3.84
IV.	Operating expenses	27.92	26.84	26.90	19.48	27.27	21.65
	Payments to and provisions for employees	19.62	16.35	18.57	11.87	18.94	13.19
	Depreciation on bank's property	0.65	0.80	0.72	0.81	0.69	0.81
	General expenses	7.65	9.69	7.62	6.80	7.63	7.65
	Total expenses (III + IV)	(100.00)	(100.00)	(100.00)	(100.00)	(100.00)	(100.00)
	Rs. million	102,554	1,814,688	186,503	4,323,901	289,057	6,138,589

Source RBI: Statistical Tables Relating to Banks in India, relevant issues

and 89.28% for all the public sector banks together. Among the interest income components, the proportion of income earned on bills is the highest, followed by income on investment, interest income on balances with RBI and others. Between 1991–1992 and 2014–2015, the relative share of income in 2014–2015 through interest on balances with RBI declined from 10.92 to 0.40% for the SBI group, from 9.48 to 1.42% for the nationalized banks and from 10.04 to 1.11% for all the banks together. This decline in the share of earnings with balances in RBI may be due to reduction in the SLR and CRR rates over the period. On the other hand, other income sources such as commissions, fees, revaluations and sale of assets have only 10–12% of the total income earnings. The State Bank and its associated banks have 12.31% through these other income sources, followed by 10.72% for other nationalized banks and 9.71% for all the banks together in group. The percentage share of commission and brokerage fees is more than the other sources of income. Approximately 50% of the source of other income of each bank group is through commission and brokerage fees. The very high proportion of interest income against the other income indicates banks' major source of earning is through lending activities. And the proportions remain more or less the same during the period 2014–2015. No major differences existed among the bank groups in terms of other sources of income.

Total Cost: In Table 6.2, total expenditure by bank group for the period 1991–1992 and 2014–2015 is given. The total expenditure of banks on interest expenditure is more than 70% of total cost for each bank group in 1991–1992. There is no change in the percentage of interest expenditure in 2014–2015. The State Bank group has expended 72.08% on interest expenditure in 1991–1992, 73.01% for the nationalized banks group and 72.73% for all the banks together. In 2014–2015, there is no change in the pattern of total expenditure except for the nationalized banks that gone up to 80.52%. The State Bank group has more or less similar share of 73.16% as in 2014–2015, and 78.35% for all the banks together. Among the interest expenditure, interest on deposit has the largest share, followed by interest on RBI and inter-bank borrowings and others. However, in 2014–2015 interest expenses on RBI and inter-bank borrowings decline to less than 3% for each bank group. The reason is the same as cited in Table 6.1, a decline in share of income earnings through balances with RBI as a result of cut in CRR and SLR rates over the period. Operating expenses on the other hand include payments to and provisions for employees, depreciation on bank's property and general expenses including miscellaneous expenditures. State Bank group incurred operating expenses of 27.92% in 1991–1992 and 26.84% in 2014–2015, respectively. For the nationalized banks, the relative shares are 26.90% in 1991–1992 and declined to 19.48% in 2014–2015. In overall, all the public sector banks together have 27.27 and 21.65% of operating expenses in 1991–1992 and 2014–2015, respectively. Maximum expenses of operating expenditure are on payments to provisions for employees. Each bank group spends only up to 1% of the operating expenses for depreciation on bank's property in each specific period. No differences were found for both the bank groups in terms of general expenses, as it was less than 10% in each period. Marginal increase was found in the payments and provisions to employees for both the bank groups.

Trends in Profitability Ratios

This section reports the trends in three profitability indicators—ROA, ROE and PM by bank group for the period from 1991–1992 to the latest data available 2014–2015. A benchmark of 5 years' average is also estimated for each of the three parameters except 4 years in the last period.

ROA across the bank groups showed that the ratio was minimum and even negative in the early part of the 90's, till 1995–1996. From the financial year 1996–1997, ROA across the banks turned positive values and reached the peak level of 1.29% in 2003–2004. During the financial period from 2004–2005 to 2010–2011, it hovered around 1% for all the public sector banks together. State Bank and its associated group reported better performance of ROA than the public sector banks. The state bank group witnessed positive values of the ROA in the early part of the 90's except in the financial year 1995–1996, in which the State Bank of Saurashtra made a loss of 48% of its total earnings. However, in the subsequent financial years, performance was improved and ROA reached the peak level of 1.34% in 2003–2004 and thereafter it remained around the value of 1%. The nationalized banks have poor performance in terms of ROA than the SBI group. After the financial sector reforms of 1991, ROA of nationalized banks had turned into negative till the financial year 1995–1996. Twelve out of the 19 banks did have loss making from their earnings in the financial year 1992–1993, and further 13 banks in 1993–1994 and declined to only 3 banks in the financial year 1996–1997. From the financial year 1996–1997, nationalized banks group witnessed a positive trend of ROAs, reaching the value of 1.27% in the financial year 2003–2004, and thereafter fluctuate around the value of 1%. During 2013–2014 and 2014–2015, the average ROA decline for each bank group which is measured as 0.56 and 0.60% for the SBI group and 0.38 and 0.33% for the nationalized banks, respectively.

ROE of the banks registered a declining trend in the first two subsequent years after the reforms, 1991 and even turned negative for the nationalized banks group. From the financial year 1996–1997, all the public sector banks recovered losses and earned 11.25% on equity. In the financial year 2003–2004, all the public sector banks reached a peak-level ROE of 25.37%. However, ROA hovered around the value of 17% in between 2004–2005 and 2010–2011. In short, the ROA of the banks after the financial sector reforms improved although there were fluctuations over the period. The performance of the State Bank group is comparatively better than that of the public sector banks. For the SBI group, the ROA remained fluctuated till the financial year 1995–1996 in which the State Bank of Saurashtra made a huge net loss. However, unlike the ROA, the ROA did not turn negative (4.55%) in this financial year. From the financial year 1996–1997, it made up its losses and reached the peak level of 28.30% in 2003–2004. Thereafter from 2004–2005, the ROE moved around the range of 18–20% till 2010–2011 and gradually declined to 14.60% in 2012–2013 and to 9.97% in 2014–2015. The nationalized banks group, on the other hand, made losses in early part of the reforms. It was from the financial year 1996–1997 that this bank group started recovering their losses with 7.91% ROA. It has reached a peak level in 2003–2004, with a value of 24.14%. ROA of nationalized banks moved around 17% till

2010–2011 and gradually declined to 6.34% in 2013–2014 and 5.95% in 2014–2015, respectively. Public sector banks together improved on ROE after the reforms.

Another determinant of profitability of banks is the PM. The PM of all the banks together was less than 2% in 1991–1992. In the subsequent period, there is a deterioration in PM of the public sector banks which remained negative till 1995–1996. In 1996–1997, it has a positive value of 3.86% and increases gradually over the period and touch the highest level of 12.75% in 2003–2004. The PM hovers around the value of 9–10% till 2010–2011 and declines to 4.13% in 2014–2015. Looking at the SBI and its group, a relative healthy picture is visible over the period except in 1995–1996, where it turns negative to −2.13%. In the subsequent periods, PM of this bank group increases gradually reaching its highest level of 13.48% in 2003–2004. In the later period, PM hovers around 10% till 2010–2011 and declines to 5.94% in 2014–2015. The State Bank group showed a constant per cent of profit after the reforms till 1994–1995. Although it made losses in the financial year 1995–1996, from the financial year 1996–1997 it recovered losses and made earnings over the period. The trend of PM for the nationalized banks is different from the SBI group. This bank group has a PM of 1.45% in 1991–1992 and turns negative in the subsequent period to till 1995–1996. In a similar pattern with the SBI group, this bank group also improves its PM gradually and reaches its peak point in 2003–2004 to 12.44%. It hovers around 9–10% till 2010–2011 and declines to 3.59% in 2014–2015. The nationalized banks group also made up its losses from 1996–1997 although there were losses in the early part of the reforms. No major differences were found in the earnings of both the bank groups except the PSBs made losses in the early part of the reforms.

Average values of profitability ratios were work out for a benchmark of 5 years and 4 years for the last period from 2011–2012 to 2014–2015 due to the availability of data. The State Bank and its associated banks group have better performance than other nationalized banks in terms of each of the ratios in each period, and the highest values are found during 2001–2002 to 2005–2006 for both the bank groups. The mean ROA hovers around 1%, around 9% for ROE and 6–7% for PM.

Moreover, trend growth rate for each of the profitability indicators is measured and the results are statistically significant. The trend growth rate is computed by regressing profitability indicator on the time trend and the equation takes the form: $Y = a + bT$, where Y represents profitability indicator and $T = (t_0, t_1, ..., t_n)$ denotes the time trend. Fitting the regression, the following results are attained:

ROA as the profitability indicator:

$$Y = -0.196 + 0.060T$$
$$(3.336)*$$
$$P = 0.003; \quad R\text{-square} = 0.336; \quad d = 1.023$$

ROE as the profitability indicator:

$$Y = -2.470 + 1.048T$$
$$(2.524)*$$
$$P = 0.019; \quad R\text{-square} = 0.235; \quad d = 1.317$$

PM as the profitability indicator:

$$Y = -3.289 + 0.693T$$
$$(3.785)*$$
$$P = 0.001; \quad R\text{-square} = 0.394; \quad d = 1.035$$

Profitability of the public sector banks grew by a margin of 0.06 in terms of ROA and is statistically significant. Similarly, the trend growth rates in terms of other profitability ratios are also statistically significant. ROA raise at the margin of 1.05 during the period from 1991–1992 to 2014–2015; PM at the rate of 0.69 basis points during the period. The growth rate of ROE is much faster than that of PM and ROA during the period.

Determinants of Profitability

Definition of variables: As discussed in the literatures, various profitability ratios are employed by the researchers in measuring bank performance. In our study, three most popular proxies of profitability, namely ROA, ROE and PM, are used. Four bank-specific variables were taken as explanatory variables. These variables are capital strength, credit quality, management of funds and operational efficiency.

The effects of bank-specific variables on profitability are also examined below.

Capital strength: It is one of the main determinants of bank performance. Banks with higher capital to assets ratio are considered relatively safer compared with lower ratios. The ratio shows ability of the bank to withstand losses. It is expected that the higher the ratio, the lower the need for external funding and therefore the higher the profitability of the bank.

H₁   Equity to total assets ratio is positively related to bank profitability

Credit quality: A higher loan loss provisions over total advances go together with a lower credit quality and hence a lower profitability.

H₂   The ratio of provisions to total loans is negatively related to bank profitability

Interest factor: The net interest rate spread is the difference between interest earned on loans, securities and other interest-earning assets and the interest paid on deposits and other interest-bearing liabilities. An increase in the value will imply a reduction in the cost of funds.

H₃   Interest factor is negatively related to bank profitability

Cost efficiency: It is defined as the ratio of operating cost to total assets. It is used to measure the impact of efficiency on bank profitability. Higher cost-income ratio is associated with lower profitability.

H₄   Cost-income ratio is negatively related to bank profitability

In this section, we examine determinants of profitability of the public sector banks using regression analysis.

Data, variables and model: The data on profitability and bank-specific variables were compiled from various reports and publications of the RBI database. Bank-wise data was used for the period from 1991–1992 to 2014–2015. Most of the data are from the annual publications of RBI, viz., Statistical Tables Relating to Banks in India and Basic Statistical Returns of Scheduled Commercial Banks in India. The sample contains 28 public sector banks comprising 8 banks of SBI and its associated banks and the rest nationalized banks. The 28 public sector banks together account for more than 90% of the total assets of all Scheduled Commercial Banks as in the financial year 2014–2015. The analysis is carried out for different bank groups—SBI and its associates, Nationalized Banks group and the public sector banks together. The determinants of profitability are—ROA, ROE and PM. These profitability ratios are expressed in terms of four bank-specific variables, namely capital strength which is measured as the ratio of equity to total assets, credit quality as defined by ratio of provisions to total advances, cost of funds expressed by ratio of interest expense to interest income and last but not the least variable is cost efficiency that is measured by ratio of operating cost to total assets. In order to examine empirically the effects of bank-specific variables on profitability, a linear regression model is fitted for each of the determinants. The regression model takes the following form:

$$
\Pi_{i,t} = \alpha + \beta_0 \, \text{Capital strength} + \beta_1 \, \text{Credit quality} \\
+ \beta_2 \, \text{Cost funds} + \beta_3 \, \text{Efficiency} + \mu_{it} \tag{6.1}
$$

where $\Pi_{i,t}$ is a measure of profitability of bank i at time t, and the variables on the right-hand side are the explanatory variables as outlined in Table 6.3 in the previous section and μ_{it} is the error term with its usual properties.

Regression Results: This section reports the regression results of profitability indicators. The results are based on the method of Ordinary Least Squares (OLS) as given in Eq. (6.1) in the previous section. Profitability indicator is expressed in terms of four ratios—capital to total assets, provisions to total advances, interest expense to interest income and operating cost to total assets. Only two estimated coefficients, namely credit

Table 6.3 A summary of dependent and explanatory variables

Variables	Description (%)	Notation
Dependent variables		
Profitability	Return on assets	ROA
	Return on equity	ROE
	Profit margin	PM
Independent variables		
Capital strength	Ratio of equity to total assets	Capital strength
Credit quality	Ratio of provisions to total advances	Credit quality
Interest factor	Interest expense to interest income ratio	Interest ratio
Operating efficiency	Operating cost to total assets ratio	Efficiency

quality and costs of fund management, are statistically significant and posses theoretically expected signs for each of the profitability indicators. The other two regression coefficients, namely capital strength and efficiency ratios, are not statistically significant. The regression results indicated that credit risk and income ratio explain profitability of the public sector banks estimated in terms of ROA, ROE and PM during the period from 1991–1992 to 2014–2015. In terms of the profitability indicator ROA, credit quality explains 0.39 and 0.70% for the cost of funds of public sector banks. For ROE, 7.7% of credit quality explains profitability and 1.5% in terms of cost of funds. Likewise, in terms of PM, credit quality explains 3.8 and 5.9% for cost of funds that define profitability during the period. We also estimated determinants of profitability by using fixed and random effect models of panel data regression. The Hausman test supported the fixed effect models. The results of FEM do support the OLS regression estimated coefficients (Tables 6.4 and 6.5).

Interest factor is one of the major determinants of profitability that is to say interest expenses in relation to interest income shaped the profit trends. It is so because non-fund banking business is negligible for Indian banks. In other words, the non-interest income in relation to non-interest expenses is very small. Hence, interest factor becomes a dominant force in profitability trend. Approximately 80% of total expenses are attributed to interest costs and about 90% of income

Table 6.4 Profitability of the public sector banks: 1991–1992 to 2014–2015 (%)

Year	Return on assets (ROA)			Return on equity (ROE)			Profit margin (PM)		
	SBI and its associates	Nationalized banks	All public sector banks	SBI and its associates	Nationalized banks	All public sector banks	SBI and its associates	Nationalized banks	All public sector banks
1991–1992	0.31	0.27	0.28	16.06	11.18	12.63	2.43	1.45	1.73
1992–1993	0.27	−2.33	−1.56	13.56	−72.23	−46.81	2.19	−23.22	−15.96
1993–1994	0.26	−2.35	−1.58	11.50	−42.68	−26.63	2.32	−24.98	−16.89
1994–1995	0.41	0.02	0.14	17.40	3.33	7.50	3.58	−0.33	0.83
1995–1996	−0.25	−0.57	−0.48	4.55	−6.33	−3.11	−2.13	−6.11	−4.93
1996–1997	0.76	0.39	0.50	19.18	7.91	11.25	6.16	2.89	3.86
1997–1998	1.15	0.66	0.81	24.75	11.72	15.58	9.04	5.17	6.32
1998–1999	0.65	0.54	0.57	15.74	9.19	11.13	5.78	2.80	3.68
1999–2000	0.86	0.53	0.63	19.96	11.22	13.81	7.64	3.86	4.98
2000–2001	0.66	0.42	0.49	15.93	7.04	9.68	6.03	2.50	3.55
2001–2002	0.95	0.68	0.76	22.63	14.47	16.89	8.96	6.21	7.02
2002–2003	1.15	1.02	1.06	25.84	19.62	21.47	11.08	9.30	9.83
2003–2004	1.34	1.27	1.29	28.30	24.14	25.37	13.48	12.44	12.75
2004–2005	0.86	0.93	0.91	17.79	15.65	16.26	9.74	10.29	10.13
2005–2006	0.81	0.85	0.84	16.48	13.92	14.65	9.63	9.87	9.80
2006–2007	0.88	0.96	0.94	18.11	16.59	17.02	10.32	10.85	10.70
2007–2008	0.86	1.03	0.98	18.10	17.69	17.81	9.14	10.71	10.26
2008–2009	0.97	0.98	0.98	20.86	17.19	18.14	10.00	9.97	9.98
2009–2010	0.98	0.97	0.98	19.46	18.03	18.40	10.78	10.83	10.82
2010–2011	0.99	0.98	0.98	18.90	17.10	17.52	10.74	10.84	10.82
2011–2012	0.88	0.84	0.85	16.30	14.46	14.89	8.78	8.66	8.69
2012–2013	0.82	0.71	0.73	14.60	11.97	12.58	8.00	7.21	7.39
2013–2014	0.56	0.38	0.42	9.67	6.34	7.11	5.52	4.06	4.40
2014–2015	0.60	0.33	0.40	9.97	5.95	6.87	5.94	3.59	4.13

(continued)

Table 6.3 (continued)

Year	Return on assets (ROA)			Return on equity (ROE)			Profit margin (PM)		
	SBI and its associates	Nationalized banks	All public sector banks	SBI and its associates	Nationalized banks	All public sector banks	SBI and its associates	Nationalized banks	All public sector banks
1991–1992 to 1995–1996	0.20	−0.99	−0.64	12.62	−21.35	−11.28	1.68	−10.64	−7.04
1996–1997 to 2000–2001	0.81	0.51	0.60	19.11	9.41	12.29	6.93	3.44	4.48
2001–2002 to 2005–2006	1.02	0.95	0.97	22.21	17.56	18.93	10.58	9.62	9.90
2006–2007 to 2010–2011	0.93	0.98	0.97	19.09	17.32	17.78	10.19	10.64	10.51
2011–2012 to 2014–2015	0.71	0.57	0.60	12.63	9.68	10.36	7.06	5.88	6.15

Note ROA data from 1991–1992 to 1996–1997 and ROE data from 1991–1992 to 1997–1998 are calculated by authors using the formula given in RBI Glossary
Source RBI: Statistical Tables Relating to Banks in India, various issues

Table 6.5 Determinants of profitability: 1991–1992 to 2014–2015

Profitability indicators	Capital strength	Credit quality	Cost funds	Efficiency	R-square	D-W statistic
Π_{ROA}	0.062	−0.394[a]	−0.70[a]	−0.104	0.816	0.988
	(0.661)	(−4.712)	(−4.557)	(−0.642)		
Π_{ROE}	2.722	−7.702[a]	−1.489[a]	0.039	0.728	1.702
	(1.127)	(3.561)	(−3.750)	(0.009)		
Π_{PM}	0.259	−3.795[a]	−0.784[a]	−2.355	0.870	1.016
	(0.318)	(−5.204)	(−5.854)	(−1.674)		

Note Figures in the parentheses are the t-values; [a]denotes level of significance at 5%
Source Estimated by authors using the OLS regression given in the previous section

originated from interest income. Higher the non-performing assets provisions in relation to total advances dampened the profitability. Thus, the coefficient of the credit quality variable is expected to be negative. Higher provisions are stipulated and attracted by higher level of bad loans indicating the poor credit quality of the banks. Credit quality is contingent on banks' internal processes of project loan appraisal and as well as effective monitoring of end-use of the credit given. The effectiveness of these two processes determines the credit quality of banks. In order to analyse determinants of profitability, both the OLS methods and the panel data regression is used. In the case of panel data—the Hausman test produces FEM as the appropriate model for the data. The results of the OLS estimates were retained in the analysis because of the similarity in both the estimated coefficients. Hence, the comment is on OLS regression model.

Conclusion

In this chapter, profitability of the public sector banks is measured in terms of ROA, ROE and PM. It is evident from the trend in profitability that banking reforms have significant impact on the performance of banks. Banks realized significant positive trend in growths of profitability, on each of the ratios selected, during the period from 1991–1992 to 2014–2015. Credit quality and cost of fund management explained profitability trend growth that was statistically significant at the conventional level.

References

Angadi, V.B., and J.V. Devaraj. 1983. Productivity and Profitability of Banks in India. *Economic and Political Weekly* 18 (48): M160–M170.

Batra, A. 1996. Bank Profitability with a Hybrid Profit Function—The Indian Case. *Indian Economic Review* 31 (2): 223–234.

Chaudhuri, S. 2002. Some Issues of Growth and Profitability in Indian Public Sector Banks. *Economic and Political Weekly* 37 (22): 2155–2162.

Demirguc-Kunt, A., and H. Huizinga. 1999. Determinants of Commercial Bank Interest Margins and Profitability: Some International Evidence. *The World Bank Economic Review* 13 (2): 379–408.

Ghosh, S. 2009. Financial Deregulation and Profit Efficiency: A Non-parametric Analysis Of Indian Banks. MRPA Paper No. 24292, https://mpra.ub.uni-muenchen.de/24292/.

Goddard, J., P. Molyneux, and J.O.S. Wilson. 2004. The Profitability of European Banks: A Cross-Sectional and Dynamic Panel Analysis. *The Manchester School* 72 (3): 363–381.

Grifell-Tatjé E., and C.A.K. Lovell. 1999. Profits and Productivity. *Management Science* 45 (9): 1177–1193.

Haslem, J.A. 1968. A Statistical Analysis of the Relative Profitability of Commercial Banks. *The Journal of Finance* 23 (1): 167–176.

Koeva, P. 2003. The Performance of Indian Banks During Financial Liberalization. IMF Working Paper, WP/03/150, pp. 1–33: (July 2003).

Loukoianova, E. 2008. Analysis of the Efficiency and Profitability of the Japanese Banking System. *IMF Working Paper*, Monetary and Capital Markets Department, WP/08/63.

Rakhe, P.B. 2010. Profitability of Foreign Banks vis-à-vis Other Bank Groups in India—A Panel Data Analysis. *Reserve Bank of India Occasional Paper* 31 (2): 49–67.

Ram Mohan, T.T. 2002. Deregulation and Performance of Public Sector Banks. *Economic and Political Weekly* 37 (5): 393–397.

Reserve Bank of India. 2015-16: Statistical Tables Relating to Banks in India, Mumbai.

Singh, S.P. 1974. Profitability of Nationalized Banks. *Economic and Political Weekly* 9 (35): M67, M69-M7.

Verghese, S.K. 1983. Profits and Profitability of Indian Commercial Banks in Seventies. *Economic and Political Weekly* 18 (48): M145–M147, M149–M157.

7

Non-performing Assets

Introduction

While the Indian banking sector showed significant resilience in the immediate spread of the global financial crisis, its impact has been marginal and tapered off gradually over the past few years. Along with the fallacious domestic growth during the period 2009–2012, the banking sector also witnessed a receding performance—slowdown in credit demand, poor asset quality and lower profitability. It showed that the slowdown in real economic activity is associated with increasing risks for banks as NPAs tend to grow steadily from 2010–2011 onwards, and its trend resists to reverse despite several corrective measures initiated. This issue of enhanced NPAs has become the focus of debate and policy challenge and the subject matter of this chapter.

Effective management of non-performing assets (NPAs) is essential for preserving the economic value of banks and stability in macroeconomic system. Banks should, therefore, put in place a strong regulatory framework so as to be able to generate reliable and quality information with regard to their asset quality management. NPAs are better controlled to the minimum, if not avoided completely, at the initial stage

© The Author(s) 2017
T.R. Bishnoi and S. Devi, *Banking Reforms in India*, Palgrave Macmillan Studies in Banking and Financial Institutions, DOI 10.1007/978-3-319-55663-5_7

of credit consideration by putting in place a rigorous and appropriate credit appraisal mechanism (Muniappan 2002).

This chapter analyses the trends, determinants and other issues of NPAs in Indian banking system. It begins with an introduction, theory of NPAs: NPAs due to asymmetric information, moral hazard and adverse selection in financial markets; or because of slowdown in macroeconomic and systemic variables. It is followed by definitions of NPAs, its classifications, various mechanisms and recovery channels introduced overtime. Next, it gives trends and profiles of NPAs at global level and also in India. Then it provides an analytical framework with conclusion.

Theory of Non-performing Assets

Two categories of factors determining NPA trends are listed in economic literature. First type of explanation lies in asymmetric information, adverse selection and moral hazards in financial markets, particularly banks. The other explanation of NPA trend is due to slowdown in macroeconomy and other systemic variables. Sometimes both factors become operative simultaneously to make NPAs more complex phenomenon to explain. These are explained below.

Information Asymmetry, Adverse Selection and Moral Hazard

The concept of information asymmetry was able to explain many diverse economic problems such as bad loan (NPAs) problem and credit rationing. In 2001, the Nobel Prize in Economic Science was awarded to recognize the excellent contributions made in information theory (Akerlof 1970; Spence 1973; Stiglitz and Weiss 1981). Their contributions were remarkable for their analyses of markets with asymmetric information and adverse selection. Each of them investigates the implications of adverse selection on the product, labour and insurance markets, respectively. Notable conclusion here is that the presence of asymmetric information problem in credit market leads to credit rationing (Stiglitz and Weiss 1981).

Banks being principal dealers in credit market and other intermediaries take themselves significant credit risks. The risk transformation by mobilizing deposits from savers and lending to deficit borrowers automatically produces risks in credit institutions. Degree of risk however varies with time, type of market and economic condition in the economy. In credit markets, the lenders' risk profile information (of a borrower's likelihood to repay) is imperfect. Borrowers, obviously, would have superior information than lenders about their own past actions, outcome of the previous projects and future intentions. Therefore, lenders always attempt to evaluate their credit risk more objectively to improve decision-making but due to constraints of cost and time, it cannot be made precise and perfectly symmetric. According to the traditional neo-classical economics, markets were 'information efficient' meaning thereby that one cannot consistently achieve returns in excess of the average market returns on a risk-adjusted basis, given the information available. More recent work by Stiglitz and others has shown that only under exceptional conditions are markets perfect and even under competitive equilibrium, credit markets may ultimately witness credit rationing owing to insufficient information, i.e. information asymmetry. Seminal contributions include: Akerlof (1970); Spence (1973) and Rothschild and Stiglitz (1976). Such information asymmetry in credit market has negative consequences as it results in adverse selection. When lenders cannot assess the risk profile of borrowers adequately, they mistake good risks as bad ones and vice versa. Banks attempt to cover the cost of insufficient information of borrowers by increasing interest rates (charging premium for extra credit risk). This leads to high cost of loans, and credit becomes expensive for low-risk borrowers, creating credit-rationing situation. On the other hand, high-risk borrowers find credit cheap given their high-risk (poor quality) projects. This phenomenon leads to high-risk credit portfolio and interest rates rise to reflect this deterioration in quality of bank assets. Higher interest rates create incentive even for good customers to take up riskier projects so as to have higher returns to compensate for higher cost of loan. Furthermore, some borrowers may have incentive not to repay, because without information sharing they can still obtain loans from other lenders. Thus, there exist problems of moral hazard (lack of penalty for non-payment) adverse selection (i.e. higher interest rates attract riskier borrowers or make borrowers take more risks) and credit rationing; i.e. given two entities with identical risk profiles, one will get a loan and the other will not. Credit information bureau has thus come into existence in India to deal with the information asymmetry issues and related consequences of adverse selection and moral hazard. Shared information allows better assessment of risk profiles of potential borrowers (deals with adverse selection) and creates incentive for borrowers to pay on time by limiting borrowers' ability to access credit from other lenders (deals with the moral hazard).

Thus, theory of information asymmetry explains the problem of rising NPAs in banking system. In a growing economy, banks keep on lending to existing borrowers and knowing more about their risk profiles. For profit maximizing objectives, banks also tend to lend to new riskier projects of existing customers and new clients with imperfect information about the quality of new ventures. Banks and customers do not share equal degree of information on the quality of projects. Projects brought for bank funding are with fictitious attractive forecast of cash flow and profits, and inherent risk of ventures is known only to borrowing firms. Banks find incentives in funding such activities in anticipation of higher return projected for such poor-quality projects. Borrower firms have tendency to poor disclosures of risk associated with bank-funded projects during different phases of business cycles in the market economy. When such projects underperform or fail to provide expected cash flow, it adversely impacts the repayment performance of loans leading to higher level of NPAs.

Macroeconomic Slowdown and Other Factors

The other variables that determine the bank NPAs are macroeconomic and systematic factors beyond the control of borrowers and lenders both. For instance, growth decline in certain sectors or economy adversely affects sales growth of corporate firms leading to fall in profits. Depressed corporate profits with cascading effects on investment, production, employment, etc., are likely to contribute to upward trend in bank NPAs. Below-mentioned various studies have documented the role of these variables in determining NPAs in India.

Banking literatures in the issues of NPAs have been reviewed in several theoretical and empirical fields from different perspectives. Most of the studies considered the issues of NPAs in terms of bank-specific internal variables as well as macroeconomic condition variables such as bank size, credit growth, accounting ratios of banks, monetary expansion, business cycle, GDP growth rate and stock return (Das and Ghosh 2003; Mohan 2004; Reddy 2004). Nevertheless, there were studies that deal particularly with the issues of NPAs in terms of legal and institutional framework variables such as shortcomings in legal and judicial systems, banking regulations, taxation policy, strong leadership and commercial orientation (Datar 2002; Reddy 2002; Dong 2002).

Ranjan and Dhal (2003) explored an empirical study of non-performing loans (NPLs) of Indian commercial banks. Their study focused on three major sets of economic and financial factors, i.e. terms of credit, bank size-induced risk preferences and macroeconomic shocks as determinants of NPAs. The study concluded that better credit culture, favourable macroeconomic and business conditions lead to lowering NPAs. On the other hand, bank size and priority sector lending produce negative impact on NPAs. In a similar way, Misra and Dhal (2010) studied management of NPAs of public sector banks for different periods. The study also concluded that terms of credit variables such as interest rate, maturity and collateral and bank-specific variables had significant effect on the banks' non-performing loans in the presence of macroeconomic shocks. Rajaraman and Vasistha (2002) in their study provided an evidence of significant bivariate relationship between an operating inefficiency indicator and the bad loans of Indian public sector banks.

In a different perspective, Rajaraman et al. (1999) analysed the variation in non-performing assets among the Indian commercial banks for the year 1996–1997. The findings showed that bank-specific characteristics such as ownership or adherence to prudential norms do not suffice to explain the inter-bank variability in NPAs, but the region of operation matters. In other words, the findings support the view that no sustainable improvement in performing efficiency of domestic banks is possible without prior improvement in the enforcement environment in difficult regions of the country.

Issues of NPAs particularly for the priority sectors lending are a matter of concern. In a theoretical framework analysis by Rajeev and Mahesh (2010), high proportion of priority sector NPAs is found as against the proportion of non-priority sectors. The role of informal organization (Self Help Group) is significant for this sector to solve the problems of non-payment as well as to improve accessibility to credit for the poor as there is possibility of financial exclusion by banks in the process of reducing NPAs.

Studies of NPAs are also not limited to bank-specific and macro-economic condition variables; rather, its scope also covers the issues on institutional and legal framework processed. Conducive legal framework is essential for solving the problems of NPAs (Dong 2002). Because of the banks' failure to take effective action, large borrowers failed to honour their repayment obligations. Strong institutional and legal framework is, therefore, essential for timely recovery of the due loans by banks. In order to contain the mounting level of NPAs, it has been suggested that a separate audit is required for NPAs and the external auditor should submit a special report (Pandey et al. 2013). Some are of the view that it appears inexplicable why the RBI did not consider it necessary to explain what lay behind the changeover from gross to net NPA as the norm. In addition, mounting or inflated figures for priority sector NPAs were due to netting procedure adopted by RBI (Shajahan 1998). Muniappan (2002) remarked that problem of NPAs was related to several internal and external factors faced the borrowers. The internal factors were in terms of diversification, modernization and inefficient management, while the external factors include recession, accidents, government policy and import duties.

Policy Definitions of Non-performing Assets

One of the major recommendations made by the Committee on the Financial System was adoption of uniform accounting practices by banks, especially with regard to income recognition, classification of

Table 7.1 Asset classification and specified period

Year ending March 31	Specified period
1993	Four quarters
1994	Three quarters
1995	Onwards two quarters
2004	90 days

assets and provisioning of unviable assets. As per the RBI guidelines, an asset, including a leased asset, becomes non-performing when it ceases to generate income for the bank. Earlier an asset was considered as non-performing asset (NPA) based on the concept of 'past due'. In that view, a 'non-performing asset' (NPA) was defined as credit in respect of which interest and/or instalment of principal has remained 'past due' for a specific period. However, with effect from 31, March 2001, the 'past due' concept has been dispensed with and the period is reckoned from the due date of payment. The specified period was reduced in a phased manner as mentioned in Table 7.1.

With a view to moving towards international best practices and to ensure greater transparency, '90 days' overdue norms for identification of NPAs have been made applicable from the year ended 31, March 2004. Effective from March end 2004, a non-performing asset shall be a loan or an advance remaining unpaid for a period of more than 90 days. The loans and advances include term loans with interest, bills purchased and discounted, advances in the form of overdraft and cash credit. In the case of agricultural loans, it is the overdue of interest and principal for a period of two harvest seasons with maximum duration of two and half years.

Asset Classification

Even though the issues of NPAs were given focus after the Narasimham Committee Report (1991), the concept of classifying bank assets based on its quality set about in 1985–1986 in which the RBI introduced the Health Code System (HCS) in banks. This system provided information regarding the quality of individual advances and the quality of credit portfolio to safeguard financial health of banks. All commercial banks were required to introduce this system, indicating the quality of individual advances under eight categories, namely satisfactory;

irregular; sick and viable; sick and non-viable; advances recalled; suit filed accounts; decreed debts; bad and doubtful debt; with a health code assigned to each borrowing account. Accordingly, the RBI classified problem loans of each bank into three categories: (i) the advances classified as bad and doubtful by bank was given Health Code 8, (ii) the advances where suits are filed or decrees obtained or both was assigned with Health codes 6 and 7 and (iii) those advances with major undesirable features are put under Health Codes 4 and 5.

Later, with the financial sector reforms, the concept of NPAs was refined in order to bring the international benchmark level. The assets of the banks and financial institutions were classified into four categories, namely standard assets, substandard assets, doubtful assets and loss assets. Further, banks were required to classify non-performing assets into the following three categories based on the period of which asset has remained non-performing and realisability of the dues: (a) substandard assets, (b) doubtful assets and (c) loss assets.

Substandard Assets: An NPA was classified as substandard for a period not exceeding 2 years. Effective from March end 2001, a substandard asset was one, which had remained NPA of a period less than or equal to 18 months. Moreover, since effective from 31, March 2005, an asset was classified as substandard if it had remained NPA for a period less than or equal to 12 months. In such cases, the current net worth of the borrowers and guarantors or the current market value of the security charged was not enough to ensure recovery of the dues to banks in full. In other words, such assets reflected credit weaknesses that jeopardize the liquidation of the debt and were characterized by losses for the banks if deficiency was not corrected.

Doubtful Assets: A doubtful asset was one which remained NPA for a period exceeding 2 years. Effective from March end 2001, an asset was termed as doubtful if it had remained NPA for a period exceeding 18 months. Further, effective from March end 2005, an asset was required to be classified as doubtful, if it had remained NPA for more than 12 months. A loan classified as doubtful had all the weaknesses inherent in assets that were classified as substandard with no possibility for collection and liquidation in full.

Table 7.2 Provisions under doubtful NPAs

Period for which the advances have remained in doubtful category	Provision requirement (%)
Up to one year	25
One to three years	40
More than three years	100

Loss Assets: A loss asset was one where loss had been identified by the bank or internal or external auditors or the RBI inspection but the amount had not been written off entirely. In other words, such an asset was considered uncollectible and of such little value that its continuance as a bankable asset was not warranted although there might be some salvage or recovery value.

In conformity with the prudential norms, RBI has prescribed provision norms based on the classification of NPAs. The main features of provisioning against the bad and doubtful assets as per RBI guidelines issued in July 2014 are mentioned in Table 7.2.

A general provision of 15% (as against 10% in July 2013) on total outstanding of substandard assets should be made without making any allowance for ECGC guarantee cover and securities available.

1. Provisions varied between 25 and 100% depending upon the period for which the advances had remained in doubtful category.
2. Loss assets should be written off. If loss assets were permitted in the books of the bank for any reason, 100% of the outstanding should be provided for out of income.

Recovery Mechanism of Non-performing Assets

Table 7.3 shows the recovery mechanism of NPAs of banks through various channels. Among the various channels of recovery available to banks for dealing with bad loans, the largest amount was recovered through the SARFAESI Act followed by Debt Recovery Tribunals (DRTs). Thus, NPAs recovered through the SARFAESI Act accounted for more than 60% of the total amount of NPAs. The highest recovery

Table 7.3   NPAs of SCBs recovered under various channels (Rs. billion)

Year	Lok Adalats		DRTs		SARFAESI Act	
	Amount involved	Amount recovered	Amount involved	Amount recovered	Amount involved	Amount recovered
2007–2008	21	2 (9.5)	58	30 (51.7)	73	44 (60.3)
2008–2009	40	1 (2.5)	41	33 (80.5)	121	40 (33.1)
2009–2010	72	1 (1.4)	98	31 (31.6)	142	43 (30.3)
2010–2011	53	2 (3.8)	141	39 (27.7)	306	116 (37.9)
2011–2012	17	2 (11.8)	241	41 (17.0)	353	101 (28.6)
2012–2013	66	4 (6.1)	310	44 (14.2)	681	185 (27.2)
2013–2014	232	14 (6.2)	553	53 (9.5)	953	253 (26.6)
2014–2015	887	43 (4.8)	3789	531 (14.0)	4705	1152 (24.5)

Note Figures in the parentheses denote amount recovered as a per cent of amount involved
Source RBI: Report on trend and progress of banking in India, various issues

channel through this Act is also reflected in terms of the ratio of amount recovered to amounts involved which remains hovered around 20% or more in the successive years as against the other channels of recovery. However, in terms of the total number of cases referred to, Lok Adalats dominated with a share of 70% or more in all the years.

Trends in Non-performing Assets

Non-performing Assets at the Global Level

A global picture of NPAs would be meaningful to see the trends of NPLs in different countries across the globe. Table 7.4 shows the non-performing loans of the selected countries. It is observed that the ratio

Table 7.4   Non-performing loans to total loans at global level (per cent)

Countries	2005	2007	2010	2011	2012	2013	2014
Japan	1.8	1.5	2.5	2.4	2.4	2.3	1.9
UK	1	0.9	4.0	4.0	3.7	2.3	2.8
United States	0.7	1.4	4.4	3.8	3.3	2.5	0.7
France	3.5	2.7	3.8	4.3	4.3	4.5	–
Germany	4.8	2.7	3.2	3.0	2.9	2.7	–
Greece	6.3	4.5	9.1	14.4	23.3	31.9	33.5
Italy	5.3	4.6	10.0	11.7	13.7	16.5	11.2
Mexico	1.8	2.7	2.0	2.1	2.4	3.2	2.9[b]
Brazil	3.5	3.0	3.1	3.5	3.4	2.9	2.9[a]
Russia	3.2	2.5	8.2	6.6	6.0	6.0	6.5[a]
China	9.8	6.7	1.1	1.0	1.0	1.0	1.1[a]
India	5.2	2.5	2.4	2.7	3.4	4.0	4.0
Indonesia	7.6	4.1	2.5	2.1	1.8	1.7	2.1[a]
Korea	1.2	0.7	0.6	0.5	0.6	0.6	–
Malaysia	9.6	8.5	3.4	2.7	2.0	1.8	1.8[a]

Notes [a]refers to as on June and [b]as on July
Source IMF: Global financial stability report, April of respective years

of non-performing loans (NPLs) to total loans for advanced countries such as US, UK, Germany, France and Japan declined over the period even though the ratio rose abruptly due to immediate response of the global financial crisis. These countries were having NPL ratio below the world NPL ratio of 4.3% in 2013. However, Greece and Italy were having high percentage of NPL ratio over the total loans and the situation becomes more serious with effect from the global financial crisis. India had a NPL ratio to total loans of 4.0% in 2014 and more or less equal to the world ratio of 4.3%. The performance of other developing countries is far better than that of India, Brazil (2.9%), Malaysia (1.8%), Indonesia (1.7%), China (1.1%) and Korea (0.6%).

Non-performing Assets of Commercial Banks

In the case of NPAs of scheduled commercial banks, there was a declining trend over the years from 1997–1998 to 2014–2015. Gross NPA ratio to gross advances of SCBs fell continuously from 14.4%

Table 7.5   Gross non-performing assets of SCBs: 1997–1998 to 2014–2015 (Rs. billion)

Year	SBI and associated banks	Nationalized banks	Public sector banks	Private sector banks	Foreign banks	Scheduled commer-cial banks
1997–1998	Not available	Not available	456.5	31.9	19.8	508.2
			(16.0)	(8.7)	(6.4)	(14.4)
1998–1999	209.1	308.0	517.1	46.6	23.6	587.3
	(15.7)	(16.0)	(15.9)	(10.81)	(7.59)	(14.70)
1999–2000	197.7	332.6	530.3	49.3	26.2	605.8
	(14.1)	(13.9)	(14.0)	(8.47)	(6.99)	(12.79)
2000–2001	205.9	341.8	547.7	60.8	31.1	639.6
	(12.7)	(12.2)	(12.4)	(8.54)	(6.85)	(11.45)
2001–2002	197.1	367.6	564.7	116.7	27.8	709.2
	(11.2)	(11.0)	(11.1)	(9.65)	5.49	(10.42)
2002–2003	170.4	368.5	538.9	133.3	28.9	701.1
	(8.7)	(9.8)	(9.4)	(9.20)	(5.38)	(9.06)
2003–2004	159.9	355.5	515.4	103.4	30.1	648.9
	(7.0)	(8.2)	(7.8)	(5.83)	(4.81)	(7.19)
2004–2005	156.2	309.8	466.0	85.6	22.3	574.0
	(5.3)	(5.4)	(5.4)	(3.8)	(3.1)	(4.9)
2005–2006	133.0	288.2	421.2	76.0	20.4	517.5
	(3.5)	(3.8)	(3.7)	(2.4)	(2.1)	(3.3)
2006–2007	126.8	262.9	389.7	91.5	24.0	505.2
	(2.6)	(2.7)	(2.7)	(2.2)	(1.9)	(2.5)
2007–2008	154.8	251.2	406.0	129.2	30.8	566.1
	(2.6)	(2.1)	(2.2)	(2.5)	(1.9)	(2.3)
2008–2009	191.1	268.0	459.2	167.9	72.5	699.5
	(2.6)	(1.7)	(2.0)	(2.9)	(4.4)	(2.3)
2009–2010	218.3	354.7	573.0	173.1	71.1	817.2
	(2.8)	(2.0)	(2.3)	(3.0)	(4.4)	(2.5)
2010–2011	281.4	429.1	710.5	179.0	50.4	940.0
	(3.1)	(2.0)	(2.3)	(2.5)	(2.6)	(2.4)
2011–2012	456.9	668.0	1124.9	182.1	62.7	1369.7
	(4.4)	(2.7)	(3.2)	(2.1)	(2.8)	(2.9)
2012–2013	627.8	1016.8	1644.6	203.8	79.3	1927.7
	(4.4)	(3.2)	(3.6)	(1.8)	(3.0)	(3.2)
2013–2014	798.2	1474.5	2272.6	241.8	115.7	2630.2
	(5.0)	(4.1)	(4.4)	(1.8)	(3.9)	(3.8)
2014–2015	735.1	2049.6	2784.7	336.9	107.6	3229.2
	(4.3)	(5.3)	(5.0)	(2.1)	(3.2)	(4.3)

Note Figures in the parentheses are the ratios of Gross NPAs to total advances
Source RBI: Statistical tables relating to banks in India, various issues

in 1997–1998 to 4.3% in 2014–2015. This descending trend of NPAs reflected an improvement in the quality of assets on account of health codes and assets classification norms under banking reforms. Nevertheless, gross NPA ratio touched its trough at 2.3% in 2007–2008 and began to look up in post-financial crisis impacting India's growth adversely. The same declining happened in the trend of NPAs of bank groups: public sector banks, private sector banks and foreign banks group. Whereas, for the public sector bank group, the ratio was the highest, with an average of 5% in March 2014–2015, for private sector banks and foreign banks, the corresponding ratios were 2 and 3.2%, respectively (Table 7.5).

Sector-Wise Non-performing Assets

From the sector perspective, NPAs of priority sectors for the public sector banks group covered 45.5% in 2000–2001, which shot up to 63.6% in 2007–2008 to fall back to below 36% in 2014–2015. Among the priority sectors NPAs, combined share of agriculture and small-scale industries was significant at an average of 35%. On the other hand, the share of non-priority sectors in total NPAs showed a declining trend up to 2007–2008, but in the years of 2008–2009 onwards deterioration of asset quality led to push up its share in NPAs of this banks group constituting more than 60%. Asset quality was more or less depended on slide in recovery in the case of non-priority sectors advances.

Regarding the sector distribution of NPAs of private sector banks group, the priority sector share contributed up to 21–30% for the entire period from 2000–2001 to 2014–2015. Within the priority sectors, agriculture and small-scale industries were big contributors claiming on average 30–40% of the total priority sector NPAs. The deterioration in the asset quality of the private sector banks group was significantly higher with a share of about 71–79% of total non-priority sectors NPAs in different years. (Tables 7.6 and 7.7)

Table 7.6   NPAs of public sector banks by sector (Rs. billion)

Year	Agriculture (i)	Small-scale industries (ii)	Others (iii)	Priority sector (i + ii + iii)	Public sector	Non-priority sector	Total NPAs
2000–2001	74	103	64	242	17	273	532
	(13.9)	(19.4)	(12.1)	(45.4)	(3.2)	(51.4)	(100.0)
2001–2002	78	106	67	251	11	303	565
	(13.8)	(18.7)	(11.9)	(44.5)	(2.0)	(53.5)	(100.0)
2002–2003	77	102	71	249	11	268	528
	(14.6)	(19.2)	(13.4)	(47.2)	(2.1)	(50.7)	(100.0)
2003–2004	72	88	78	238	6	257	501
	(14.4)	(17.6)	(15.5)	(47.5)	(1.2)	(51.2)	(100.0)
2004–2005	73	78	83	234	5	238	477
	(15.2)	(16.4)	(17.4)	(49.1)	(0.9)	(50.0)	(100.0)
2005–2006	62	69	93	224	3	187	414
	(15.0)	(16.7)	(22.4)	(54.1)	(0.8)	(45.1)	(100.0)
2006–2007	65	58	106	230	5	152	386
	(16.9)	(15.1)	(27.5)	(59.5)	(1.3)	(39.3)	(100.0)
2007–2008	83	58	112	253	3	142	397
	(20.8)	(14.6)	(28.2)	(63.6)	(0.8)	(35.6)	(100.0)
2008–2009	57	70	116	243	5	193	440
	(13.0)	(15.9)	(26.4)	(55.2)	(1.1)	(43.7)	(100.0)
2009–2010	83	115	110	308	5	259	573
	(14.5)	(20.1)	(19.2)	(53.8)	(0.9)	(45.3)	(100.0)
2010–2011	145	143	124	412	3	298	710
	(20.4)	(20.2)	(17.5)	(58.1)	(0.4)	(41.9)	(100.0)
2011–2012	227	178	157	562	32	563	1125
	(20.1)	(15.9)	(14.0)	(50.0)	(2.9)	(50.0)	(100.0)
2012–2013	280	284	105	669	0.0	890	1559
	(18.0)	(18.2)	(6.7)	(42.9)		(57.1)	(100.0)
2013–2014	n.a.	n.a.	n.a.	792	0.0	1375	2167
				(36.5)		(63.5)	(100.0)
2014–2015	n.a.	n.a.	n.a.	959	0.0	1712	2671
				(35.9)		(64.1)	(100.0)

Note Figures in the parentheses denote percentage to total. n.a. refers to not available

Source RBI: Report on trend and progress of banking in India, various issues

Table 7.7   NPAs of private sector banks by sector (Rs. billion)

Year	Agriculture (i)	Small-scale industries (ii)	Others (iii)	Priority sector (i + ii + iii)	Public sector	Non-priority sector	Total NPAs
2000–2001	3	10	5	18	1.2	45	64
	(5.0)	(15.6)	(8.0)	(28.6)	(1.9)	(69.5)	
2001–2002	4	15	6	25	0.3	91	117
	(3.8)	(12.7)	(5.3)	(21.8)	(0.3)	(77.9)	
2002–2003	5	13	6	24	0.9	93	119
	(4.5)	(10.6)	(5.5)	(20.6)	(0.8)	(78.6)	
2003–2004	5	13	8	25	0.7	78	104
	(4.4)	(12.2)	(7.4)	(24.0)	(0.7)	(75.3)	
2004–2005	5	10	8	22	0.4	66	88
	(5.3)	(11.0)	(8.6)	(24.9)	(0.5)	(74.7)	
2005–2006	5	8	10	23	0.0	55	78
	(6.6)	(10.3)	(12.3)	(29.2)	(0.1)	(70.8)	
2006–2007	9	6	14	29	0.0	64	92
	(9.3)	(7.0)	(14.9)	(31.2)		(68.8)	
2007–2008	15	7	13	34	0.0	96	130
	(11.3)	(5.0)	(10.0)	(26.3)		(73.7)	
2008–2009	14	7	15	36	0.8	132	169
	(8.5)	(4.0)	(9.1)	(21.6)	(0.4)	(78.0)	
2009–2010	20	11	16	48	0.0	126	174
	(11.6)	(6.6)	(9.4)	(27.6)		(72.4)	
2010–2011	22	13	14	48	2	132	180
	(12.1)	(7.2)	(7.5)	(26.8)	(0.8)	(73.2)	
2011–2012	22	17	12	51	0.0	132	183
	(11.8)	(9.4)	(6.7)	(27.9)		(72.1)	
2012–2013	22	20	11	52	0.0	148	200
	(10.9)	(9.9)	(5.3)	(26.0)		(74.0)	
2013–2014	n.a.	n.a.	n.a.	61	0.0	167	227
				(27.0)		(73.0)	
2014–2015	n.a.	n.a.	n.a.	72	0.0	244	316
				(22.8)		(77.2)	

Note Figures in the parentheses denote percentage. n.a. refers to not available
Source Reserve Bank of India. 2000-01 to 2015-16. Report on trend and progress of banking in India, various issues

Distribution of Non-performing Assets by Bank

Distribution of NPAs by bank was analysed for the period from 1995–1996 to 2014–2015. Frequency distribution of all public sector banks on the basis of ratio of gross NPAs to total advances was made to find out the level of risk faced by banks during these years. Initially, banks were operating with very high risk as indicated by high NPA ratio in the absence of any strict regulation and internal risk management process relating to loan quality. From 1995–1996 to 1998–1999, most of the public sector banks were found in high-risk category as these were found in high-range NPA ratios, namely 10–15% and beyond this range. Out of the 27 public sector banks, 20 banks had high-risk NPAs range of 10–15 % and above in 1995–1996. In the 2003–2004, most of the banks (15 banks) gradually shifted and concentrated in the range of below 10% NPA ratio. Between 2004–2005 and 2006–2007, NPAs declined for all public sector banks to range of 3–5% range, and majority of banks were operating in this risk range. For example, banks were able to contain these high-risk NPAs in 2007–2008, and it was almost in normal low range for all banks, except for two banks, namely Central Bank of India and SBI, that were having NPA score of more than 3%. In the financial year 2008–2009, all the 27 public sector banks had NPAs up to 3% range. The gradual shift in NPA ratio by banks, converging to 3% and even lower range, showed that banks have made an improvement in their asset quality over these years, on account of fresh assets quality regulation and also strengthening internal process of loan risk management. However, from 2009–2010 onwards, there is a slight increasing trend in the NPA ratio of banks specifically from 2011–2012 to 2014–2015, in which NPA ratio has increased for nine banks to the range of 5–7% as compared to only one bank at this level in the previous year. This is affected by the global crisis in terms of slowdown of growth process of Indian economy. In brief, it showed a drastic improvement in the NPAs risk of all the public sector banks as a result of the financial sector reforms but post-financial crisis banks were again exposed to high risk of NPAs especially from

Table 7.8   Frequency distribution of banks by gross NPAs to total advances ratio

Year	Up to 3%	Above 3–5%	Above 5–7%	Above 7–10%	Above 10–15%	Above 15–20%	Above 20%
1995–1996	0	0	1	1	10	5	10
1996–1997	0	0	0	2	7	10	8
1997–1998	0	0	1	2	10	7	7
1998–1999	0	0	2	1	9	10	5
1999–2000	0	0	2	2	15	6	2
2000–2001	0	0	3	5	13	3	3
2001–2002	0	0	5	7	10	4	1
2002–2003	0	2	6	9	8	2	0
2003–2004	0	5	7	11	3	1	0
2004–2005	4	10	9	4	0	1	0
2005–2006	9	14	4	1	0	0	0
2006–2007	21	7	0	0	0	0	0
2007–2008	26	2	0	0	0	0	0
2008–2009	27	0	0	0	0	0	0
2009–2010	22	4	0	0	0	0	0
2010–2011	24	2	0	0	0	0	0
2011–2012	17	9	0	0	0	0	0
2012–2013	11	14	1	0	0	0	0
2013–2014	4	12	9	0	1	0	0
2014–2015	1	12	11	2	0	0	0

Source Calculated by authors based on RBI: Statistical tables relating to banks in India

2011–2012 onwards. Recent trend of NPAs of banks was shifting in successive years to high range with no sign of reversal (Table 7.8).

Analytical Framework and Results

It is worthwhile to look for economic explanation of the above trend in NPAs. For this, it is plausible to examine the link between the high NPAs of banks and slowdown in the economy. Deterioration in the asset quality of banks was associated with slowdown in the growth of the economy that existed in the recent past. The hypothesis thus formulated was that slowdown in economy did not lead to high NPAs or to say high ratio of NPAs of banks was not directly related to real GDP growth rate; rather, it is due to asymmetric information and adverse selection. The hypotheses thus formulated are:

H_o slowdown in the economy is not associated with higher level of NPAs of banks.

H_1 slowdown in the economy is associated with higher level of NPAs of banks.

Data and methodology: The data for this analysis was compiled from the various reports and statistical data published by the RBI for various years. Data on NPAs for each bank group were analysed with the sample period from 1997–1998 to 2014–2015 and for individual bank from 1995–1996. However, in the analysis of NPAs by sector, sample period was restricted from 2000–2001 to 2014–2015. The bank groups taken for the analysis were public sector banks group, private sector banks group, foreign banks group and all scheduled commercial banks. Foreign banks group was excluded in sector analysis for its marginal and negligible contribution in the priority sector advances and also for non-availability of relevant data. Data on annual real GDP growth rate and primary sector growth rate were taken from the Economic Survey Report for the sample periods chosen. Since data on real GDP growth rate by the category of priority and non-priority sectors were not available, analysis was restricted to agriculture credit of the priority sectors and corresponding annual growth rate of primary sector. It used simple statistical tools such as percentages, descriptive statistics and correlation. Further, regression was fitted to test the validity of results produced by the correlation and descriptive statistics.

In descriptive statistics of NPAs for each bank group, high mean values with high-standard deviations implied fluctuation in the trend owing to differential impact of slowdown except for foreign banks group which operated in niche market. This is supported by the individual-level bank data, which shows large variations in the ratio of NPAs of the individual banks in the same group. As expected, slowdown impact as well as information asymmetric problem affected banks vividly and discretely. Further, negative values of kurtosis show flatter distribution, which has moderately skewed among banks (Table 7.9).

Table 7.9   Descriptive statistics of NPAs of SCBs

Bank group	Mean	Std. deviation	Skewness	Kurtosis
SCBs	6.36	4.53	0.82	−0.95
PSBs	5.41	6.60	0.14	−0.88
Private	4.91	3.31	0.65	−1.44
Foreign	4.27	1.84	0.40	−1.08

Table 7.10   Correlation coefficient between growth rate of real GDP and NPA ratio by bank groups: 1997–1998 to 2014–2015

GDP growth rate and NPAs of SCBs	−0.63**
GDP growth rate and NPAs of PSBs group	−0.47*
GDP growth rate and NPAs of private sector banks group	−0.65**
GDP growth rate and NPAs of foreign banks group	−0.65**
Agriculture growth rate and NPAs in agriculture for SCBs	0.06
Agriculture growth rate and NPAs in agriculture for PSBs	0.04
Agriculture growth rate and NPAs in agriculture for private sector banks	0.17

Note *denotes significant at the 0.5% level. And ** at 0.01% level

Table 7.11   Result of regression analysis

Independent variables	Coefficient	Std. Error	T-statistics	R-square	F-value	Remark
NPA ratio for SCBs	−0.232	0.096	−2.405* (0.031)	0.29	5.784*	Significant
NPA ratio for PSBs	−0.207	0.087	−2.372* (0.033)	0.29	5.626*	Significant
NPA ratio for private sector banks	−0.342	0.137	−2.506* (0.025)	0.30	6.278*	Significant
NPA ratio for foreign banks	−0.577	0.229	−2.522* (0.024)	0.31	6.359*	Significant

Dependent variable: Real GDP growth rate
Sample period: 1997–1998 to 2012–2013

Note *denotes significant at 5% level

Correlation was estimated between the real GDP growth rate and the NPAs for each bank group, namely public sector bank group, private sector banks group, and foreign banks group and scheduled commercial banks together for the period 1997–1998 to 2014–2015. All correlation coefficients were found significant at the 5 and 1% levels. The negative correlation coefficient supported the hypothesis that slowdown in the economy was associated with positive trends in NPA ratios of banks. However, at the NPAs of sector level produced positive statistically insignificant correlation coefficient indicating no substantial relationship with variables chosen (Tables 7.10 and 7.11).

Negative regression coefficients, as expected in theory, supported the validity of correlation results highlighting inverse relation between the real GDP growth rate and NPA ratios of banks. All the estimated coefficients possess negative signs consistent with theoretical arguments, and the corresponding *t*-values were found significant at 5% level. To say it clearly, on an average as the real GDP fell by 1%, NPA ratios of the SCBs increased by 23%; for the PSBs by 21%; for private banks and foreign banks group by 34 and 58%, respectively. Regarding goodness of fit for the overall regression, *F*-values were significant at the 5% level. Therefore, the null hypothesis that slowdown in the economy was not associated with high NPA ratio stands rejected. In other words, deterioration in the quality of assets of banks attributed to macroeconomic slowdown in Indian economy. However, at times there might be asymmetric information relevant to explain the trends in NPAs.

Needless to mention here that detailed analysis of GDP growth on the NPAs of banks might be useful. Also, there was a need to analyse by incorporating other macroeconomic variables apart from GDP growth, which would give more clarity on issues related to NPAs of banks.

Conclusion

The study was an attempt to find out the determinants of high NPAs of the banks. Bank group-wise analysis of NPAs was carried out based on the hypothesis that there was no correlation between slowdown in the economy and high NPAs of banks and rather it is an asymmetric information phenomenon. Empirical analysis tested the validity of null hypothesis that there was no association between high-risk NPAs of banks and slowdown in economy stands rejected. Further, when the same analysis was carried out for sector level NPAs, results did not support the hypothesis. This might be due to data constraint, as desired data on real GDP growth rate for priority and non-priority sectors was not given. Further analysis of agriculture growth rate and NPAs in agriculture sector reveals statistically insignificant result. Despite these limitations, the study was a preliminary work relating to NPAs, and there was a need to conduct detailed empirical analysis of the effect of growth of the economy on NPAs.

NPA control, recovery and management were an integrated continuous process. In credit market, adverse selection is recurring pervasive phenomena. Mitigating adverse selection was possible by allowing loans to be extended to safe borrowers who had previously been priced out of the market, resulting in higher aggregate credit. Containing the moral hazard was also a challenging task in the financial sector, given the frequent political interventions in the forms of loan waiver schemes, postponement in loan recovery, etc., in the recovery of bank credit. So it is necessary to design mechanism mitigating moral hazard by either incentivizing borrowers to repay or increasing the borrowers' cost of defaulting as non-payment with one institution would result in sanctions from all others. This would encourage debt repayments and a more efficient recycling of credit. Reducing information monopoly is another effective measure which would result in lowering of interest costs for the borrower. Reducing over-indebtedness as overly extended borrowers would now receive less credit. Equally, long-term strategy has to have lowering poverty and improving the distribution of income (Sinha 2012). It is to be noted that better risk management and credit evaluation mechanism would be required to prevent loans turning into non-performing assets.

References

Akerlof, G. 1970. The Market for "Lemons": Quality Uncertainty and the Market Mechanism. *Quarterly Journal of Economics* 84 (3): 488–500.

Das, A., and S. Ghosh. 2003. Determinants of Credit Risk. In the Conference on Money, Risk and Investment. *Nottingham Trent University*, November.

Datar, M.K. 2002. Redefining the Debtor-Creditor Relationship: NPA Ordinance. *Economic and Political Weekly* 37 (37): 3786–3789.

Dong, He. 2002. Resolving Non-performing Assets of the Indian Banking System. *MRPA* Paper No. 9758, July.

International Monetary Fund. 2015. Global Financial Stability Report, April, Washington DC.

Misra, B.M., and S. Dhal. 2010. Pro-cyclical Management of Banks' Non-performing Loans by the Indian Public Sector Banks. BIS Asian Research Papers.

Mohan, R. 2004. Finance for Industrial Growth. *Reserve Bank of India Bulletin*, Speech article, March.

Muniappan, G.P. 2002. The NPA Overhang—Magnitude, Solutions, Legal Reforms. Lecture at *CII Banking Summit*, April, Mumbai.

Pandey, S.J., G.T Vishakha, and Bipin Deokar. 2013. Non-performing Assets of Indian Banks—Phases and Dimensions. *Economic and Political Weekly* XLVIII (24), June.

Rajaraman, I., and G. Vasistha. 2002. Non-performing Loans of Public Sector Banks—Some Panel results. *Economic and Political Weekly* 37 (5).

Rajaraman, I., Sumon Bhaumik, and N. Bhatia. 1999. NPA Variations Across Indian Commercial Banks: Some Findings. *Economic and Political Weekly* 34 (3–4): 161–163, 165–168.

Rajeev, M., and H.P. Mahesh. 2010. Banking Sector Reforms and NPA: A Study of Indian Commercial Banks. Working Paper 252, *Institute of Social and Economic Change*.

Ranjan, R., and S.R. Dhal. 2003. Non-performing Loans and Terms of Credit of Public Sector Banks in India: An Empirical Assessment. *Reserve Bank of India Occasional Papers* 24 (3).

Reddy, P.K. 2002. A Comparative Study of Non Performing Assets in India in the Global Context—Similarities and Dissimilarities, Remedial Measures. Working Paper, *IIM Ahmedabad*.

Reddy, Y.V. 2004. Credit Policy, Systems, and Culture. *Reserve Bank of India Bulletin*, March.

Reserve Bank of India. 2000-01 to 2015-16. Report on Trend and Progress of Banking in India, Various Issues.

Rothschild, M., and J.E. Stiglitz. 1976. Equilibrium in Competitive Insurance Markets: An Essay on the Economics of Imperfect Information. *The Quarterly Journal of Economics* 90 (4): 629–649.

Shajahan, K.M. 1998. Non-performing Assets of Banks: Have They Really Declined? And on Whose Account? *Economic and Political Weekly* 33 (12): 671–674.

Sinha, A. 2012. Striking a Balance: Credit Penetration and NPA Management—Role of Information Sharing. *RBI Bulletin*, April.

Spence, M. 1973. Job Market Signaling. *Quarterly Journal of Economics* 87 (3): 355–374.

Stiglitz, J.E., and A. Weiss. 1981. Credit Rationing in Markets with Imperfect Information. *The American Economic Review* 71 (3): 393–410.

8

Information Technology in Banking System

Introduction

Over the past 25 years, accelerated computerization and use of advanced technology has radically transformed the way Indian banking institutions function now. As a result of Narasimham Committee recommendations and the RBI's initiatives relating to computerization and technology in banks relating to Information Technology (IT) adoption, banks have gradually shifted from prevalent traditional labour-intensive manual methods of banking operation to most modern electronic and software-driven technology-based banking business. Information technology became deeply embedded part of banking process in India.[1] This chapter evaluates the role of technology in banking industry in India and its impact on banks' performance and efficiency. This analysis was based on the secondary data relating to public sector banks from the Reserve Bank of India.

Information technology offered tremendous potentials to benefit in terms of speed, accuracy, safety and efficiency with which volume of banking business being handled now. Recognizing urgent need of technology in banks, The Reserve Bank of India proactively constituted

© The Author(s) 2017
T.R. Bishnoi and S. Devi, *Banking Reforms in India*, Palgrave Macmillan Studies in Banking and Financial Institutions, DOI 10.1007/978-3-319-55663-5_8

committees and working groups, namely the Rangarajan Committee 1 and Rangarajan Committee 2 in the 1980s for bank computerization, Saraf and Barman Working Groups in the 1990s and 2000s for technology adoption for settlement and clearing payment and current Working Group on Financial Technology, to explore the new paradigm of financial technology and its application in banks. RBI has also set up the Institute for Development and Research in Banking Technology (IDRBT) in 1996 and, recently, established the Reserve Bank Information Technology (ReBIT) Pvt Ltd, conducting studies and advanced research experiments on cyber security and developing cutting edge capabilities for supervising financial technology usage in the banking sector.

The technology has become indispensable in the production, delivery and management of banking services. Information technology-based production techniques results in improvement in productivity. This is also true in the case of banking sector. The role of technology is significant in the modern financial system (Rangarajan 2011). In fact, it is unthinkable to imagine the current financial systems without electronic fund transfers, ATMs, Internet banking and other innovative software applications in banking services facilitated by information technology. Firms required new technologies to receive productivity gains as well as to increase scale economies. Technology has been helping in delivering affordable financial services with greater efficiency without compromising on levels of safety, security and reliability (Padmanabhan 2012).

Rapidly changing technology in banking in the forms of software applications, computers and servers, Internet, cloud computing and storage has ushered in new paradigm that is pervasive in very core of industry for solutions that are not only faster and cheaper, but that also offer greater security and efficiency. Technology tends to reduce the operational cost of the banks as well as time taken in completion of transactions. Technology revolution in the Indian banking sector can be traced back with computerization of a few key account-related functions, processing information gathered from paper-based document and that too also limited to some main branches by using ledger-posting machines. After 1990, IT began to penetrate in the most of functional areas in the financial services industry. Branch automation and other customer-related services were facilitated with the use of IT in Indian banks. Until the 1990s, one could make payments through two predominant means of cash and cheque. Subsequent years witnessed inter-bank connectivity through network-based operations, adoption of Core Banking Solution (CBS), use of ATMs and innovations such as mobile banking, Internet or phone banking, mobile banking unit and pre-paid cards that brought transformation in the Indian banking system. These technological advances benefitted customers and banks in ease of doing banking transactions. Banks reaped gains of the cutting costs in the delivery of these services to maintain their existing market shares. According to Berger (2003), improvement in IT infrastructure helped in risk management and its control, reducing the costs of integration, speed of banking processes and other related problems. The major benefits of technology use in the banks were centralization of several processes such as customer information, centralized transaction process, centralized accounting process, basic MIS and real-time information availability. Electronic transfer of payment on real-time basis is a landmark change in the Indian financial system as electronic-based payment system is superior to paper system in terms of traceability, efficiency, speed and safety.

Role of Information Technology in Banking: Select Studies

Technology revolution was responsible for the spread of IT by leaps and bounds in banking sector—integration all processes into central location and unprecedented increase in banking products and services that were offered on the scale of operation. Economic literatures in the field of financial technology were not able to keep pace with innovative developments in IT and its impact on working of Indian banks. Since the scope of research in technology use in banking was very wide and new areas to explore were numerous, thus, the debate on technology in banking continued. In fact, idea of banking business without IT applications seems to be absurd as pervasive IT in ordinary process of transactions impacting efficiency. Some of the studies found positive impact of technology on the performance and structure of the industry. Others noted inconclusive results or even indicated negative impact of technology in banking. For instance, Berger (2003) analysed effects of technological progress on the performance of US banking industry and its structure and found an increase in overall productivity, improved quality and extended range of banking services. Issues on the scale, geographic spread, and mergers and acquisitions were also incorporated in the model to see the effects of technology on these variables. The study found positive results for consolidation of banks as the profit efficiency of the banks was improved. Kolodinsky et al. (2004) explored the factors that contributed to popularity of three different forms of e-banking technologies of US banks. The study found that e-banking technologies could not be aggregated into a single category, and thus, 'one size fits all' did not work. Rather, the use of e-banking depended upon saving of time, decrease in errors, improving inaccurate accounting and manipulation of data, etc. In a different perspective, Ho and Mallick (2010) examined the effects of investment in IT in the banking sector. The results challenged popular evidence of IT, making a negative effect on profitability. This negative effect on the performance of banks was attributable to the competition effect of IT investment both theoretically and in empirical sense that firms competed for market shares. The result was similar to the findings of Beccalli (2007) which stated that there was a little connection between IT investment and bank profitability or efficiency, indicating the profit paradox. Similar evidence was given by Loveman (1994) that reported no significant contribution of IT expenditure in productivity of the firms. One possible reason for the insignificant impact of IT investment was that firms competed for market share and for retaining the number of customers and not charged the full cost for setting up new technology. Issues of risk and uncertainty arising from financial technology were highlighted in a study by Krishnamuthy (2006) and it suggested that banks should adopt such a strategy in which risks and innovation in banking products moved parallel and simultaneously.

The above studies on technology in banking have employed different variables given the structure of the industry and identified the various benefits from the IT innovations in banks.

Technology Spread and Intensity in Payment System

Commercial banks also have an important function of payment clearing in addition to financial intermediation. Though responsibility of payment clearing lies with RBI, it conducts itself in major cities and in other cities with the help of public sector banks. The Reserve Bank continued in its endeavour to facilitate the alignment of banking sector with innovations in technology by improving its own information technology infrastructure, implementing new applications and initiating steps for further adoption of technology in the banking sector. Several initiatives for infrastructure enhancement included introduction of Magnetic Ink Character Recognition (MICR)-based cheque processing, implementation of the electronic payment system such as Real-Time Gross Settlement (RTGS), Electronic Clearing Service (ECS), National Electronic Funds Transfer (NEFT), Cheque Truncation System (CTS), Mobile Banking System, etc. Introduction of such technologies has had significant benefits to the customers and banks. Banks computerization moved very fast as all bank branches were computerized in 2013 as against 86% computerized branches in 2007. All the bank branches implemented Core Banking Solution (CBS) by the end of 2013 as against not more than 45% CBS branches in 2007. For the SBI group, 100% coverage was recorded for completion of both the CBS and computerization process. This was so because IT in banks were guided either by the need for creating competitive advantages (strategic) or by the operational requirements of a bank (Ho and Mallick 2010) (Table 8.1).

The number of branches of public sector banks has increased to 89,711 in 2014–2015 as against 62,211 in 2010–2011 and 47,833 in 2005–2006, recorded 28.6% of the total branch expansion during these years. The growth in the installation of ATMs is also significant

Table 8.1 Computerization in public sector banks: 2013

Category	2007	2008	2009	2010	2013
Fully computerized branches (%)	85.6	93.7	95.0	97.8	100.0
Core banking solution	44.4	67.7	81.4	90.0	100.0

Source RBI: Report on trend and progress of banking in India

supplementing the functions of branches. In March end of 2014–2015, the number of ATMs installed/operating touched 69,652, five times more than its figure at 12,608 in 2005–2006. The growth in the number of ATMs installed enhanced capacity of banks and convenient banking advantage for customer and thus improving the ratio of ATMs to number of bank branches. The percentage of number of ATMs installed to number of bank branches expands continuously from 26.4% in 2005–2006 to 80% in 2010–2011 and 78% in 2014–2015. The public sector banks set up and operated 45% off-site ATMs of the total ATMs installed during 2014–2015. This growth in the percentage of ATMs shows significant shift towards advanced technology creating positive impact owing to render convenience, better service and quality products to the customers. The coverage of the automated teller machine network and the facilities being provided by the banks through the ATMs is increasing. In 2015, about 44% of the ATMs were located in rural and semi-urban centres (Table 8.2).

The total turnover under various payment and settlement systems witnessed a phenomenal increase by 100% between 2010–2011 and 2015–2016, i.e. in terms of volume from 49 million transactions in 2010–2011 to 98 millions in 2015–2016. Simultaneously paper-based transactions were on decline. The Systematically Important Payment System's (SIPS) share in the total turnover accounted for more than 90% in 2015–2016 as against 53.8% in 2008–2009. The SIPS continued to show rising trend over the share of RTGS accounts since 2010–2011.

The total paper clearing system decelerated in its value and volume of transactions gradually to be discontinued later, because of the shift of paper-based transactions to electronic modes of payment. The contribution of MICR in both value and volume of transactions declines to zero

Table 8.2   Branches and ATMs of public sector banks

Year	No. of branches	No. of ATMs installed	On-site (in %)	Off-site (in %)	Percentage of off-site to total ATM	Percentage of ATM to branches
2005–2006	47,833	12,608	52	48	47.8	26.4
2006–2007	49,666	16,329	63	37	37.0	32.9
2007–2008	52,880	21,788	59	41	40.8	41.2
2008–2009	55,438	27,277	64	36	36.3	49.2
2009–2010	58,825	40,680	58	42	41.5	69.2
2010–2011	62,211	49,487	60	40	39.8	79.5
2014–2015	89,711	69,652	54	46	45.6	77.6

Source RBI: Report on trend and progress of banking in India

in 2015–2016 as against its substantial share in 2010–2011. On the other hand, the share of Check Truncation System (CTS) to the total paper clearing system increased from 14.2% of value in 2010–2011 to 85.4% in 2015–2016 (RBI Annual Report, 2015–2016).

The RTGS system, since its inception in March 2004, has witnessed a steady growth in both value and volume terms over the period. These significant figures of RTGS registered impressive growth rates as compared to paper-based payment systems that were declining steeply. During 2015–2016, the RTGS processed around 98 million transactions valued at rupees 824 trillion. As on 30, April 2016, the number of RTGS-enabled bank branches were more than 120,506 (Table 8.3).

The total retail payment system includes cheque clearing, retail electronic fund transfer and card payments. The electronic clearing service-credit processed 3142 million transactions at value around Rs. 91,408 billion in 2015–2016—approximately eight times more in volume and value transacted in 2010–2011. Relatively, share of ECS-credit and ECS-debit gradually slipped down over these years. As against this, NEFT increased in importance in volume and value terms of payment clearing. It was 40% in volume and over 90% in value of payment cleared in 2015–2016 (Table 8.4).

The use of card-based payments rose from 502 millions in volume in 2010–2011 to 2707 millions in 2015–2016—more than five times, because of greater acceptability by merchants and infrastructures

Table 8.3   Total paper clearing system and growth of RTGS

Item	Volume (million)		Value (Rs. billion)	
	2010–2011	2015–2016	2010–2011	2015–2016
CTS	160.4	958	14,391.2	69,889
	(11.6)	(87.0)	(14.2)	(85.4)
MICR clearing	994.6	0	68,621.0	0
	(71.7)		(67.7)	
Non-MICR clearing	232	138	18,329.1	11,972
	(16.7)	(13.0)	(18.1)	(14.6)
Total paper	1387	1096	101,341	81,861
clearing	(100)	(100)	(100)	(100)
RTGS	49.3	98.3	484,872.3	824,578

Note Figures in parenthesis represent percentage share
Source RBI: Annual reports, various issues

Table 8.4   Retail electronic funds transfer systems

Type	Volume (million)		Value (Rs. billion)	
	2010–2011	2015–2016	2010–2011	2015–2016
ECS-Credit	117	39	1817	1059
	28.8	1.3	15.2	1.2
ECS-Debit	157	225	737	1652
	38.7	7.4	6.2	1.8
EFT/NEFT	132	1253	9392	83,273
	32.5	41.3	78.6	91.1
(IMPS), (NACH)	0	1517	0	5424
		50.0		(5.9)
Total retail electronic clearing	406 (100)	3034 (100)	11,946 (100)	91,408 (100)

Notes IMPS Immediate Payment Service, *NACH* National Automated Clearing House; Figures in parenthesis represent percentage change over previous year
Source RBI: Annual reports, various issues

available for payment clearance. Credit cards exceeded the debit card use over the past 5 years. A new payment mode such as prepaid instruments also gradually emerged as an important instrument in 2015–2016, like to be greater in demand with mobility of population in space and income.

A comparison of paper-based transactions and electronic mode of payments shows that the percentage share of paper-based transaction in total volume and value both continued a declining trend over the period.

Table 8.5   Growth in electronic and paper-based payments

Items	Volume (million)		Value (Rs. billion)	
	2010–2011	2015–2016	2010–2011	2015–2016
Credit cards	265	785	755	2407
Debit cards	237	1174	357	1589
Prepaid instruments	0	748	0	488
Total card payments	502	2707	1112	4484
	(100)	(100)	(100)	(100)
Paper-based transactions	1387	1096	266,303	81,861
	(37.7)	(13.6)	(64.8)	(31.5)
Electronic transactions	2296	6945	114,357	177,752
	(62.3)	(86.4)	(35.2)	(68.5)
Total	3683	8041	410,660	259,613
	(100)	(100)	(100)	(100)

Source RBI: Annual reports, various issues

The volume of electronic mode of transaction dominated the paper-based system in 2010–2011 and 2015–2016. Its relative position almost reversed in past 5 years in value terms as electronics transactions rose from 35.2% of the total retail payments in 2010–2011 to 68.5% of value transactions in 2015–2016. It is likely that the switch from paper to electronic payments was fuelled in large part by IT advances that reduced the costs and increased the availability and convenience of electronic payments (Table 8.5).

Information Technology Use and Bank Performance

The raw data on the technology in banking industry show that overtime there was changes in the use of technology by the banks. Introduction of variety of instruments in the payment and settlement system is expected to reduce operational costs as well as more transactions at the given network framework. In this section, we will analyse the linkage between technology use in banking services and performance of the public sector banks. The performance of the banks is measured in terms of accounting ratios as these ratios reflect the conduct of functioning of the banks. Profit per employee and business per employee are the two productivity ratios. ROA and ROE are used as a measure of profitability of banks and cost as a ratio of total assets is used to determine the cost condition of the firms. All the ratios show significant performance during the period from 2001–2002 to 2012–2013. Profit per employee and business per employee have increased over the period. This is no exception for the profitability ratios. Not much change is found in the case of interest cost but operating cost continues to decline gradually during the period.

Correlation is work out to find out the nature of relationship between the tech-savvy variables (Branches and ATMs) and the performance indicators. Branches and ATMs variables are positively related to the productivity variables—profit per employee and business per employee, with R-square having more than 0.90 in terms of profit per employee and 0.98 for the business per employee and which are statistically significant at the 5% level. No correlation is established in the case of profitability ratios; the respective R-square values are very low and are negative. Negative correlation is found in the case of growth in total assets and the IT variables, but not statistically significant. In terms of the cost variable, positive correlation is found between IT variables and interest cost to total assets ratio. The values of correlation are 0.59 (significant at 5%) for ATMs and 0.64 for the branches, respectively. But both the correlation coefficient signs do not produce theoretically excepted sign. However, in the case of other cost parameter, the correlation coefficients (-0.55 for branches and -0.50 for ATMs) produce expected signs, which are negative. The negative correlation between the number of branches and ATMs with the operating cost to total assets ratio shows that firms compete for their existing market shares and they will not charge the full costs of using new technology. This is also evident from the values of the Herfindahl-Hirschman Index (HHI) values where market structure shows oligopolistic in nature. The HHI value in terms of total assets continues to decline from 0.12 in 2001–2002 to 0.10 in 2004–2005 and further to 0.08 in 2012–2013, showing the presence of competition among the firms for market shares (Table 8.6).

Table 8.6 Correlation coefficient between branches, ATMs and performance indicators

Item	Branches	ATMs
Growth in total assets	−0.32	−0.36
Profit per employee	0.92*	0.91*
Business per employee	0.99*	0.98*
ROA	−0.22	−0.24
ROE	−0.31	−0.32
Interest cost/Total assets	0.64*	0.59**

Note * and ** refer to significant at 5 and 10% level

Conclusion

Information technology heralded great opportunities to improve the scale and efficiency of the banks. Technology in banking has enabled banks to undertake vivid activities in terms of mode of production and delivery of voluminous financial services with quality, speed and safety to the customers. Electronic mode of transaction has dominated the paper-based system in value terms even though the later has still higher coverage in volume of transactions. Association between use of financial technology and performance of the banks was reflected in correlation presented. statistically significant correlation coefficients were found for productivity ratios and technology use. Correlation coefficient between interest cost and technology use gave theoretically opposite signs but values were statistically significant. This means that technology use and interest cost of were unrelated. Equally important aspect technology spread and intensity was that it might not boost profitability and opposite may be possible.

Technology innovation enabled the authorities to promote the cause of financial inclusion (Gupta 2011). The biggest challenges of Indian banking relate to the extension of the coverage of banking services to the remotest parts of the country. Technology provides the scope of affordable financial inclusion through mobile banking, as today more than 800 million mobile connections are in place. Moreover, use of Smart cards/ATMs allowed the people to access transactions in a secured way regardless of time and place. However, with the complexity of the modern banking system, it is essential that the issues of fraud, hacking, computer virus, etc., should be addressed. For this, the RBI has already set up Reserve Bank Information Technology private limited, a subsidiary to develop advances technologies to meet these challenges. Issue of IT governance needs to be incorporated in the corporate governance of the firms for better compliance, accountability, transparency in data flows and better information system.

Notes

1. **Committees and Working Groups set up by the RBI:**
   a. Committee on Mechanisation in the Banking Industry (1984) Chairman: Dr. C. Rangarajan.
   b. Committees on Communication Network for Banks and SWIFT implementation (1987) Chairman: Shri T.N.A. Iyer.
   c. Committee on Computerisation in Banks (1988) Chairman: Dr. C. Rangarajan.
   d. Committee on Technology Issues relating to Payments System, Cheque Clearing and Securities Settlement in the Banking Industry (1994) Chairman: Shri W.S. Saraf.
   e. Committee for proposing Legislation On Electronic Funds Transfer and other Electronic Payments (1995) Chairperson: Smt. K.S. Shere.
   f. Working Group on Cheque Truncation and E-Cheques (2003) Chairman: R.B. Barman.

References

Beccalli, E. 2007. Does IT Investment Improve Bank Performance? Evidence from Europe. *Journal of Banking & Finance* 31 (7): 2205–2230.

Berger, A.N. 2003. The Economic Effects of Technological Progress: Evidence from the Banking Industry. *Journal of Money, Credit, and Banking* 35 (2): 141–176.

Gupta, S.K. 2011. Financial Inclusion—IT as Enabler. *Reserve Bank of India Occasional Papers* 32(2).

Ho, S.J., and S.K. Mallick. 2010. The Impact of Information Technology on the Banking Industry. *The Journal of the Operational Research Society* 61 (2): 211–221.

Ilyina, Anna, and R. Samaniego. 2008. Technology and Finance. *IMF Working Paper*, No. WP/08/182.

Kolodinsky, J.M., J.M. Hogarth, and M.A. Hilgert. 2004. The Adoption of Electronic Banking Technologies by US Consumers. *The International Journal of Bank Marketing* 22 (4): 238–259.

Krishnamurthy, M. 2006. Product Innovation in Banking Industry. *Professional Banker* 8 (6): 51–55.

Loveman, G. W. 1994. An Assessment of the Productivity Impact of Information Technologies. In *Information Technology and the Corporation of the 1990s*, T. J. Allen and M. Scott Morton (Eds.), Oxford University Press.

Padmanabhan, G. 2012. Technology Enabled Transformation in the Financial Sector. Keynote address at the GM/CIOs Conference, *Institute for Development & Research in Banking and Technology* (IDRBT), Hyderabad, 17 December.

Rangarajan, C. 2011. Role of Technology in Development of Banking. *Institute for Development and Research in Banking and Technology.*

RBI. 1984. *Committee on Mechanisation in the Banking Industry.* Chairman: Dr. C. Rangarajan.

RBI. 1987. *Committees on Communication Network for Banks and SWIFT Implementation.* Chairman: Shri T.N.A. Iyer.

RBI. 1988. *Committee on Computerization in Banks.* Chairman: Dr. C. Rangarajan.

RBI. 1994. *Committee on Technology Issues Relating to Payments System, Cheque Clearing and Securities Settlement in the Banking Industry.* Chairman: Shri W.S. Saraf.

RBI. 1995. *Committee for Proposing Legislation on Electronic Funds Transfer and Other Electronic Payments.* Chairperson: Smt. K.S. Shere.

RBI. 2003. *Working Group on Cheque Truncation and E-Cheques.* Chairman: R.B. Barman.

9

Summary and Conclusions

Introduction

This chapter provides a summary of main points of study and offers insight into potential areas of further banking reforms leading to consolidation and restructuring, eventually raising performance. It relates to current banking structure and reforms, competition and concentration, consolidation and restructuring, cost efficiency, productivity, profitability, non-performing assets and information technology use. The RBI's adopted go-slow approach in banking reforms due to its conservative attitude and also in order to keep pace with gradual macroeconomic reforms. Hence, notable drastic turnaround was not visible in any aspects of the Indian banking over the past 25 years.

Banking Structure

The global financial crisis of 2008 put a question mark on financial stability and degree of financial reforms carried out for this purpose for 2 decades across countries of the world. It was a reflection of inherent

© The Author(s) 2017
T.R. Bishnoi and S. Devi, *Banking Reforms in India*, Palgrave Macmillan Studies in Banking and Financial Institutions, DOI 10.1007/978-3-319-55663-5_9

weakness of banking systems in advanced and other economies alike in terms of their capacity to cope with the challenges of globalized world and prompted many countries to review and redesign their banking structures. In view of this, it is important to review the banking structure in India as well for its optimality, efficiency and other performance parameters for which banking reforms were progressively implemented during past a quarter century. RBI prepared a futuristic-oriented discussion paper relating to banking structure in 2013.[1] Indian banking reforms of past 25 years were strengthen its structure and consolidation with a U-turn in performance. The evidences presented here can be meaningful input in future banking reforms for consolidation and restructuring in order to benefit from so far insufficiently accomplished scalability, competition, technology optimization, with a motive to serve financial needs of fast-growing and globalizing economy so that the digital payment system and financial inclusion objectives are attained (RBI Annual Report 2013–2014). Banking reforms carried out over the past 25 years have had notable achievements and failures to redefine priority areas of reforms and weigh strategy thereof for further restructuring the banking system. Camron criteria of optimal structure are helpful to analyse developments in Indian banking sector, namely (a) density—ratio of number of bank branches/offices to either population or area, (b) size of banking system relative to macroeconomy—ratio of bank assets to GNP or wealth, (c) size distribution of banks within banking system—market share indicating degree of oligopoly or monopolistic power, and (d) geographical concentration—regional distribution of bank branches, credit and deposit.[2] These are emphasized for maximum productive efficiency, allocative neutrality and the absence of exploitation by adopting ethical practices and maximum responsibility to technological changes and market-based demand of the society. Though relative size of India's banking system improved with reference to its own past record, it did not attain height enough to match with China and advanced countries. Density in terms of population coverage by branch at aggregate level has reached appreciable level below 11,000 but rural, semi-urban areas and backward regions including entire eastern India need much to improve on this yardstick. A bank branch is expected to cover about 20,000 population and can cater in its operational area to deliver financial services cost effectively if not cost efficiently. Many areas and regions have higher population per branch than this estimated ideal coverage.

Features of Indian banking structure evolved over the decades were less consistent with indicators of optimal banking structure as enumerated above, i.e. high concentration of financial assets with the public sector banks, greater regulation and controls, peak level of SLR and CRR, imposition of directed credit programs and investments—all made banking system rigid and inflexible with high cost of intermediation-affected profitability of banks. Because of high non-performing assets, fragile financial health of the institutions and low quality of banking services, there was an urgent need for improving efficiency, productivity and profitability of the banking so as to enable them to withstand challenges of globalization.[3]

With deregulation of interest rates and significant reduction of variable reserve ratios, not only asset-portfolio underwent a change for better quality, but also productivity and profitability of banks also improved. Most of the Indian banks, irrespective of ownership and size, do niche area or specific sector-based lending operation, thus rendering competition less relevant or moderate in urban area. Rural areas remained under-banked with some of them even unbanked. Absence of banking competition in rural and semi-urban areas required coordination among cooperatives, regional rural banks and commercial banks. High entry barriers coupled with concentration of banking assets in public sector banks with common decision-making power with central government alone, Indian banking industry appeared to be oligopolistic in nature. State Bank Group and five big banks commanded a share of over 45% of assets of all scheduled commercial banks in 2015. Post-reform banking branch scenario found to tilt in favour of urban and metropolitan areas, already networked suffice and other areas reported shrinkage over the years. Successive and continuous fund transfer from rural to urban and further to metropolitan areas was another perturbing trend as seen from data on low to high credit-deposit ratios in such population groups, despite stipulation of 40% of credit-deposit ratio for rural branches. Cost constraints caused saturation in branch expansion and ATMs networks. Unitary ratio of ATMs to branches displayed unprecedented technology penetration and modern methods of banking anywhere, anytime banking service. Credit allocation according to priority sectors stipulations contributed substantially in diversification of assets portfolio and growth but because of government intervention it became constrained source of bank income and profitability.

Consolidation through selective mergers and acquisition, marginal privatization and few new entries of banks did not change the landscape of the Indian banking. Mergers and acquisitions helped only private banks realized inorganic growth. Public sector banks indeed were instrumental in the execution of compulsory takeovers and amalgamations, to support the RBI policy to weed out sick banking units or financially distressed banks. Privatization of banks met with political resistance for the reasons of suspicious intentions and complicity with private interests. Failure of privatization of public sector banks well known as sale of bank equity was more or less limited to about 20% or less for all these years. Undoubtedly, new banks' success to scale up remained uncertain to realize so far. Bank credit outstanding reveals uneven allocation among sectors given the contribution of each activity in output, GDP and employment in the economy.

In sum, banking structure needed a review of ownership and autonomy, consolidation strategy by incentivizing more mergers and amalgamations, restructuring network of branches and ATMs. Many ATMs often found with functional disorders or often empty without cash in rural, semi-urban areas and needed upgradation in software and further servicing along with timely and adequate replenishment of cash to make their smooth operation. Restructuring of Indian banking system will be a positive step in the direction of accelerating economic development and financial inclusion. For this, government ownership limiting to 50% of equity, tie-up with differential banks for deposit mobilization, credit processing, payment clearing and outsourcing various other business processes, amalgamation of all regional rural banks into five entities on the geographical advantage-such as western, eastern, southern, northern and central, mergers of small banks to form a couple of medium-scale bank are some of the suggestions that can be evaluated for their feasibility and macro economic implications.

Banking Reforms

Narasimham Committee Report so-called Report of the Committee on the Financial System set the text and tenure of financial reforms including banking reforms in November 1991. Since then, banks have completed 25 years of banking reforms, long enough to attain the intended objectives and realize tangible results in their functional autonomy, flexibility, better record of performance, etc. Main objectives of banking reforms were financial stability and efficiency of banks so as to accomplish sustained economic growth and development. The Committee report starting with an overview of deficiencies and defects in prevalent banking system provided a blueprint of what was needed to be done to bring changes to improve the system. The major recommendations included deregulation of bank entries for competitive environment, liberalization of interest rates to eliminate subsidy, reduction in variable reserve ratios lower enough to release resources, recapitalization to improve net worth, prudential regulation adding transparency and disclosures in balance sheet and profit and loss accounts—income recognition and provisioning against non-performing assets, strengthening governance and recovery mechanism of bad loans, etc. All the recommendations were introduced with modifications and changes made for consistency with Basel norms wherever applicable at different point of time. Entry barriers were liberalized to make room for entry of private banks including foreign banks. New bank licensing was issued in 12 cases to improve competition and restructure institutional composition but some of them miserably failed to achieve the breakeven level and forced to merge with other banks. Now licenses are made available on tap subject to compliance with pre-set norms. Entry of differential banks is a novel experiment in India to test its potential, given low penetration of banking in rural and semi-urban areas. However, promotion of massive digital payments can make them relevant and popular among banking customers. Minimum equity capital requirement for new bank license was gradually raised from initial Rs. 1000 millions to Rs. 5000 millions in 2016 with additional condition of 40% holding with promoters alone. It is not a big deterrent for fresh entry of banks and more licenses may be demanded in years to come. It is equally relevant to highlight the need for review of other criteria for their inadequacy such as 40% promoters' contributions, foreign holdings in voting equity capital, eligibility and management quality benchmarks for new entrant banks.

The other important change was slashed variable reserve ratios that were hiked earlier to support the government borrowings at subsidized rate to finance fiscal deficits and also to control the inflationary pressures. In post 1993–1994, fiscal deficits gradually began moderating and inflation pressure subsidized and therefore, reduction in CRR and SLR was called for to improve the balance sheet of the banks. CRR was brought down from peak level to 4% over the years and can be reduced further to the minimum level of 3% of demand and time deposits if price environment stabilized at a very moderate level. Likewise, SLR was reduced from its peak at 38.5–20.75% close to the statutory minimum in 2015. This drastic change in policy ratios benefiting banks from funds released consequent to such variations. Besides, policy reforms will facilitate much-needed development of bond market in India. Benefits of minimum CRR and SLR may be sustained in future provided fiscal deficit is adhered to the budgetary targets so as to make public borrowing modest in years to come and inflation targeting becomes successful.

Regarding the prudential regulation, the RBI has issued guidelines successively, on the basis of Basel norms, relating bank capital adequacy, asset classification, income recognition, disclosure and transparency in balance sheet, assets and liability management, risk control and non-performing assets, corporate governance, etc., during past 25 years. Banks were enjoined to adhere to the stipulations to add transparency, accountability and best governance practices. Since 1994, Board for Financial Supervision has been engaged in performing monitoring function of inspection and surveillance to safeguard the health of financial institutions and consolidating the accounting system.

Since 1991–1992 onwards, banks began complying with the minimum capital ratio. But given the high NPAs of Indian banks, the capital maintained fell short of the adequacy norms. Banks are not insulated against the risks of macroeconomic shocks and recessionary danger. So

far the capital norms were set either to prevent bank failure and promote banking stability or to reduce losses to the depositors. This is a
very narrow approach in the sense that it controls the risk appetite of
banks and did not serve the purpose of strengthening net worth. Banks
were expected to operate through multinational routes in global market to seize better opportunities available. Incentive-based capital norms
will be the right approach. In this context, international experience of
capital mobilization for a healthy and growing bank may be useful.

Though Indian banks were given NPA norms for guidance in regard
to assets classification, there have been ups and downs in NPA ratios
due to the factors beyond the control of the banks. NPA ratio can be
minimized by experimenting with various options which included uniform application of the asset classification norms at each bank level.
These options are flexible corporate debt restructuring mechanism,
development of market for debt securitization and setting up of asset
reconstruction companies. This will contribute to minimizing provisioning requirement—prevent the erosion of net worth of banks and
repayment discipline in loan market.

Consolidation and Restructuring

Restructuring and consolidation has moved at slow pace given the
potential for disruptions in the existing scheme of banking industry.
Few mergers of small and weak banks with the large ones were the one
type of strategy in the past 25 years. In response to opening new bank
licensing policy, a dozen new entries were made and only few succeeded
to make a viable business. Many of the new banks either were merged
with others because of their non-viability or unable to operate profit-
ably to survive. Only half of a dozen banks mainly from public sector
institutions (IDBI and UTI) or big business houses such as Kotak and
Mahindra could make a growth to attain the size. In the case of those
merged entities, there was hardly any substantial impact on the profitability or augmentation of capital or growth of banks merged with. There
was also insignificant impact of such a strategy on consolidation and
restructuring of banks. Greater privatization, more new entries backed

by established corporate institutions can amend existing structure for financial inclusion.

Concentration and Competition

The Indian banks have apparent low concentration associated with lack of competition. Low concentration is appeared to be not real because the government-owned banks controlled over three-fourths of the financial assets and 90% of branches. Though efforts were made in the reforms package to enhance competition and diffuse concentration, the progress remains disappointing slow and creeping. This included select cases of mergers and acquisitions for consolidation; new entry for competition; new international benchmark as a service practice; liberalization of interest rates for competitive interest rates environment, etc. The significance of bank concentration is often cited by regulators across the world for banking stability. But it is antidote to bank competition. Promoting competition was one of the objectives of financial reforms as well as necessity for economic growth. The competition can be in various forms: price based and non-price based. Reserve Bank has been issuing guidelines for the banks to prevent high charges of interest rates on advances to high-risk activities. Besides, bill discount rate of the State Bank of India serves as a benchmark rate for the other banks to follow. In view of these practices, the interest rates on either deposits or loans vary in a very short range without much visible competition. Among the non-price competition, there is a very little product differentiation to mention, given standard service delivery benchmarks for all banks. Empirical data suggest that banking in India is akin to oligopolistic markets defined by features such as few dominant firms, high interest spread (scarcity rent), high entry barriers, lack of open competition, limited product differentiation coupled with homogeneous services delivered, etc. The oligopoly banking system carries a greater systematic risk with potential crisis in the financial market. Thus, competition remains static and concentration changes marginally during the reforms era.

Performance

Cost Efficiency and Productivity: Most of the banks were operated at a size-generating economies of scale in most of the years after reforms. These banks also attained minimum average cost in select years. Even small banks realized economies of scale in that era. This implies that minimum efficient size (optimum size) was at a small scale which was possible to realize even for a new entrant bank. Among the sources of economies, wages and salaries and other operating costs were major items. Minimum efficient size is estimated at the deposit of Rs. 190,000 million in 2014–2015, and all public sector banks were within this size range. This became a cutoff size for new entrant banks for sustaining profitable business. Large banks benefitted more from the cost economies than the small banks over the years. This is also supported by the results of positive total factor productivity growth enjoyed by all the banks. Large banks benefited from gains of scale efficiency and small banks from that of technical efficiency for these years.

Profitability: The profitability of public sector banks showed a significant positive trend during the period from 1991–1992 to 2014–2015. Larger banks realized greater cost efficiency and managed credit quality following good governance. As a result, profitability record of large banks was better than that of their counterparts. Higher NPAs have been big drag on the profitability more for public sector banks.

Non-Performing Assets: Non-performing assets after the reforms showed downward trend in successive years till 2008–2009. In post-global crisis, it has taken a reverse trend eroding the banks' net worth, disrupting recycling of funds and raising a series of concerns related to uniform compliance at bank level of NPA norms and asset classification. Fluctuations in NPAs were on account of asset classification, provisioning requirement, etc. However, NPAs in post 2008–2009, recession in growth remained major factor to reckon with added problem of asymmetric information. Though each bank has a common exposure to recession, asymmetric information problem varies by bank due to the internal unique procedures of asset management. In the context of NPAs control and recovery by banks, mitigating adverse selection problem and containing moral hazard is a challenging task. Reducing information gaps and improving the discipline of repayment can contribute to long-term strategy in NPAs management.

Information Technology: Technology in banking services serves as an important tool in increasing further scope of financial inclusion for the masses that remained financially excluded in villages and remotest part of the country. Over the period, banks have been adopting new techno-centric approach in delivering its services in the form of mobile banking, Internet banking, Smart cards/ATMs, etc., regardless of time and place. Electronic mode of transaction has dominated the paper-based system in value terms even though the later has still higher coverage in volume of transactions. Besides, its role in increasing efficiency in the delivery of financial services is widely acknowledged, even though cost of using technology is high but is an integral part of banking operation. In modern banking, issues such as fraud, hacking and computer virus remained a big challenge. The Reserve Bank of India has been updating its policy in technology use and also set up Reserve Bank Information Technology private limited, a subsidiary to develop advances technologies to meet all these challenges.

Policy Suggestions

On the basis of its features, current banking structure can characterized as oligopolistic in nature and thus far from ideal optimum for the fast-growing Indian economy of 1.2 billion population. Because of cost constraints and geographical spread of economic activities in vast areas, density of commercial banks in rural and semi-urban areas remained very low leaving many gaps to serve. These gaps exhibiting financial exclusion are possible to correct with technology penetration in service delivery and choice of appropriate banking model, involving a proper balance between in-house operations and outsourcing business processes. It needs further reforms to restructure branches and business for reason of efficiency and competitive organizational environment, minimizing of information asymmetric problem and strengthening recovery mechanism to keep NPAs under control, enforcing greater transparency and disclosures compliance for uniformity in assets quality rating in financial statements, upgrade of ATMs, computerization and technology software for real-time bank service delivery. Challenges of financial globalization are not restricted to competition in marketplace alone but related to host of other issues such as risk assessment and cyber security, competition in urban segment and coordination in credit of rural markets, product innovations, governance-related best banking practices and service delivery bench-marks. Suitable amendments in banking regulation consistent with new developments in banking sector might be desired for sustaining growth dynamism of Indian economy. Incentive-based norms rather supervision-led regulation may contribute to liberal credit regime to replace the pre-vailing system of credit constrained coupled with credit rationing with complete focus on risk aversion in banking activities (D'Souza 2000).

Raising profitability of the banking activity is a serious challenge for all banks even in the absence of competition. Considerable economies in the cost were generated because of technology spread and penetration but improvement on return on asset has been facing a constraint due to high variable reserve ratios and priority sector credit targets. As a con-sequence of market orientation in banking reforms, banks have gained autonomy and freedom in practice to break from rigidity and inflexibil-ity in conduct. Balance sheet and income of banks were constrained by the regulatory intervention. Therefore, solution lies in the lower SLR in proportion to reduction in fiscal deficits. Bank must move away from the investment-centric balance sheet to a more diversified assets port-folio generating market linked return if not very high yield. Imposition of 20% SLR as minimum safety ratio is appeared to be high as against free banking regime of many countries as mentioned in Chap. 2, opt-ing for complete elimination of SLR requirement. It is not impossible if the government budget becomes a low deficit or balanced budget. Moreover, relative size of Indian banking has grown many times rela-tive to that of the 1960s when these were made as minimum mandatory ratios, specifying 20% SLR and 3% CRR norms. Banking liabilities in relation to GDP are likely to exceed 100% in the next couple of years, and public debt needed to create certain economic infrastructures was opened for private investment under economic reforms. In view of these developments, high variable reserve ratios that impacted return on bank assets cannot be justified. Case for retaining CRR becomes weak in view of liquidity for banks is available from multiple sources other than RBI in Indian financial markets. The reduction in these ratios will release resources to be deployed in the form of credit to private sector, and thus, the substantial high rate of return earned on such assets will improve profitability and productivity of banking industry. What is needed is to identify the intent as either economic or prudential regulation where the former may be emphasized more for competitive pricing of credit with efficiency in allocation and latter for ensuring the health and efficiency of the banking system (Polizatto 1990).

Regarding the compliance of non-performing assets norms, there appear to be manipulations in some of the banks if not all having high NPAs in such cases. In the current environment, bank management lacks incentives for efficient credit allocation and quality control of the assets. Safety of loan assets can be ensured by way of better risk assessment methods, improving information set about the projects quality and customers' creditworthiness, monitoring the end-use of credits and incentivizing the efficiency of credit allocation. In this context, credit rating agencies, credit bureaus and other related institutions need to be strengthened for producing high-quality information and surveillance mechanism for better outcome. Besides, new institutions to monitor end-use credit, asset seizing and custodians, inventory management of bank funded assets, etc., need to be set up. There is a view that capital inadequacy due to high NPAs is one of the reasons for slow growth in credit, affecting adversely macroeconomic environment. Abovementioned measures can be a good substitute for new supervision-based regulation of NPAs. In sequence of proposed ideas for experiments, the system of tranche called the Structured Early Intervention and Resolution as proposed by Benston and Kaufman (1993) may be useful to consider for it. Wholesale credit seems to be more risky than retail credit. Corporate loans in the wholesale market and individual loans in retail market were normally assumed the same risk weight despite the fact that credit risk between corporate firms and between individual clients will be at variance. Therefore, the recovery mechanism of such loans must be designed to align with past profile of borrowers' and inherent risk in activity or assets funded.

Potential of mergers and acquisitions in Indian banking landscape as well as in financial service sector is tremendous. In the case of past mergers, there were scarce gains in profitability, a discouraging trend. However, this strategy might produce gains if the strategic rationale in terms of premium price paid to the shareholders of merged entity and integration between merged and merged with is handled effectively to generate fruitful outcome. Merging of financial service firms with banks may help in attaining the inorganic growth and cost-effective expansion of business. In addition to efficiency effect of mergers and acquisitions, the post-merger revenue effect may be positive because combined firms market share tends to be larger than pre-merger period producing disproportionate gains in revenue. A related positive revenue effect may be possible to achieve if the firm is able to acquire distribution channels for broadening and deepening assets' market segments as well as avail strategic option of diversification. If the product range widens after mergers, revenue economies of scope by cross-selling get generated. A related issue is that it is a guarantee against 'too big to fail' because of the enlarged scale through mergers and acquisitions possible if the merged institutions become international with multiple diversification of businesses (Walter 2004). Some of the small commercial banks suffering from muted growth; regional rural banks with consecutive losses; and financial fragile urban cooperative commercial banks are possible candidates for M&As in next decade, if restructuring of banking is expedited as it should happen in public interest. These entities either amalgamate among each other or merge with medium or large size banks on synergy potential available from such mutual transactions. Suitable legal amendments can be made as a part of further banking reforms.

Some suggestions in each of the chapters already given are not repeated here.

Notes

1. RBI (2013).
2. Camron (1972) (Ed) p. 9.
3. RBI (1991).

References

Benston, G.J., and G.G. Kaufman. 1993. Improving the FDIC Improvement Act: What was Done and What Still Needs to be Done to Fix the Deposit Insurance Problem. In *Reforming American Financial Institutions and Markets*, ed. G.G. Kaufman. Boston: Kluwer Academic Publishers.

Camron, R. 1972. *Banking and Economic Development—Some Lessons of History.* New York: Oxford University Press.

D'Souza, Errol. 2000. Prudential Regulation in Indian Banking. *Economic and Political Weekly* 35 (5): 287–298.

Polizatto, V. 1990. Prudential Regulations and Banking Supervision. *The World Bank, Policy Planning and Research Working Papers*, WPS 340.

Reserve Bank of India. 1991. *Report of the Committee on the Financial System.* November, Mumbai.

Reserve Bank of India. 2013. *Banking Structure in India—The Way Forward.* Mumbai, India: Discussion Paper.

Walter, Ingo. 2004. *Mergers and Acquisitions in Banking and Finance What Works, What Fails, and Why.* New York: Oxford University Press.

Index

© The Editor(s) (if applicable) and The Author(s) 2017
T.R. Bishnoi and S. Devi, *Banking Reforms in India*, Palgrave Macmillan Studies in
Banking and Financial Institutions, DOI 10.1007/978-3-319-55663-5

Printed by Printforce, the Netherlands